AUSTRALIA'S DEMOCRACY

AUSTRALIA'S DEMOCRACY

A SHORT HISTORY

John Hirst

ALLEN&UNWIN

Curriculum
CORPORATION

First published in 2002

Copyright © Commonwealth of Australia, 2002

Australia's Democracy: A Short History is Commonwealth copyright. Requests and inquiries concerning reproduction and rights should be addressed to the Manager, Legislative Services, AusInfo, GPO Box 1920, Canberra ACT 2601.

This publication is a reproduction of a Commonwealth Department of Education, Science and Training funded publication titled *History of Australian Democracy.*

Australia's Democracy: A Short History was supported by funding from the Commonwealth Department of Education, Science and Training under the *Discovering Democracy* programme.

The views expressed here are those of the author and do not necessarily represent the views of the Commonwealth Department of Education, Science and Training.

Allen & Unwin
83 Alexander Street
Crows Nest NSW 2065
Australia
Phone: (61 2) 8425 0100
Fax: (61 2) 9906 2218
Email: info@allenandunwin.com
Web: www.allenandunwin.com

Curriculum Corporation
PO Box 177
Carlton South Vic 3053
Australia
Phone: (61 3) 9207 9600
Fax: (61 3) 9639 1616
Email: sales@curriculum.edu.au
Web: www.curriculum.edu.au

National Library of Australia
Cataloguing-in-Publication entry:

Hirst, J. B. (John Bradley), 1942– .
   Australia's democracy: a short history.

   Bibliography.
   Includes index.
   ISBN 1 86508 845 5.

   1. Democracy—Australia—History. 2. Voting—Australia—
   History. 3. Australia—Politics and government. 4.
   Australia—Social conditions. I. Title.

321.80994

Set in 10.25/13 pt New Baskerville by Bookhouse, Sydney
Printed by Brown Prior Anderson in Melbourne

10 9 8 7 6 5 4 3 2 1

Preface

Australians can't get enough books on the history of bushrangers and sport. It is surprising that until now this very successful democratic country has not possessed a single history of its democracy. Why this is so is one of the puzzles this book tries to answer. The book is in two parts. The first provides a narrative account from 1788 to 2000; the second is a series of interpretative essays.

For a number of years the Commonwealth government has been encouraging civics education in the schools and the wider community. This book is part of that program. I am indebted to my colleagues of the Civics Education Group for their encouragement and support, and particularly to Stuart Macintyre.

My thanks are also due to Judy Brett, who allowed me to read her work on the Liberals; to Alex McDermott and Jeremy Sammut, who helped me with the research and discussed their findings with me; to Joan Rydon, who advised me on electoral systems; to John McMillan, who spoke to me on his own role as legal reformer.

As always, the staff at the Mitchell Library in Sydney and the La Trobe Library in Melbourne have been very helpful.

John Iremonger of Allen & Unwin believed in this project as soon as he heard of it. It has been a pleasure to work again with the man who has done so much to promote the understanding of Australian society.

David Kemp, the former federal Minister of Education, gave strong support to the civics education program. It was his idea that there should be a single-volume history of democracy in Australia.

Some minor alterations have been made to a few of the documents reproduced in the book. Those wanting to quote from them exactly should check the originals.

The use of the term 'Aborigines' in this book is contextual. Nowadays, the preferred term for the indigenous people of Australia is 'Aboriginal people'.

J.H.

Contents

CONTENTS

PART I

Making a democracy

ONE

Rights without votes, 1788–1850

How important is the right to vote? How does it compare with the advantages of living under a government that can't lock you up without allowing you a fair trial, that can't stop the criticisms of the media, that can't control the judges, that itself has to obey the law? These things are an important part of what we understand by democracy.

Australians had the advantage of living under governments like this long before anyone had the right to vote. This was because Australia was colonised by people from Britain, which was the first country in Europe to have a government that respected rights and liberties. In Britain there was a king, but unlike other monarchs he had to rule through a parliament. Yet Britain was not a democracy: at the time Britain settled Australia only one man in ten had the right to vote, and no woman had the franchise. Voters were men possessing a certain amount of property.

Though political rights were restricted, every man and woman in England, rich and poor, had the same legal rights. Their homes could not be invaded by the police, unless the police had a warrant from a court; if they were arrested they had to be put on trial in open court; and if they were to be punished severely they had to be found guilty by a jury. Everyone had the right to petition the king for mercy. Ordinary English people knew their rights and were proud of them.

DEMOCRACY IS MORE THAN VOTING

Imagine a country in which at free, compulsory elections 90 per cent of the electorate votes for the Nationalist Party. That party, with the continuing support of most of the people, suppresses all other parties, imprisons their leaders, closes down opposition newspapers, forbids the speaking of any but the alleged 'national' language, imposes the state religion on everybody, and forces the University to teach from a 'national point of view'. Such a country is in no sense a democracy. The fact that 90 per cent of the population completely support the Government's actions does not make the country a democracy. It only makes the tyranny more terrible.

Eugene Kamenka, 'What is democracy?', *The Australian Highway* July 1958, p. 40

The great landowners of England ruled the country through the parliament. They were strong supporters of the independence of the law. They had passed an Act which said that though the king could appoint the judges, he could not dismiss them; only parliament could dismiss a judge. By insisting on the independence of the law and the legal rights of subjects, the landowners had limited the power of the king.

Founded in law

English people carried their rights with them when they went to English lands overseas. But in Australia Britain created a colony like no other—it was to be made up of convicts, people who by definition had lost their rights. At first the plan was to govern New South Wales by military power, but it seems that Lord Sydney, the minister in charge, did not like this. He was an old-fashioned supporter of the rights of Englishmen and did not want to depart from the normal processes of the law, even in dealing with convicts. Before the first fleet sailed it had been decided that English law was to operate in the new colony.

Australians know nothing of Lord Sydney, even though his name is attached to the first and largest city of their country. If he was responsible for the decision to ditch the plan for a military government, he made one of the most significant decisions in

Australia's history. The law, the traditional protector of English liberty, did not have to be re-established in this oddball society: it was there from the start.

If you had poked your head inside the tent where the first criminal court was sitting on 11 February 1788, you might have thought it was a military court. The judge and the jury were military officers, dressed in their uniforms. There were six jurymen instead of 12, and they and the judge voted together on guilt and innocence and on punishment. But they were administering English law, even though none of them was trained in the law. The accused was innocent until proven guilty (even though most of the accused were convicted criminals under sentence); witnesses were cross-examined by the accused and the court; if the evidence was weak, the accused went free.

The same military judge presided over the civil court. At its first session, two convicts, Henry and Susannah Cable, brought an action against the captain of a ship for losing their luggage. The couple had met in an English jail; they had had sex in jail and their first child was born in jail. They got married just after they landed in Sydney. Their action against the ship's captain was successful: he had to pay them the value of the luggage they had lost. In England this case could not have happened. Convicts in England could not own property, could not bring an action in court, and could not give evidence in court. Lord Sydney's decision to allow the law to operate in New South Wales immediately brought amazing consequences. Convicts had to be given the same legal rights as free people.

If the law was to control the affairs of a society where three-quarters of the people were convicts, then convicts had to be allowed to give evidence in court—otherwise the courts could not establish the facts of the cases before them. If convicts were to be taken to court for stealing, then convicts had to have the legal right to own property, because the property stolen by convicts often belonged to other convicts. At the first sitting of the criminal court one convict was found guilty of stealing another convict's bread, worth tuppence.

Of course, convicts were made to work for other people; in this sense they were not free people. But if they were to be punished for not doing their work properly, they had to be taken to court. Masters could not punish their convict servants themselves. In court the convicts could give their side of the case, to which usually the court did not pay much attention. But if a convict claimed that his master was not feeding him properly or that he had hit him, the court gave more attention to what the convict said.

The planners of this colony used international law to decide how the Aborigines should be treated. If the native inhabitants of a territory lived settled lives and owned their lands, Europeans could occupy their territory only by making a treaty with them. When the British government was considering sending its surplus convicts to a site in West Africa, the plans for this settlement included making a treaty with the local owners.

When the government sent the convicts to New South Wales instead, it decided that it did not have to make a treaty with the Aborigines. The government knew that the Aborigines were hunters and gatherers, not farmers, and that they did not live in villages. From this information it wrongly concluded that they did not own their lands. It acted on the assumption that the land was 'terra nullius', belonging to no-one.

Aboriginal law was also ignored. Theoretically the Aborigines were to be protected by English law. That law was bent a long way to give convicts legal rights; it was not bent at all for the Aborigines. They were not allowed to give evidence in court. As they were not Christians, it was thought they would not understand that God would punish them if they did not tell the truth. So if settlers attacked and killed Aborigines they were safe, provided that they did not give evidence against each other. The Aborigines could not tell the court what had happened.

In 1799 white settlers were for the first time brought before the criminal court on a charge of murdering Aborigines. Three Aboriginal boys came to the Hawkesbury to return the gun of a settler killed by the Aborigines. Spurred on by the wife of the man who had been killed, a group of settlers murdered two of these messengers and buried them. The military officer on the Hawkesbury and the local constable got to hear of this and they had the bodies dug up. The evidence they collected could be admitted in court.

In their defence, the settlers told the court how many of their neighbours had been attacked and killed by Aborigines. They said that soldiers had been sent out to kill Aborigines when they attacked the settlers (which was true), so why was their action murder? The court found them guilty, but was divided over punishment. Three officers (including Matthew Flinders, the explorer) wanted to flog them and set them free. Four did not want to take responsibility for any punishment and asked the governor to send the case to London.

Governor Hunter was in a bind. He knew that the settlers had done more killing than the Aborigines, but he knew how unpopular it would be to punish settlers for killing Aborigines. He agreed to let the case go to London and the settlers to go home. In London the government decided that, as it was so long since the offence, the settlers should not be punished, but the British policy of protecting Aborigines still stood! The settlers drew a different lesson.

Convict society

Every Australian knows that convicts were brutally flogged. This was the standard punishment for male convicts who neglected their work or committed new crimes. If the crime was rated as serious the convict was sent to a harsh penal settlement like Norfolk Island or he was hanged. These punishments are in our eyes so barbaric that to talk of convicts' rights seems like a sick joke and convict society nothing other than a cruel oppression.

The punishments were severe, but everything else about this settlement was slack. It is often called a jail, but it was not at all like a jail, if a jail is thought of as a place of strict discipline and control. It was more like the jails of England at the time the convicts left it—people being put behind their walls but no-one caring much about what went on inside them. Henry and Susannah Cable were not unusual in starting a family in jail.

Putting men and women together is not the way to run a strict institution. Women convicts were sent to New South Wales because the government thought it cruel and unnatural to create an all-male society—which shows that their thinking about punishment was very different from our own. Women were given lighter work and after the early years were not flogged. Their chief purpose was to be sexual partners to the men—officers and soldiers as well as convicts. The children of these unions were free subjects with all the rights of English people, even though one or both parents were convicts.

As no-one had been sent to supervise the work of convicts, Governor Phillip had to put convicts in charge of other convicts. Very quickly these convict overseers hit on a method to get the

7

> ## THE FIRST DEMONSTRATION: GOVERNMENT FARM, PARRAMATTA, DECEMBER 1791
>
> Many of the convicts there not having any part of their weekly ration left when Tuesday or Wednesday night came, the governor directed, as he had before done for the same reason, that the provisions of the labouring convicts should be issued to them daily. This measure being disapproved of by them, they assembled in rather a tumultuous manner before the governor's house at Parramatta on the last day of the month, to request that their provisions might be served as usual on the Saturdays. The governor, however, dispersed them without granting their request; and as they were heard to murmur, and talk of obtaining by different means what was refused to entreaty (words spoken among the crowd, and the person who was so daring not being distinguishable from the rest), he assured them that as he knew the major part of them were led by eight or ten designing men to whom they looked up, and to whose names he was not a stranger, on any open appearance of discontent, he should make immediate examples of them. Before they were dismissed they promised greater propriety of conduct and implicit obedience to the orders of their superiors, and declared their readiness to receive their provisions as had been directed.

David Collins, *An Account of the English Colony in New South Wales* London, 1798, Vol. 1, pp. 192–3

convicts to work. They set a daily task: so much land cleared, so many bricks made; and when that was completed the convict was free to leave. If a convict worked hard, he might have to work only till lunchtime. In their 'own time' in the afternoon, the convicts could take extra work and earn money. Later, when the convicts had to work for the whole day, their masters had to pay them a small wage because they were losing their outside earnings.

The convicts stuck up for themselves and were in a good bargaining position because there was no-one else to do the work. They protested to Governor Phillip himself about the size of the daily task on the government farms, and he was forced to reduce it.

The early governors had no orders from Britain about the punishment of the convicts, so it was not against government policy to make convicts overseers. Whenever a new job had to be done, governors looked for a convict to do it. Convicts were used as

Scene of the first demonstration, 1791: the Government Farm, Parramatta

policemen, lawyers, teachers, doctors, architects and artists (a job for the forgers!). They were promised a pardon if they did their job well or even given one before they started. In picking on skilled convicts for responsible jobs, the governor didn't care what crime they had committed or how long their sentence was.

In 1801 Governor King introduced the ticket of leave, which gave convicts their freedom so long as they behaved themselves—an Australian invention which was later the model for the probation system. Tickets were given to convicts who could get their own living, and convicts who were gentlemen were given tickets as soon as they left the boat.

Convicts with rights; convicts with wages; convicts in top jobs; convicts free on arrival—where would it end? With ex-convicts being rich! After 30 years the ex-convicts owned as much of the colony as the free settlers. Every convict could get a small farm when his time was up, but this was not the route to great wealth. The rich ex-convicts got their start by working for the officers, who were the first traders. They then branched out on their own and became also shipbuilders, whalers, bankers and large landowners.

9

The largest house in Sydney 1810,
owned by ex-convict Simeon Lord,
who made his first money selling
rum for an officer

Ex-convicts could not have become wealthy if they had not possessed the same economic rights as free settlers: the right to start a business, to sue for debt, to own property. The ex-convicts also depended on an important local right: to have convicts work for them. The women among the ex-convict business people enjoyed these rights as well and were much more independent than they would have been in England.

Under English law, convicts did not regain all their rights after they had served their time, and even a pardon did not restore all rights. This was ignored in the colony. A pardon made you fully free and convicts who served out their time received a certificate of freedom (another local invention), which gave them 'all the rights and privileges of free subjects'.

Lachlan Macquarie, the fifth governor (1810–21), thought no position should be denied to ex-convicts. He invited rich ex-convicts to Government House dinners and balls and made three of them magistrates. Ex-crims were now judging crime! The rich free settlers were very angry. They regarded themselves as far superior to the ex-convicts, no matter how rich these were, and now the governor

Mary Reibey, ex-convict businesswoman

was treating them as equal to themselves. The governor ignored their protests. He thought them a fussy, whingeing lot: it was the enterprising ex-convicts who had made the place; if free settlers didn't like ex-convicts, let them go elsewhere.

Macquarie had uncovered the logic of this strange settlement and made it into a principle. Convicts and ex-convicts were not to be oppressed: the colony belonged to them.

Challenging the governor

For more than 30 years the governor alone ruled the settlement. He made all the decisions and his orders were the local law, which was added to English law. The judges were officers under his command and he chose the six military officers to be the jury at criminal trials.

The governor was also in charge of economic development, as he had the power to allocate land, trading opportunities and convict workers, and the right to sell produce to the government store. Keeping sweet with the governor was important for success.

Convicts were part of this politics of winning the governor's favour. As British subjects they had the right to petition the King, which in New South Wales meant the right to send their requests to the governor. They asked him for permission to marry, to have

11

wives sent out from Britain, to be reassigned so they could live near their partner or children, and to receive a pardon or a ticket of leave. Their petitions had more chance of success if they could get a respectable person to support it, such as their master or a minister of religion.

The only people who could afford to quarrel with the governor were those who had good connections back in Britain. They used their influence to attempt to get his policy changed or to get him sacked. John Macarthur, the pioneer sheepman, boasted that he was responsible for the recall of several governors.

The only institution in the colony that could stand up to the governor was the military. Though officially under his command, the military was part of a larger institution, the British army, with its own traditions and connections. One of its traditions was that you made up for being in some awful outpost by making money. The officers were the colony's first traders, and their chief business was supplying convicts and ex-convicts with rum. The governors wanted to limit the rum trade because drunken convicts committed new crimes, and to get drunk ex-convict small settlers went into debt and lost their land. The officers resented the governor's interference and more or less ignored his orders.

Governor Bligh (1806–09), like his two predecessors Hunter and King, upset the officers by attempting to control their business activities, and he offended the property holders of Sydney with his plans for the redesign of the town. Authority in his hands looked threatening, for he was short-tempered and foul-mouthed. His mistake was to mess with John Macarthur. When Bligh thought he had Macarthur cornered, Macarthur got the military to march on Government House and arrest the governor. For a time the military became the government.

The British government could not allow this rebellion to succeed, though it dealt fairly gently with the rebels. It sent Macquarie to re-establish lawful authority. The rebellious soldiers were recalled and replaced by men of Macquarie's own regiment. That reduced the chance of conflict between governor and military. However, when in turn Macquarie's regiment was replaced, trouble erupted again. The new regiments refused to be bound by the governor's policy of accepting ex-convicts at Government House. They pointedly did not invite them to the officers' mess, which they declared to be the true setter of society's standards. Macquarie was incensed at this insubordination.

 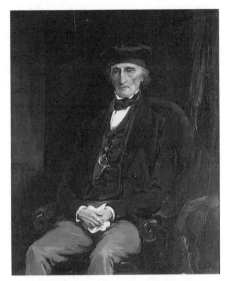

Governor Macquarie (left) and Judge Bent

Macquarie was generous to the ex-convicts and devoted himself to improving the colony, but he was a true autocrat. He thought New South Wales would advance only if everyone agreed with him, and he saw opposition to himself as treachery. On occasions he used his power arbitrarily. When three free men broke his rules by entering the Government Domain, he had them flogged without trial.

The institution that successfully challenged Macquarie was the law. In his time the judges were properly trained lawyers, not military amateurs. Officially they were still under the governor's command, but they fought against this as a threat to the independence of the law and their status as judges. When Judge Jeffrey Bent arrived in 1814 to take charge of the civil court he was dismayed to find that the lawyers who would be appearing before him were ex-convicts. He refused to admit them. Macquarie thought this was cruel to the lawyers and an obstruction of justice, because without ex-convict lawyers the court's work could not be done. He requested Bent to allow them in at least until free lawyers arrived from England. A governor interfering with a judge made Bent see red. And what a request it was! In no other place in the king's dominions, said Bent, would the purity of the law be stained by the admission of lawyers who had themselves broken the law. He refused the governor's request and closed his court. It stayed closed for two years while the dispute was referred to Britain.

Meanwhile the judge refused to pay toll on the Parramatta Road. He claimed that taxes could not be levied on the say-so of a governor. Taxes could be levied only by a representative assembly. This was a principle of the English constitution: no taxation without representation. The judge was summoned to appear before a magistrate's court for non-payment of the toll. He did not show up.

The British minister for the colonies, Earl Bathurst, decided that Bent had carried his opposition to the governor too far and sacked him, but he did not support Macquarie's argument in favour of ex-convict lawyers. There were now sufficient free lawyers, and the ex-convicts were not to practise.

The next judge warned Macquarie quietly that he agreed with Bent that the governor did not have power to levy taxes. Macquarie asked the minister in London for advice. The minister referred the question to the government's legal advisers, who came to the same conclusion as the judges. If Englishmen abroad were to be taxed without representation, there would have to be a British Act of Parliament taking the right of representation from them. As no such Act had been passed, the rule of the governor of New South Wales was illegal. Even a convict colony had to be governed by the rule of law.

Macquarie was now in great danger. As soon as he returned to England, anyone who had been made to pay his illegal taxes could take him to court and sue for damages. He pleaded with the government for protection. The government passed a special Act of Parliament to make legal all that had been done in New South Wales.

Then in 1823 another Act of Parliament reformed the government of the colony. The governor could no longer pass laws on his own; he would have to put his proposals to a small council whose members would be appointed by the British minister. The governor was still to be in charge; the council members could not propose laws. The council was given the right to tax. There was to be a chief justice, who would be entirely independent of the governor. No law could be passed by the council unless the judge had declared that it was consistent with the laws of England, so far as the circumstances of the colony allowed.

The colony was still to receive convicts, so it would not be allowed an elected assembly or the usual jury system, but now its government was on a proper legal basis.

Britain tries toughness

The British government at first took no interest in what happened to the convicts in New South Wales: the important thing was that they were out of the way. Their punishment was to be exile.

After 1815, with the end of the long wars with revolutionary France, the British economy went into recession and the armed forces no longer soaked up the unemployed. Crime increased and the government was under pressure to get tough on crime. The critics wanted to know how transportation to New South Wales could deter crime when convicts lived well and ex-convicts made fortunes. There was growing support for the new idea of turning prisons into well-run and tightly disciplined institutions, where punishments would be adjusted to fit the crime and prisoners would be reformed. With a network of new prisons, the unscientific approach of shipping criminals out of the country could be abandoned.

In 1819 the British government sent a one-man commission of enquiry to New South Wales to see whether punishment could be tightened up or whether transportation should be stopped. Commissioner John Bigge opted for tightening up, which then became the policy the government followed. The special deals and soft options were to cease. All convicts were to work; they were not to receive wages; after serving a certain proportion of their sentence they were to be eligible for a ticket of leave, but only if they had been well-behaved. To check who was well-behaved, central records were to be kept. To scare convicts into being well-behaved, Norfolk Island and the other penal settlements were to be made truly terrible.

The government also decided to reshape the colony's society. It was not to be a place where ex-convicts rose to prominence. Macquarie's policy was rejected. Convicts were not to be given land when their time was up. More free settlers were to be encouraged to migrate so that they would be the largest group and masters of most of the convicts. To create a proper English society, the Church of England was to be made not only the official but the wealthiest church: it was to receive one-seventh of all new land.

The system did become tougher for convicts, though masters still gave special rewards to skilled and responsible convicts. Reducing the influence of ex-convicts would take time. The government did not propose to remove their legal rights. Indeed, as the validity of some of their pardons had been questioned in the courts, the 1823 New South Wales Act re-established their rights. The government could not leave ex-convict business people defenceless. No-one proposed to remove their right to have convicts work for them.

At the same time as the British government was trying toughness, young William Wentworth returned to his native land. He had a very different vision for its future. He wanted it to have proper courts, with 12 jurymen instead of a military jury, and an elected assembly instead of the governor and his small nominated council. Under his plan, ex-convicts would have the right to sit on juries and to vote for the assembly. As ex-convicts were in a majority, they would control the colony. The free settlers, who gave themselves such airs, would be nowhere.

Wentworth himself was not an ex-convict. His father was almost a convict. He came from a good family, but when he was in London training to be a doctor he mixed with a wild crowd and took to highway robbery. He appeared in court several times and was lucky to escape conviction. At the end of his third trial, he told the court that he was voluntarily going to the new convict colony. The funds to get him out of the way had been supplied by a distant relative, Lord Fitzwilliam, the head of an old landed family. On the voyage out, D'Arcy Wentworth took Catherine Crowley, a 17-year-old convict, as his sexual partner. Young William was conceived on the boat.

To have a convict mother in early New South Wales was no great shame. William Wentworth grew up confident and proud because his father was the largest landholder in the colony and related to a lord. It was only when he was in London studying law that William learnt that his father had been charged with highway robbery. Now he felt that his family's honour was stained. At the same time John Macarthur refused him permission to marry his daughter. He came back to New South Wales with a great ambition: to be the fighter for his country's liberties and to be avenged on the free settlers who dared to look down on him and his father.

His political supporters were the ex-convicts. They were not particularly upset at military juries or the absence of an assembly;

after all, in the colony as it was, they had made their fortunes. What riled the richer ex-convicts was the social exclusion that the free settlers practised against them. As business people they had constant dealings with each other, but the free settlers would not invite ex-convicts to their dinners or balls. What made it more riling was that some of the ex-convicts came from higher-class families and were better educated than the free settlers.

A movement of former criminals demanding political rights has an image problem. Nevertheless, this movement did have several things going for it. First, Wentworth himself, who was big, loud, witty and fearless. Second, the principle that the British government could not deny—that Englishmen abroad should govern themselves. Of course there were obvious reasons why this colony should not govern itself, but the ex-convicts explained to the government that they were respectable and wealthy people, not a lawless rabble. They had their own agent in London, who got to speak to the officials in the Colonial Office and even the minister himself. Third, opinion in Britain was running in favour of extending political rights. A conservative government still ruled, as it had done for nearly all the years since the colony was founded, but liberal reformers who wanted to give political rights to middle- and

---

JOHN MACARTHUR LISTS WENTWORTH'S SUPPORTERS, 1820S

sentenced to be hung since he came here
repeatedly flogged at the cart's tail
a London Jew
Jew publican lately deprived of his licence
auctioneer transported for trading in slaves
often flogged here
son of two convicts
a swindler—deeply in debt
an American adventurer
an attorney with a worthless character
a stranger lately failed here in a musick shop
married to the daughter of two convicts
married to a convict who was formerly a tamborine girl
attending county wakes and fairs

Quoted in A.C.V. Melbourne, *Early Constitutional Development in Australia* Brisbane, 1963, pp. 131–2

EDWARD EAGAR, AN EX-CONVICT LAWYER, DESCRIBES THE REV. SAMUEL MARSDEN, LEADING FREE SETTLER, 1822

A man descended from the lowest ranks in life, brought up to the trade of blacksmith, of a narrow inferior education, of coarse vulgar habits and manners, accustomed to no better society than the original confined unimproved society of New South Wales, and who, were it not for the accidental circumstance of his obtaining the appointment of Assistant Chaplain of New South Wales at a time when it was more of discredit than honour to hold such a situation, would to this day have remained in that obscurity, out of which, neither his birth, education, talents or manners gave him any right to emerge.

Quoted in
John Ritchie,
*The Evidence
to the Bigge
Reports*
Melbourne,
1971, Vol. 2,
pp. 235–6

working-class people were becoming more influential. Some of the reformers in the British parliament spoke up for the ex-convicts.

When Wentworth returned to the colony in 1824 he brought with him his friend Robert Wardell, a fellow lawyer, and a printing press. The two men launched the *Australian*, the first independent newspaper in the colony. Very soon it was running the first anti-government campaign. Its target was Governor Darling (1825–1831), whose instructions were to run a tight and tough convict system.

Darling was very disturbed when two soldiers serving in the colony openly committed a robbery because they believed they would be better off as convicts. Darling decided to make an example of Sudds and Thompson: he amended their seven-year sentence to work on the roads in chains. In the parade ground on a hot day they were stripped of their uniforms and the chains were riveted onto them. A special iron collar was added to the normal leg chains. Sudds was already ill, and a few days later he died in hospital.

Wentworth and the *Australian* went to work on Darling. They accused him of altering the sentences illegally, of creating a cruel punishment—of murdering Sudds. Everything Darling now did was criticised. Wentworth threatened that as soon as the governor returned to England he would have him charged with murder.

Wentworth's political message was that this tyrant was in charge only because the colony was denied its own assembly.

In 1826 another newspaper, the *Monitor*, began. It was run by a kindly religious man, E.S. Hall, who was appalled at the convicts' suffering on the road gangs and at the penal settlements. These were the places that the British government wanted to be harsh. Hall ferreted out information on what was going on in them (it was not always accurate) and filled his paper with stories of starvation and brutal floggings.

Darling thought the world had gone crazy: in a convict colony newspapers were operating freely; they were criticising the governor and his administration; and the convicts were reading the papers! He was afraid that the convicts would be encouraged to rebel. The Colonial Office shared his view and encouraged him to pass tough laws to control the press. But when he tried, Francis Forbes, the new chief justice of the supreme court, stood in his way. Every act of the local council needed his approval.

Darling's first plan was to require that newspaper editors apply for licences to publish. Forbes said that under English law there was a right to publish without getting permission. Darling then

GOVENOR DARLING AND CHIEF JUSTICE FORBES ON RIGHTS, 1827

Governor Darling

The people are taught by the newspapers to talk about the rights of Englishmen and the free institutions of the mother country, many of them forgetting their actual condition. Besides, although this is an English colony, there is no similarity whatsoever in its composition to that of England.

Quoted in David Neal, *The Rule of Law in a Penal Colony* Melbourne, 1991, p. 27

Chief Justice Forbes

Without trial by jury, without the corrective power of an assembly, without one single popular right, the people of this country naturally regard the Supreme Court as their only protection against absolute power.

Quoted in C.H. Currey, *Sir Francis Forbes* Sydney, 1968, p. 241

tried to put a tax of four pence a copy on each newspaper. This was the same tax as in England. The tax was designed to make the papers more expensive so that poor people could not buy them. Forbes found even this proposal illegal on a technicality. In assessing whether local laws were in accordance with English law, Forbes had plenty of leeway. The laws could be varied to fit the circumstances of the colony. But Forbes saw the colony in a very different way from Darling. He was a liberal who did not like the governor's wide powers, and he used his position to stop the governor muzzling the liberal press. The result was a press that was freer in the convict colony than in England.

The editors could be prosecuted for libel. Darling mounted six successful cases against Hall for libelling government officials. However, the prison to which he was sent was run in the old-fashioned way, and Hall continued to edit his paper and create new libels from his cell. Darling also took away Hall's convict workers. Hall appealed to the supreme court and Forbes ruled that the governor did not have this power. It was a threat to the right to

Governor Darling and Chief Justice Forbes

own property if the governor could take away the convicts necessary to work it.

Darling's final attempt to silence Hall was to pass a law banishing from the colony an editor twice convicted of libel. This was in accordance with English law; even Forbes accepted it. However, the English law was being repealed just as Darling was passing his. Darling's law was disallowed in London.

The governor carrying out Britain's tough policy faced a tough opposition: Wentworth and the ex-convict party, a free press defending convicts and ex-convicts, the courts, even change within Britain itself.

The age of reform

Wentworth held a great party at his harbourside mansion when Governor Darling sailed home. He had made life very difficult for the governor, but he had not persuaded the conservative government in Britain to agree to the constitution he wanted. His hopes rose when the liberal reforming party in Britain—the Whigs—came to power in 1830. The new government moved quickly to give middle-class people the vote and to give the new towns more members of parliament. The 1832 Reform Bill, as it

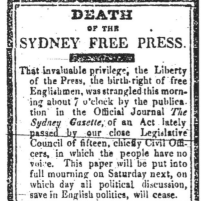

The Monitor *and the* Australian *greet Darling's law to banish editors*

was called, was passed after a tremendous struggle when it looked as if reform might fail and be replaced by revolution.

The new government sent a new governor to New South Wales, Richard Bourke (1831–37), the first liberal governor. He supported the claims of the ex-convicts. It was the British government that would decide whether to grant a local elected assembly, but there was something the governor could do. In 1828 the British government had decided that the question of juries could be settled by the Governor's Council. Bourke introduced into his council a Bill to allow normal juries in criminal trials, with ex-convicts having the right to be jurymen. All the free-settler members of the council were opposed. Bourke could count on the votes of the officials of his government, who made up the other half of the council; with these and his own casting vote the measure just got through.

Bourke's greatest liberal measure concerned religion. In Britain the Whig government was thinking about removing the religious injustice practised in Ireland. Though most of the Irish were Catholics and poor, they were made to pay money to the official Protestant Church of Ireland, which they did not attend. Bourke came from Ireland and knew first-hand the bitterness this caused. In New South Wales a quarter of the people were Catholic. Bourke decided to end the policy of favouring the Church of England and to give funding on the same basis to the Church of England, the Presbyterians and the Catholics—or, broadly, to the churches of the English, the Scots and the Irish.

In the event the Whig government put Irish churches in the 'too hard' basket, but it did approve Bourke's policy for New South Wales. It was amazing that, in a convict colony run by Protestant Britain, Catholics were to be treated the same as Protestants. Religious equality was established in Australia long before it was in Britain.

Bourke's 1836 Church Act was his own idea. No-one in the colony had requested it. Of course, Presbyterians and Catholics welcomed the downgrading of the Church of England; but none of the churches would have proposed giving government money to its rivals: each thought that it alone taught the truth. This is an example of a wise ruler being able to settle community conflict better than the community itself.

The argument over the colony's future constitution became very bitter in Bourke's time. The free settlers were furious with the governor for supporting the ex-convicts. If ex-convicts could sit on juries, what could be said against giving them the vote? The free settlers ran a campaign in Britain to have Bourke recalled and against the granting of an assembly. If an assembly was granted, they said, ex-convicts should not vote for it. The ex-convicts and their liberal supporters, sensing they were close to victory, set up the Australian Patriotic Association, which paid for an agent to advocate their cause in Britain. The association was not a democratic body. To join cost one pound; to elect members to its committee you had to give at least five pounds, a very high amount. In the assembly that Wentworth was proposing there was to be a property test for the vote.

The Whig government was no keener to grant an assembly than its predecessor. It was faced with conflicting demands from the colony and it did not seem sensible to give self-government to a bitterly divided community. Ministers looked at the issue many times but always postponed it.

This government took two very important decisions about the colony's social make-up. In 1831 it started a scheme to send free workers to the colony. The funds for their fares were to be raised by selling land in the colony rather than giving it away. The

Richard Bourke, first liberal Governor

provision of this new labour force enabled the government to take the second decision in 1839, to stop transportation to New South Wales. Neither of these policies had been requested from the colony. The government introduced them because it thought a society relying on convict labour could never be healthy. It had also accepted the new thinking that transportation was not the way to deter crime and reform criminals.

In 1834 the Whig government had abolished slavery throughout the British empire. The anti-slavery campaigners then turned their attention to the oppression and cruelty suffered by indigenous peoples in British colonies. The British government for the first time put pressure on the governor of New South Wales to protect the Aborigines from the settlers.

This task fell to George Gipps (1838–46). It was an almost impossible task. The sheep and cattle men were advancing rapidly into new territory. They were not buying their land; they were just squatting on it—hence their name, squatters. The Aborigines fought against the men who had invaded their lands, but the invaders were determined not to let Aborigines stand in their way.

TWO VIEWS OF THE ABORIGINES

Governor George Gipps, 1839

As human beings partaking of our common nature—as the original possessors of the soil from which the wealth of this country has been principally derived—and as subjects of the Queen, whose authority extends over every part of Australia—the Natives of this colony have an equal right with the people of European origin to the protection and assurance of the law of England.

A large sheep owner, 1826

One of the largest holders of sheep in the colony maintained at a public meeting at Bathurst, that the best thing that could be done, would be to shoot all the Blacks and manure the ground with their carcases, which was all the good they were fit for! The women and children should especially be shot as the most certain method of getting rid of the race.

Quoted in
R.H.W. Reece,
*Aborigines and
Colonists*
Sydney, 1974,
pp. 176, 111

Killings went on that no-one heard about. The Aborigines were still not allowed to give evidence in court.

On the northwest frontier in 1838, a group of stockmen, convicts and ex-convicts, went on the hunt for Aborigines. At Myall Creek station they killed at least 28 Aborigines—men, women and children. They had been camped and working on the station; they had not been spearing cattle. When the overseer returned he found the pile of bodies. He alerted the authorities, and with his evidence the men were brought to trial. The jury—an ordinary jury of 12 men—found them not guilty. But Governor Gipps was determined to punish them. He put them on trial again and this time the jury did convict. The governor then had to withstand a strong campaign that these white men should not hang for killing blacks. Gipps would not give way and seven men were executed. Their deaths did not change things on the frontier. Aborigines were still killed, and the killers were not brought to trial. Britain's new concern for Aborigines could have little impact when so many people thought that killing Aborigines was no crime. And Britain itself wanted the colony's wool, and wool could be produced only if Aboriginal lands were taken.

In 1840 transportation to New South Wales ceased. The free settlers were now less concerned about an elected assembly, even if ex-convicts were allowed to vote for it. They already slightly outnumbered convicts and ex-convicts. The numbers of convicts and ex-convicts would now fall and those of free migrants and the Australian-born would rise. James Macarthur, son of John, decided he should now work with Wentworth; as rich men they had a lot in common. So in 1842, without objection from the free settlers, the British government set up a new, partly elected Legislative Council. One-third of its members were to be appointed and two-thirds would be elected. Ex-convicts could be members and vote for it so long as they met the property qualifications.

This divided society had faced two dangers. The free settlers might take control and deprive ex-convicts of political rights. Or the ex-convicts might get control and provoke a furious backlash from the free settlers. By giving power to neither group the British government had done well. It had not always seen the issue so clearly; sometimes it thought it should give more local control, but then it dithered and delayed and the governor was left in charge. Then it had acted to end transportation and the problem went away. It was able to make political rights the same for free settlers

S.T. Gill born England 1818—died Australia 1880
The avengers c 1871
Watercolour 38.7 x 64.1

S.T. Gill The Avengers

and ex-convicts, which was what their legal rights had been from the beginning.

The demand for self-government

Though they now had a partly elected Legislative Council, the colonists of New South Wales did not rule themselves. This council could pass laws, but they could be vetoed by the governor or the Colonial Office. Nor could it pass laws on all subjects: control over land, which was a crucial issue in a new country, was kept by Britain.

The government of the colony consisted of the governor and his officials—the colonial secretary, the treasurer, the attorney-general and so on—who were appointed by the Colonial Office and were always from Britain. They sat in the council as nominees of the governor. The colonists had to pay for their salaries, but they could not alter them. If the council could have controlled the officials' salaries, they could have controlled the officials. That's what Britain did not want; the government was responsible to the Colonial Office, not the colonists.

In 1842 New South Wales covered all of eastern Australia, including the territory that is now Victoria and Queensland. Tasmania (which was then called Van Diemen's Land) had been separated from New South Wales in 1825. Convicts were still being sent there; more and more convicts, as they were no longer to be sent to New South Wales. Tasmania continued to be ruled by a governor and a nominated council.

The same system of government operated in the two colonies that had been established without convicts, Western Australia and South Australia. There were only a few thousand colonists in Western Australia which was founded in 1829. The settlement had stagnated and almost collapsed. The soil around Perth was poor and the colonists had difficulty finding anything to grow and sell. South Australia, founded in 1836, was doing better. The soil around Adelaide was good for wheat growing, and copper had been discovered not far inland.

South Australia was unique among Australian colonies in that its founders had designed their colony as a model society, not just a place to dump convicts or make money. They adopted the plan of selling land rather than giving it away, so that settlement would remain concentrated and orderly. They would not need convicts because the funds from the land sales would pay the fares of respectable young married couples to form the workforce. All churches were to be equal, which was to be achieved by giving no government money to any of them. And they would govern themselves. The British government promised they could do this when the population reached 50 000. But long before that figure was reached, the colonists were asking Britain to be allowed to elect members to the Governor's Council.

During the 1840s demands for more local control of local affairs came from South Australia, Tasmania and New South Wales. The chief battle occurred in New South Wales. Wentworth was the leader of the elected members of the council, still pursuing his ambition to give his birthplace its full measure of British freedom, though becoming more conservative in his views. He had a wonderful arena in which to work. The governor had to call the Legislative Council if he wanted laws passed and expenditure approved, which gave Wentworth the chance to make speeches, register protests, criticise the governor's officials, and hold up proceedings.

In Tasmania and South Australia even nominated councils could be troublesome. The governor nominated men of standing because he wanted his council to be well respected, but these leading colonists were quite ready to defy the governor. In South Australia they walked out of the chamber, leaving the council without a quorum and unable to do business. In Tasmania six councillors resigned and left Governor Wilmot unable to pass his budget until he had appointed new men, whom he had a hard time finding. The 'patriotic six' were heroes.

The issues that divided the colonists from the governors and the British government were various. In South Australia Governor Robe upset many colonists by introducing Governor Bourke's policy of giving money on the same terms to all churches. They wanted no government grants and a separation between Church and State. In Tasmania the colonists came to hate the convict system. The colony was flooded with convicts, many more than it could absorb. They were now worked in government gangs rather than being assigned to the settlers—and yet the settlers were taxed to cover the great cost of the police and gaols necessary to run the system. And they did not have votes for the council that passed the tax.

The Statue of Wentworth in the University of Sydney which he founded

WILLIAM CHARLES WENTWORTH

In New South Wales the squatters came close to rebellion when Governor Gipps tried to make them pay more rent for their land. This too was taxation without representation. It was tyranny! The squatters, though they were wealthy and held great tracts of land, got lots of support from the rest of the community.

The desire to control land policy was the chief force behind the demand for full self-government in New South Wales. The big landholders and squatters were the largest group among the elected members of the Legislative Council. They managed to make Gipps back off from his proposals and to persuade the British government to give them some security over their lands. They would have liked to be declared the owners of the lands they had taken. The British government would never agree to that; instead it allowed them to have long leases on their land. Once they had acquired them in 1847, they were not so passionate about self-government. Wentworth of course did not give up his campaign.

The British government was, in principle, in favour of allowing colonists to govern themselves. It would happen when their numbers were greater, when their communities were more settled, when their convict past was further behind them, when they were more mature. The colonists, on the other hand, wanted their British rights now.

From 1846 the minister for colonies was the 4th Earl Grey. He took the job very seriously. As a young minister in the Whig government of the 1830s he had been closely involved in the decisions to send free workers to New South Wales and stop transporting convicts. He would certainly not agree to self-government until he thought the time was ripe. The fact that the colonists were asking for it was no evidence that they were ready for it. He was particularly suspicious about the demand to hand over land policy to the colonists. He saw no reason why the first-comers should take control of the land; the land had to be managed as a resource for the whole empire and access to it left open for generations of new migrants. It was Grey who had reluctantly agreed to give the squatters their leases, but he had insisted that the Aborigines keep the right to hunt over their lands.

In 1850 Grey allowed South Australia and Tasmania to have partly elected councils, like the one in New South Wales. Victoria was to be separated from New South Wales and have a council of the same sort. But Grey did not give in to the demand for full self-government. All the new bodies were to operate under the same limitations as the New South Wales council. At the first elections in South Australia, 'no State aid' to churches swept the field. In Tasmania the winning cry was 'no more convicts'.

Grey made the no-convict cry into a national cause by attempting to reintroduce convicts to the mainland. Grey said these convicts were not real convicts: they had spent some time in the new prisons and hence were reformed! He called them exiles. The squatters were prepared to take them, as they had difficulty getting labour in the bush. Nearly everyone else was opposed to the scheme. An anti-transportation campaign emerged, led by merchants and professional people in the towns with strong support from working people.

The Tasmanians now had allies. They organised a national campaign by sending delegates to conferences in Melbourne and Sydney. The movement adopted an Australian flag and issued solemn protests and appeals to the British people to save them from the crime and shame that Grey was heaping on them. They took oaths not to employ convicts and to give their support and money to any who suffered in the cause.

They were imitating the American colonists in their fight with Britain 80 years before, but the Australian colonists did not want to be rebels. They were confident that Britain would eventually listen to their cry. At their great meeting in Mort's warehouse in Sydney, the republican John Dunmore Lang wanted to add to their declaration that if all else failed they would take up arms, appealing 'to God and the world as to whether we shall not have right and justice on our side'. This was the crisis moment for the movement. The support of wealthy, respectable people would disappear if this was added. Lang agreed to withdraw his suggestion.

The flag of the Australasian anti-transportation league (their activities extended to New Zealand)

PROTEST AGAINST TRANSPORTATION

Resolutions adopted at meeting of 4000 people at Circular Quay, Sydney, when the 'Hashemy' arrived with exiles

We, the free and loyal subjects of Her Most Gracious Majesty, inhabitants of the city of Sydney and its immediate neighbourhood, in public meeting assembled, do hereby enter our most deliberate and solemn Protest against the transportation of British criminals to New South Wales.

FIRSTLY.—Because it is in violation of the will of the majority of the colonists, as is clearly evidenced by their expressed opinions on this question at all times.

SECONDLY.—Because numbers among us have emigrated on the faith of the British Government, that transportation to this colony had ceased for ever.

THIRDLY.—Because it is incompatible with our existence as a free colony, desiring self government, to be made the receptacle of another country's felons.

FOURTHLY.—Because it is in the highest degree unjust, to sacrifice the great social and political interests of the colony at large to the pecuniary profit of a fraction of its inhabitants.

FIFTHLY.—Because being truly and devotedly attached to the British Crown, we greatly fear that the perpetration of so stupendous an act of injustice by Her Majesty's Government, will go far towards alienating the affections of the people of this colony from the mother country.

For these and many kindred reasons, in the exercise of our duty to our country—for the love we bear our families—in the strength of our loyalty to Great Britain—and from the depth of our reverence for Almighty God—we protest against the landing again of British convicts on these shores.

Sydney Morning Herald, 12 June 1849

Grey was stubborn. The huge protests at Circular Quay in Sydney when a ship of exiles arrived led him to suspend further shipments, but he would not abandon his right to send convicts to New South Wales and Victoria. Convicts were still flowing to Tasmania. Not even Grey dared to send exiles to South Australia, though it did join the national movement against him.

Susan Fereday *Launceston VDL Aug 10 1853*
Cessation of Transportation Celebrations 1853
Watercolour and ink 20.3 x 28.7 cm

Celebrating the end of transportation, Launceston 1853

Then in the winter of 1851 gold was discovered in New South Wales and Victoria. Everyone could see that it would be stupid to transport convicts to goldfields—except Grey. His policy was abandoned only because in 1852 his government lost office. The new minister of the colonies did not know much about Australia, but he knew how to get a quiet life. He announced that transportation of all sorts would cease and that the Australian colonies (except Western Australia) could be fully self-governing. Western Australia was so poor that it had requested convicts to be sent there.

The rights and liberties that the colonists had sought were British, and they got the right to govern themselves without breaking from Britain. They were a new society, but they had not had to think in new ways about politics. As they moved to take control of their own affairs, they would depart from British practice.

Votes for men, 1850–1880

In the 1850s the colonists had to decide how they would distribute political rights among themselves. In 1852 Britain gave them permission to draw up their own constitutions to provide for self-government. Nearly all the colonists wanted their constitution to be a British constitution. Under the British constitution (which was a set of practices, not a single document) legal rights among men were equal, but political rights were very unequal. Most colonists wanted political rights to be wider than in Britain, but if rights were extended too far would their constitutions cease to be British?

The British constitution

The rulers of Britain thought that equal legal rights depended on political rights being unequal. Legal rights and freedoms could operate only in a stable society, and in their eyes the secret of Britain's stability was that it gave different groups in society different political roles.

From one family came the monarch. In the 1850s this was the much-loved Queen Victoria, happy with her husband and producing many children. She mostly ruled according to the advice of her ministers, but she still had some say in who they were, and they could not take the Queen for granted.

The royal family was the first among the noble families of the aristocracy, the great landowners of the country. The heads of these families, the lords, earls and dukes, had the right to sit in one house of parliament, the House of Lords. With them sat the bishops and the two archbishops of the Church of England.

The second house of parliament was the House of Commons. Its members were commoners: that is, they were not noble, but they were not common and ordinary. Most of the members were landowners closely connected to the aristocracy. To vote for them you needed to own a certain amount of property or to be paying a certain amount of rent. Since the great Reform Bill of 1832, middle-class men had the vote. Nearly all working-class men did not.

The standard explanation of how this arrangement produced a stable society was that government was composed of three elements—monarch, lords and commons—with none having full power; they checked and balanced each other. There was a popular element in the constitution—the election of members of the Commons—but if the Commons became too popular the balance would be upset. If working men, who were the great majority, controlled the Commons, they would sweep lords and monarch away, rob the rich of their property and plunge the country into chaos.

If that political model and that thinking was all that Britain had to offer, Australians would have had very few options in planning their own future—unless they struck out on their own. But in Britain itself there was a massive protest at the British constitution.

In the 1830s and 40s huge numbers of working people challenged their exclusion from political power. The middle class had got the vote in 1832 only because of monster demonstrations in favour of reform. Most of the demonstrators were working people, but when parliament agreed to reform itself they were still excluded. They felt betrayed and rallied behind their own program for reform, which they called the people's charter. The supporters of the charter were called Chartists.

The charter was a very radical document. It had six points:

- manhood suffrage (votes for all men);
- secret ballot (voting to take place in secret);
- equal electoral districts (the same number of voters in each electorate);
- payment of members of parliament (so poor men could be elected);

- no property qualification for members (anyone to stand for parliament);
- annual parliaments (an election every year).

The Chartists planned to win these changes by presenting to parliament petitions signed by millions. They were determined to remain a peaceful and lawful movement. Three times they presented their petition and each time the parliament ignored them. It did not even discuss their demands. The aristocracy and the middle class were united in thinking that they were a revolutionary threat. The constitution gave rights according to property and birth; the Chartists wanted to give the same rights to all. There could be no concessions.

What could the Chartists do? They discussed going on strike until their demands were met, starting a financial crisis by withdrawing their savings from the banks, spending their money only at shops that would support them—and armed rebellion. The supporters of rebellion said moral force would never work; only physical force would make parliament take them seriously. Some 'physical force' men attempted armed uprisings, which were all easily put down. The rebels were caught and tried and sent to Australia as convicts.

The movement involved hundreds of thousands of people. All working people would have come under its influence even if they were opposed to it. For the first time ordinary people were organising peacefully to stake their claim to be citizens. They refused to be 'the poor' who were to be ruled by their betters.

This movement in Britain is an important part of the history of Australia. The working people who came to Australia as migrants in the 1830s, 40s and 50s had been educated in democracy. This did not mean that the new country would automatically become democratic. The Chartists got their support in Britain because in hard times the workers in the new factories and workshops were close to starvation. In Australia, even in hard times, workers lived much better and had less need to worry about politics. The men who came to dig for gold in the 1850s were much more interested in a new rush than in a new political movement. And in Australia the squatters, landowners and businessmen did not want to see power pass to the people, though they were less frightened of them than the property owners of Britain. In Australia there were not millions of people living in desperate poverty.

Chartism was an encouragement to democracy in Australia—

An Adelaide Democrat Opposed to Democracy

Fifty working men met in an Adelaide hotel in November 1855 to form an association to watch over the debates on the new constitution.

Mr Morris proposed:
That the meeting now proceed to form the Association and the following be suggested as the leading principles thereof:
• Manhood suffrage (for both houses).
• Vote by ballot.
• House of Assembly to be elected every three years.
• Electoral districts based on population.
• The upper house to be elected by the whole colony; members to serve for six years, half to retire every three years.
Let us stand by the men of our choice whom we have sent to the Council. If they kept closely to their principles and were backed by popular opinion, we will certainly obtain all we wish for. All the great liberal measures which have been passed in England were carried by the popular voice.

This association is not a Chartist, Radical, or Democratic one, or one to be called by any of those ugly names, but an association which must watch over the formation of a Constitution which will secure prosperity and civil and religious liberty to us and our children.

Register
8 November
1855

and also a great handicap. Just as they were in Britain, Chartism and democracy were dirty words in Australia. Those who wanted to advocate democratic changes had to say they were not democrats or Chartists, otherwise they would be branded as un-British and disloyal to the mother country.

Democracy's odd supporters

In 1850 Australia did not look like a country that would rapidly become democratic. In eastern Australia nearly all the good land was held in large estates or squatting leases. Their owners were in charge of the country's chief industry—wool making—and looked

Re-creating England in New South Wales: the landed estate of Thomas Mitchell, surveyor-general and explorer

set to become a landed ruling class, like the one in England. In the New South Wales Legislative Council, which had been partly elected since 1842, owners of large estates and squatters predominated. Their leader was William Wentworth, who had been struggling for self-government for 30 years. In his youth he was a radical, but now he was increasingly conservative.

The first Australian organisation of democrats was formed in Sydney in 1848, the year of the last great Chartist demonstration in Britain and a year of revolutions in Europe. The Sydney democrats were inspired by these movements, but their own organisation was orderly, timid and small. Its activists could fit comfortably in the back room of Henry Parkes's toyshop, which was their regular meeting place.

Parkes had come to Australia as an assisted migrant and had struggled to find his feet. At first he had taken common labouring work. Now he was practising his trade; on his lathe he carved toys out of bone to go on sale in his shop. Before he left England he had joined in the great demonstrations in Birmingham to persuade parliament to pass the Reform Bill of 1832.

Most of the activists were migrants who had been involved in reform and Chartist movements in Britain. Their followers, too, were chiefly migrants. The young men born in Australia were not very interested in politics. They were keen about sport and drinking. They had no direct experience of working people being hungry and rich and powerful men ignoring their cries for reform.

The democratic activists took their democratic principles seriously, which meant they were in principle republicans. Democracy and republicanism were then closely connected. If you believed that political rights should be equally shared you could not agree that one person should be monarch by right of birth. But of course the democrats could not be too open about their republicanism because most colonists were very loyal to the Queen.

There was one bold republican in the colony—a Presbyterian minister, the Reverend John Dunmore Lang. In 1850 he called for the complete freedom and independence of Australia. Henry Parkes told Lang he would gladly serve in such a noble cause. But the movement soon petered out. Once Britain gave the right to self-government, republicanism had no point for most people.

The democrats' own organisation did not last longer than a year. But it was surprisingly influential. It organised a public meeting in Sydney to discuss the franchise. The democrats did not dare to demand that all men should have the vote for fear that they would be denounced as Chartists. The meeting sent off a petition to the British government asking that the property qualification for voting for the Legislative Council be lowered. The lowest qualification then for the vote was the paying of 20 pounds a year in rent. The democrats asked that this be halved to 10 pounds. This was a clever move, because 10 pounds was the existing English rate established by the Reform Bill in 1832. This would not look like a radical request. In fact it was because property values were much higher in the colony. A 10 pound franchise in Sydney would give the vote to most working men who rented a house.

This petition would normally have got nowhere. It happened that it had a very able advocate in London. This was Robert Lowe, a lawyer who had just returned from New South Wales after making his fortune. In the colony he had been active in politics and turned against Wentworth and the squatters. The democrats had helped him to get elected to the Legislative Council, though he made clear

*Rev. John Dunmore Lang,
Presbyterian minister and
republican*

to them that he was not a democrat. Now back in London he took up their petition and found an irresistible argument in its favour. He said that rich ex-convicts had the vote and the decent free working man who had just arrived did not. The qualification had to be lowered to reduce convict influence!

At this time parliament was considering the Bill that gave partly elected Legislative Councils to South Australia, Tasmania and Victoria (which was to be separated from New South Wales). The House of Commons had already passed the Bill, with the existing 20 pound franchise in New South Wales to apply to all Australian elections. When the Bill reached the House of Lords, the franchise was halved to 10 pounds. Lowe's argument had worked. This is the only time the House of Lords has proposed a *widening* of political rights. It had picked Australian democracy out of the gutter.

Wentworth and his conservative friends were appalled. The Sydney democrats were astonished and delighted. Parkes was now running his own newspaper, the *Empire*. In it he crowed that Wentworth could not denounce the House of Lords as Chartists and democrats.

39

Wentworth still had a weapon up his sleeve. The electorates would have to be reorganised now that Victoria had been separated from New South Wales. The council gave very few seats to Sydney and other towns, where opposition to the squatters was strongest; most of the seats went to the country, which got much more representation than it was entitled to on a population basis.

Then elections were held. Wentworth ran for his old seat of Sydney, where once he had been a popular hero. Now he was known as the supporter of the squatters and the resumption of transportation. He boldly told the new 10 pound electors that he would never have given them the vote. He only just scraped home. There were three members elected for Sydney, and he came third.

In 1851 there were Legislative Council elections in New South Wales, Victoria, Tasmania and South Australia. In all the colonies property values (and hence rents) were higher than in Britain, so many more people were eligible to vote. In New South Wales the democrats had requested a wider franchise. The other colonies received it without any agitation at all. Though the franchise was widened, ordinary people could not consider running for election. There was no payment for members of the council. The councillors were chiefly pastoralists and large landowners, with some business and professional men.

In the next few years the voting qualifications in Australia were transformed without human intervention. With the goldrushes, the price of everything skyrocketed—including property and house rents. This was most marked in Victoria and New South Wales where gold was found, but South Australia shared in the boom. Only in Tasmania did property values stay the same; in fact, they began to fall as the colony became an economic backwater. As prices rose, more and more people qualified for the vote. In Sydney, Melbourne and Adelaide the occupant of the cheapest house became eligible to vote. The House of Lords had set a low qualification and inflation had made it worthless. What odd supporters democracy in Australia had!

Now that the electorate was widening rapidly, some conservatives began to see advantages in widening it still further. The conservatives could hope to find supporters among people who did not own property or pay rent—the servants in their homes and clubs, the men who ran their sheep and cattle stations, the young clerks who worked in their offices and lived in lodgings. To include these in the electorate the test would have to be the amount of salary earned

THE WIDENING OF THE ELECTORATE IN NEW SOUTH WALES

Percentage of adult males possessing the vote

	1850	1851	1856
Sydney	34	48	95
Other towns	26	33	68
Counties	16	25	47
Total settled areas	21	33	63
Squatting districts	—	12	23
Total colony	—	**28**	**55**

Note: The changes between 1850 and 1851 were the result of the lowering of the qualifications by the House of Lords. Between 1851 and 1856 (the first election under responsible government) the changes were the result of inflation and the additions Wentworth made in 1853. Of these inflation was the more important overall.

J. Hirst, *The Strange Birth of Colonial Democracy*, Sydney, 1988, p. 100

or the amount spent on board and lodging. Conservatives hated the thought of manhood suffrage, but they helped to push closer to it. It was a desperate ploy: they were halting democracy by giving more people the vote.

Making constitutions

In 1852 the British government indicated that the Legislative Councils could draw up constitutions under which the colonies would be self-governing. The constitutions were to be British, so there had to be two houses of parliament. To match the House of Commons there would be a Legislative Assembly; to match the House of Lords, a Legislative Council (the same name as the old partly elected house that was being replaced).

The government would no longer be the governor and his officials. There would be ministers and a premier, who would be members of parliament. Ministers would have to have the support of a majority in the Assembly. This is the system of responsible government—ministers would be responsible to parliament.

41

New South Wales

In New South Wales Wentworth took the lead in framing the new constitution. Since he did not want 'to sow the seeds of a future democracy', he insisted that the British model would have to be closely followed.

Wentworth thought the electorate was already too democratic; he attempted to make it more conservative by adding to it boarders who paid 10 pounds a year and those who earned salaries of 100 pounds a year. These would be the voters for the Assembly. Most electorates for the Assembly were to be in the country; Sydney and other towns were to have very few. This arrangement was made especially hard to change: electorates could be altered only if two-thirds of the Assembly agreed.

There were to be no elections for the Legislative Council. Like the House of Lords, it would be made up of men from a superior social order. Wentworth claimed that New South Wales had such a group in the great landowners and squatters. At first, councillors were to be nominated by the governor for life, but gradually the pastoral families were to be made into an aristocracy by the monarch. Then there would be lords in New South Wales and a true House of Lords. Wentworth realised that there would be opposition to this scheme, so it could be altered only by a two-thirds vote in both houses.

How to create upper houses had been a long-standing problem in British colonies. Everyone agreed that colonial constitutions should imitate the British, but in colonies there was no aristocracy to make a House of Lords. There had been talk of creating an aristocracy in Canada, so Wentworth wasn't the first with this idea. In Canada and other colonies with self-government the councils were made up of men nominated for life by the governor. These had not worked well. Councillors looked like favourites; they did not have the standing of British lords, who came from old and noble families and were not chosen by anyone.

Despite the difficulties with nominated councils, the British government refused to allow them to be elected. That would increase the popular element and destroy the balance that a British constitution required. But around 1850 British opinion began to shift. Trying to copy when you couldn't copy properly was perhaps silly. Let the colonial constitutions fit colonial circumstances. Sir John Pakington, the minister for colonies who gave permission for

Australian self-government in 1852, said Councils had to be nominated. But shortly afterwards he was replaced and the next minister, the Duke of Newcastle, was happy for Councils to be nominated or elected. So from the old world came the word that the new world could be different.

Wentworth's constitution had plenty of support in the Legislative Council; outside, it ran into fierce opposition. This movement was led by business and professional men who were liberals, not democrats. They objected to Wentworth setting up the squatters as a ruling class and giving so little representation to Sydney and other towns. The democrats joined in this protest and organised the meetings and rallies. They had more thoroughgoing criticisms but they had to keep them quiet.

It was a democrat, Daniel Deniehy, who made the best attack on the scheme for local lords. What would they put on their coats of arms, he wanted to know. For the Macarthurs it would have to be a keg of rum! He made fun of lords in Australia by calling them a 'bunyip aristocracy'. Very soon Wentworth dropped the plan for an aristocracy, but he would not agree to an elected upper house. The councillors would be nominated by the governor.

Most migrants hated nomineeism, as they called it. What they wanted to escape was a society where 'getting on' depended on your birth or your relatives or who you knew or being known at

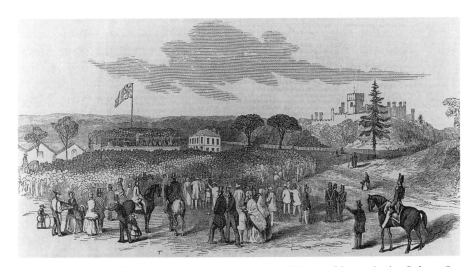

The great public meeting protesting at Wentworth's constitution Sydney 1853

court. They did not want a society of equals, but every man should have a chance to get on without favouritism. The liberals did not want a democratic upper house; it could be made up of substantial men of property elected on a narrower franchise than the Assembly.

Wentworth denounced his critics as democrats, Chartists and republicans. They had an easy answer to this: the British minister for colonies was happy with an elected upper house, so who was Wentworth to say that an elected upper house was un-British? The liberals proclaimed that they were better Britons than Wentworth and just as loyal. Their upper house would be a more independent body and more like the House of Lords than a group of nominees.

It was unfortunate for Wentworth that the Chartist bogey no longer worked so well. In the 1850s British Chartism did a great service to democracy in Australia by disappearing. The last great rally took place in London in 1848. The 'hungry' 1840s were over, the 1850s were prosperous. Chartism was dead.

As soon as that threat was past, middle-class reformers in Britain began to support further political change: more people should get the vote, but not everyone; more electorates should be given to the towns, though not exactly in proportion to their population; perhaps the secret ballot could be tried. Leading liberal politicians in parliament gave their support. The government actually introduced a new Reform Bill to parliament, though it did not get very far.

That did not matter. Britain was no longer constitutionally frozen. The liberals in New South Wales attacked Wentworth's scheme of Assembly electorates by pointing out that Britain was considering giving more representation to the towns. They felt that Britain was heading in the direction they wanted to take; Wentworth was boasting of being British, but his Britain was disappearing.

Parkes made sure that the *Empire* gave large coverage to the new reform movement in Britain. His brief flirtation with republicanism was over. He used this new movement to show Lang that republicanism was not necessary for New South Wales. Britain was itself widening the definition of liberalism, so democratic reformers in the colonies could get most of what they wanted under a 'British liberal' label. Then they would not have to frighten the colonists with talk of democracy and republicanism.

Wentworth knew that the trend of opinion was against him.

A LOYAL OPPOSITION TO WENTWORTH'S CONSTITUTION

The new constitution—Great open air meeting

This was the most orderly and determined, if not the most numerous, body of colonists ever assembled for a political purpose.

The object of the meeting was to enter a public protest in the face of the whole civilised world against the obnoxious clauses of the new Constitution Bill. The principal features of the measure at which this opposition was raised were: the proposal to confer hereditary colonial titles and to distribute the seats in the Legislative Assembly principally among the squatting and thinly inhabited districts of the country.

A large platform was erected on the site selected and the British flag waved over the speakers.

At about half-past one o'clock Mr J.B. Darvall MLC came forward and said: You are met together, not to resist the law, or for any unlawful purpose whatever; nor do you entertain disloyalty in your hearts, whatever may have been said of you in another place. [Loud cheers.] You are assembled together under a national flag of which you are all justly proud. Three cheers, then, for the British flag. [The whole of the audience then united in three enthusiastic cheers for the British flag.] Gentlemen, you are met today for the purpose of petitioning her Majesty the Queen. Three cheers, then, for your beloved Queen. [Three loyal and enthusiastic cheers were then given.] Gentlemen, there is one thing more. You are met to protect your glorious Constitution, to insist upon it that the law under which you and your children will live, shall be conformable with that form of government so long and so happily enjoyed in your fatherland. [Loud cheers.] For that glorious constitution, one cheer more. [Three prolonged cheers were then given for the British Constitution.]

Mr John Gilchrist J.P. said: The opinions of the colonists have been treated with contempt, and the cry of democracy and republicanism raised against them. In the face of which I assert that a more loyal and more patriotic people does not exist in any part of her Majesty's dominions. We must now petition the Queen and we have every reason to expect success from the opinions expressed by some of the most influential of Her Majesty's Ministers . . .

Empire,
7 September
1853

Except for the scheme to make colonial lords, his constitution passed through the Legislative Council; it was in London that he feared it might come unstuck. He took himself off to London to defend it. The minister for colonies, Lord John Russell, had received petitions from the liberals and democrats against the constitution. He was reluctant to override the Legislative Council, but he did want to make sure that the colonists could change their constitution readily. He was worried about the provisions that required two-thirds votes to make key changes. He overrode them in a clever way: he inserted a clause allowing any part of the constitution to be changed by ordinary majorities—including the two-thirds provisions.

Wentworth was furious at the British government for making it so easy to remove the safeguards against democracy. When the constitution went home, he did not go with it.

Only in New South Wales was there a social group well-established and confident enough to attempt setting itself up as a colonial aristocracy. There was no Wentworth in the other colonies.

HENRY PARKES ANSWERS DR LANG'S CALL FOR 'FREEEDOM AND INDEPENDENCE'

Dr Lang is quite right in his abstract principle. An essentially popular and democratic government is no doubt the best for any country; but when the habits of a people are once formed, it is a mere waste of energy to attempt to change them. Such a government as he proposes to establish here could only be achieved by a revolution.

It is not probable that a sudden severance of these colonies from the mother country will ever take place; but it is certain that the growth of popular power is silently working out a revolution in the mother country and is exercising at the same time an influence which is being felt at the farthest extremities of the empire, and that the complete realisation of all our views of local self-government will be a natural and inevitable consequence. We think freedom and independence may be achieved without disintegration, and we had rather agitate for possibilities than lose our time in chasing a phantom.

Empire,
1 February
1854

In Victoria, Tasmania and South Australia the new constitutions provided for elected upper houses.

Victoria

Victoria's constitution was drawn up in 1853 when the goldrush was in full swing. No-one took much notice of what the Legislative Councillors were doing. They were rich men who had come before the goldrush. For the Assembly, men earning salaries of 100 pounds a year were added to the electorate of 10-pound a year renters. The Council, designed as a check on the Assembly, was to be elected by substantial property owners. The property had to be worth 1000 pounds or a rental value of 100 pounds per year (10 times the qualification for the Assembly). To be a member of the Council you had to own property worth 5000 pounds—almost as much as a millionaire today.

This Legislative Council was at least not made up of nominees. But it was a more effective check to democracy than Wentworth's Council. As Wentworth himself explained, if the Council kept on rejecting a popular measure, the governor could create new members. The House of Lords had agreed to pass the 1832 Reform Bill only after the government threatened that it would ask the King to swamp it with new members. If the Victorian Legislative Council blocked popular measures, nothing could be done. There was no way of resolving deadlocks between the two houses. When the rushes were over and the diggers became more interested in politics, they were to find the Council always blocking their way.

Diggers did not own landed property or pay rent or receive salaries. But the men responsible for the colony's new wealth were not entirely excluded from the new constitution. Diggers who took out an annual digging licence were to be allowed to vote for the Assembly. Very few diggers took out annual licences. Nearly all took the monthly licence and complained that it cost too much.

Protests over the licence reached a crescendo at Ballarat late in 1854, when the constitution was in London waiting approval. The diggers objected not merely to the amount of the licence (which had to be paid whether they found gold or not) but to the way the system was enforced. A corrupt low-class police force was always hounding them to show their licences. The diggers wanted

THE RESOLUTIONS OF THE DIGGERS AT BAKERY HILL, BALLARAT, NOVEMBER 1854

As reported by Governor Hotham to the Colonial Office

At a meeting held on Bakery Hill, in the presence of about 10,000 men, on Saturday, November 11, 1854, the following were adopted as the principles and objects of the Ballarat Reform League:—

- That it is the inalienable right of every citizen to have a voice in making the laws he is called on to obey. That taxation without representation is tyranny.
- It is the object of the league to place power in the hands of responsible representatives of the people to frame wholesome laws and carry on an honest Government.
- That it is not the wish of the league to effect an immediate separation of this colony from the parent country, if equal laws and equal rights are dealt out to the whole free community; but that, if Queen Victoria continues to act upon the ill advice of dishonest ministers, and insists upon indirectly dictating obnoxious laws for the colony, under the assumed authority of the Royal prerogative, the Reform League will endeavour to supersede such Royal prerogative by asserting that of the people, which is the most royal of all prerogatives, as the people are the only legitimate source of all political power.

Political changes contemplated by the Reform League:—

1. A full and fair representation.
2. Manhood suffrage.
3. No property qualification of members of the Legislative Council.
4. Payment of members.
5. Short duration of parliament.

Immediate objects of the Reform League:—

- An immediate change in the management of the gold fields, by disbanding the Commissioners.
- The total abolition of the diggers' and storekeepers' licence tax.

'Further Papers Relative to the Discovery of Gold in Australia' *British Parliamentary Papers*, 1854–5, Vol. 38, pp. 70–1

the licence fee and the licence system removed, but as their protest grew its aims widened. The Ballarat Reform League adopted almost all the Chartist points. Its secretary was John Humffray, who had been a Chartist in Wales.

The debate about methods which had divided the Chartists in

Britain was repeated at Ballarat. A minority of the diggers, including many of the Irish, wanted to take up arms. A physical force Chartist proclaimed:

Moral persuasion is all a humbug.
Nothing convinces like a lick in the lug.

Humffray was a moral force man and to the last, even as the rebels were being sworn in by their leader Peter Lalor, he argued against violence. He was speaking from a tree stump when four diggers pointed their pistols at him and said he must join them. He said, 'Put down your guns, mates. The government is more afraid of you with a newspaper in your hand than a revolver'.

The rebel diggers built a stockade at the Eureka lead. Above it flew their flag of the Southern Cross without a Union Jack. On Sunday morning, 3 December 1854, when the diggers were asleep, the soldiers stormed the stockade. They took only 10 minutes to capture it. Thirty diggers and five soldiers died.

Most of the diggers had not supported the rebellion, but they were angry at the slaughter and at the regime that had led to this trouble. Humffray immediately re-emerged to demand that the

Charles A. Doudiet: *Swearing allegiance to the Southern Cross 1854*
Collection: Ballarat Fine Art Gallery

The rebel diggers at Ballarat take the oath under the flag of the Southern Cross

rebels not be punished and that the goldfields be reformed. Peter Lalor, who had lost an arm in the fighting, was in hiding. Governor Hotham insisted that the rebels who had been caught be tried for treason, but juries in Melbourne acquitted them.

The governor did accept that the goldfields had to be reformed. Only a handful of diggers were now taking out licences. A royal commission recommended that the licence system be dropped and the money needed to run the goldfields be raised by an export duty on gold. The new permission to mine would be a 'miner's right', to cost only 1 pound and to last for a year (the old licence cost 1 pound for a month). All the diggers would now hold annual licences, and so they were all eligible to vote. Again, without the formal qualifications being changed, there was a huge increase in the number of voters. The new system virtually established manhood suffrage because any man willing to spend a pound could become a voter.

Though the new constitution was soon to come into operation, the existing partly elected Legislative Council was enlarged to enable the goldfields to elect eight members. Peter Lalor and John Humffray were elected unopposed for Ballarat. In less than a year the rebel leader had become a Legislative Councillor.

Early in 1856 this expanded Council established the secret ballot as the method of election to be used when the new constitution came into force. All the new goldfields members voted for the ballot. This was the first point of the Charter to be adopted in Australia.

The supporters of the secret ballot in Britain wanted to protect voters from being pressured to vote in a certain way by their employers and landlords or the local lord. This was less of a problem in Australia because people could make a living without having to please their 'betters'. Some conservatives feared that in Australia, with many more people voting, it would be the better-off who would be put under pressure by working men. Their support helped to get the secret ballot accepted.

Australian elections had been like Britain's in that lots of alcohol was consumed and riots often occurred. When voting occurred in public, the state of the voting was known throughout the day. If votes were close, supporters of the rival candidates would rush off to find voters who had not voted, give them plenty of grog, fill out a voting paper for them, and then steer them to the voting table. Meanwhile they would do all they could to stop the other side finding voters and getting them to the polls. So the other argument for the secret ballot was that it would make elections more orderly, as no-one would know what was happening until it was all over. And buying drinks to secure votes would stop because a candidate would scarcely give voters drink unless he could check that they did actually vote for him.

The ballot had been discussed in Britain for decades; now in Australia an actual plan to implement it had to be worked out. It was not easy. With open voting, the voter wrote out on a piece of paper—any piece of paper—the name of the candidate he wanted to vote for and signed his name. To save voters the trouble of doing this, the candidates' supporters would provide papers already written out. This was also a help to those who could not write. The voter took his paper to the returning officer, who read it, checked with the voter that he did want to vote as his paper said, and then recorded his vote against his name on the list of people entitled to vote.

The obvious way of making elections secret was to have the voters drop their papers in a locked box and count them at the end of the day. But then their signatures would be on the papers, and the counters could see for whom they had voted. The breakthrough idea was to have the government print ballot papers with the names of the candidates on them. The voters would strike out the names of those they did not want to vote for. It would be very hard to identify a voter just from crossings out. Those who could not write could work the system, so long as they could read. Those who could not read were allowed to ask the returning officer for help.

But what if candidates produced ballot papers that looked exactly like the government's, or got hold of some of the government's and distributed them to their supporters? To stop this trick, the returning officer put his initials on the back of the ballot paper. The voter had to fold the ballot paper so that the initials were on show as he dropped the ballot into the box. Only ballots with initials were valid.

What if someone pretended to be a voter? When the real voter showed up, there would be no way of knowing which of the ballots in the box was the illegal one. So the returning officer also wrote on the back of the ballot paper the voter's number from the list of voters.

This plan was developed by one of the Legislative Councillors, Henry Chapman, who had worked for political reform in England. Before coming to Victoria he had been Colonial

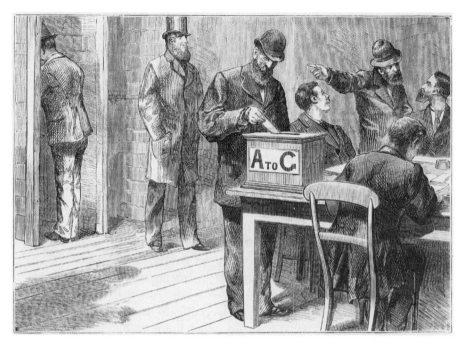

The operation of the secret ballot: an Australian invention

Secretary in the Tasmanian government and lost his job for
opposing transportation. His plan worked well. The other colonies
adopted it soon after Victoria. Britain copied it in 1872.
In America the scheme was called 'the Australian ballot' and was
widely adopted in the late nineteenth century as a way of stopping
political corruption.

Tasmania and South Australia

Like Wentworth, Governor Denison of Tasmania and Governor
Young of South Australia thought a British constitution could not
have an elected upper house.

Governor Denison tried to persuade the Colonial Office in
London and the Legislative Council in Hobart that the new
Legislative Council must be nominated. They both disagreed with
him. The Colonial Office told the governor that an elected upper
house was acceptable and that is what the Legislative Council
created. It was not as exclusive as Victoria's: the voters were to own

property worth 50 pounds a year. For the Assembly salary earners were added to the existing voters, as in New South Wales and Victoria, and another likely conservative group was included—university graduates, doctors, lawyers and military officers.

Governor Young of South Australia kept secret the message from the Duke of Newcastle that in the new constitutions the upper house could be elected or nominated. The Legislative Council reluctantly accepted a constitution with a nominated upper house. Then the secret got out and Councillors and colonists were furious with the governor. They sent off petitions to London asking that the new constitution not be approved.

The minister for colonies, Lord John Russell, accepted the colonists' complaints. He decided not to put the constitution to parliament for approval. He ruled that the colonists were to have the chance to draw up another constitution, but only after elections had been held for the elected members of the Council. The minister wanted to be sure this time that the Council reflected the people's views.

South Australia was the only colony where an election was held on the issue of what sort of constitution the colony should have. There was great interest in the election. Enrolment to vote, like voting itself, was voluntary. Many new people got themselves on the roll. At the first election in 1851 the number of men on the roll amounted to 35 per cent of the colony's adult males. For this election the figure was 74 per cent—a huge increase. This was an indication that the rent and property qualifications now kept very few people off the roll.

'No nominees' carried all before it at the election. The successful candidates were all in favour of an elected upper house and a widening of the franchise, and most were in favour of the secret ballot. The radical George Kingston—a very different figure from the conservative Wentworth—took charge of framing the constitution. Kingston was a fiery Irishman who had arrived with the first settlers as assistant surveyor to Colonel Light. He had become rich as a director of the Burra copper mine, but he was a rich man on the popular side. There had been battle to control the mine. A syndicate of shopkeepers had won out against a syndicate of rich landowners.

Kingston advanced a plan for a thoroughly democractic constitution, though he did not use that word. Nothing like it was put forward in the other Legislative Councils. He wanted manhood suffrage for both houses of parliament. The difference between them would be that the upper house would be elected by the whole colony, and its members would serve for longer terms (nine years) and be over 35 years old.

Most of the members supporting an elected upper house had not wanted one like this. They did not want pure democracy and no protection for property. Kingston was forced to compromise. If he agreed to have property holders elect the upper house, there would be no objection to manhood suffrage for the lower house. The property franchise set for the upper house was the same as Tasmania's—the property was to be worth 50 pounds per year—but, unlike the Victorian and Tasmanian provisions, people renting houses could vote for the South Australian upper house so long as their rent was at least 25 pounds per year.

The South Australian constitution was the most democratic of them all. In this well-ordered society, where small farming was more important than squatting and there were no diggers and ex-convicts, the leaders of society were less worried about popular power than those in Victoria and New South Wales. They were also proud to be shaping a new, model society. In 1851 theirs was the first country in the British Empire to separate Church and State.

Three of the Chartist points were embodied in the South Australian constitution: manhood suffrage, no property qualification for members of the Assembly, and the secret ballot. The plan for the ballot followed Victoria's, except that voters were to put a cross in a box beside the candidate they preferred.

Altering the constitutions

In South Australia and Tasmania the constitutions drawn up in the 1850s remained unaltered for years. There was little to complain about in the South Australian constitution. In Tasmania the rent and property tests for the Assembly excluded most working men from the vote, but they did not complain. Men of any spirit left the island for the mainland. The rent test for the Assembly was lowered from 10 pounds to 7 pounds in 1870, but this did not make the electorate wider. It merely gave the vote back to men who had lost it because of the fall in property values.

In these two colonies the men who had drawn up the constitutions continued to be elected to the new parliaments. The move to the new system of responsible government was made without much disruption. In New South Wales and Victoria things were very different. Liberals with democrats in support took charge of the Assemblies and formed governments. Conservatives found it harder to get elected to the Assemblies. The constitutions were altered in a democratic direction.

These colonial constitutions could be altered by parliament. The provision that a two-thirds vote was required for some alterations in New South Wales was ditched by the first parliament.

Manhood suffrage and the abolition of property qualification for members of the Assembly were carried in Victoria in 1857; these two reforms and the ballot were carried in New South Wales in 1858. Manhood suffrage was now scarcely a radical measure, since so many people already had the vote. In Victoria its introduction was used to make it harder for diggers to vote. With their miner's right they could vote in any electorate where they happened to be. With manhood suffrage a voter had to be resident in an electorate for three months before he was eligible to vote.

Conservatives opposed manhood suffrage, for it signified to them that the colonies were on the road to ruin, even though they were gearing up to defend the provisions that would stop power really passing to the people. Liberals too had their doubts about it. To the disgust of the gold-diggers, Peter Lalor opposed it.

PETER LALOR EXPLAINS HIS OPPOSITION TO MANHOOD SUFFRAGE

It is assumed by my friends that previous to my election I was an ultra-democrat, but now I take an opposite course from selfish motives, and consequently that I am degraded, and unworthy of being trusted.

I would ask these gentlemen what they mean by the term 'democracy'. Do they mean Chartism, or Communism or Republicanism? If so, I never was, I am not now, nor do I ever intend to be a democrat. But if democracy means opposition to a tyrannical press, a tyrannical people, or a tyrannical government, then I have been, I am still, and I ever will remain a democrat.

Quoted in Geoffrey Serle, *The Golden Age*, Melbourne, 1963, p. 260

Because conservatives were opposed to manhood suffrage and liberals had doubts about it, limitations were placed on its operation. It still excluded some men—those whose work took them from place to place. When it was adopted in New South Wales and Victoria, the right to qualify to vote by the holding of property was not removed. This meant that property owners could vote in every electorate where they owned property. This was called plural voting.

In Victoria from 1863 a further limitation was put on manhood suffrage. The official reason for this was to make the voting roll more accurate. Many working men got on the roll and then left the district. On voting day someone else could vote in their name. Candidates were good at spotting these opportunities. The problem could have been fixed by appointing more officials to run the system, but that was expensive. Instead voters who owned no property had to register themselves regularly and pay 1 shilling to obtain an 'elector's right', which they had to show to prove their identity before they could vote. A shilling then would be what you earned for an hour's work—say, $10–15 today. But those who owned property did not have to register or pay. Their names went on the roll automatically from the list of ratepayers kept by local government bodies.

Well before manhood suffrage was adopted, all the players realised that how electorates were distributed was more important than the extension of the franchise. Over this issue there was much more struggle. Liberals and democrats managed to remove the gross favouritism towards the country, but electorates were still not equal. Conservatives did not want that, but country liberals and democrats were also worried about giving too much power to the capital cities.

In no colony was payment of members established. The Victorian Assembly was in favour of it, but the Council rejected it. Without payment, only a limited range of people could be MPs. Conservatives and most liberals were opposed to payment. They thought that members of parliament should be independent men not looking to get paid for public service. Parliamentarians dressed like English gentlemen with frock coats and top hats and so set themselves apart from the men who voted for them.

The limitations on Australian democracy should not be stressed too much. By the standards of the day, the Assemblies were democratic bodies. However, above them with almost equal powers were the Legislative Councils, which were far from being democ-

An elector's right: paying to acquire the vote

ratic. The Council in New South Wales was nominated by the governor; in Victoria it was elected by property holders. Once there were liberal governments in New South Wales they could advise the governor to make new appointments to the Council, but he did not have to follow their advice. Liberal governments in Victoria could do nothing if the Council blocked them.

Even though the constitutions had been amended in a democratic direction, 'democracy' remained a dirty word. Liberals and democrats talked instead of 'widening' the franchise or making it 'more liberal', and of increasing 'popular rights' or the 'democratic element' in the constitution. Liberals were glad to talk this way because it made them look good without committing them to democracy. Democrats talked this way to help their cause, but it put limits on what they could ask for—and perhaps they did not want to ask for more. They did not proclaim that the people were sovereign and demand that a constitution be formed on that basis. Queen Victoria was sovereign over Australia and the people of Australia were British subjects. A British constitution simply could not be thoroughly democratic.

57

DEMOCRACY BY ACCIDENT

Anon,
Democratic
Government in
Victoria,
Melbourne,
1868

It is a misfortune that the people of Victoria acquired all the privileges of democracy without that wholesome struggle for democratic
principles which is needed to make any popular government sound
or secure. To have arrived at manhood suffrage without having
achieved it was a bad introduction to the practical art of self-ruling.
The democratic form of government came in fact to Victoria less by
choice than by accident.

If there had been a long stuggle to establish manhood suffrage,
democratic principles might have been proclaimed, but, as we have
seen, so much of the extension of the franchise happened without
any effort by the colonists. The British Chartists organised and got
nowhere; with virtually no organisation the Australian democrats
reached the Chartist goals.

If Britain had stood against political change, Australians would
have been forced to think in new ways. But Britain had taken up again
the process of reforming itself, and every decision of the British
government about Australian affairs in the 1850s helped liberals
and democrats. Conservatives who wanted an aristocratic element
in Australian constitutions were undermined by two progressive
British aristocrats, the Duke of Newcastle and Lord John Russell.

From 1859 there was a new colony in Australia. Queensland was
separated from New South Wales. The British government ruled
that it should adopt the New South Wales constitution as it then
was. This meant that, without the people of Queensland being
consulted, the new colony would acquire manhood suffrage and
the secret ballot—and a Legislative Council nominated by the
governor. However, the chief justice of New South Wales, a conservative, ruled that the voting qualifications had to be those in the
original constitution, not in the constitution as it had been
amended. This was not what the British government had intended.
So the Queensland Assembly was elected on broad property and
rent qualifications until 1872, when manhood suffrage was
introduced.

Struggle and shame

The liberals and democrats in New South Wales and Victoria did not change their constitutions for the principle of the thing. They had the squatters in their sights. They wanted to increase popular power so that they could rewrite the land laws to allow ordinary people to have access to the land.

There was much more interest in the land question than in manhood suffrage and equal electorates. Elections were fought over it. Ministers and ministries were destroyed when they failed to solve it. In Victoria a sort of alternative parliament met down the hill from the real one to discuss it. This was the Land Convention, which was modelled on the great meetings of the Chartists in Britain. Delegates were sent to the Convention from every large town and goldfield. They were elected at public meetings which gave them their instructions. The Convention was to draw up a land policy that it hoped the parliament would adopt. The people were now organised to demand change.

In the late 1850s the demand for land reform became more and more radical. The radical reformers treated the great pastoral industry as if it had no right to exist. The squatters had pinched the people's land and they should be sent packing. The people should be allowed to enter their holdings without notice and select a farm. This was the policy of selection before survey. Anyone who stood against a radical land law had trouble getting elected to the Assemblies. Conservatives were the first to disappear, and then some of the liberals. Business and professional men wanted the land to be more closely settled and developed, but they were unhappy at a savage attack on an industry that was important to the prosperity of their communities.

New, more radical parliamentarians were elected, often quite poor men, not well educated, who got elected by shouting 'The land belongs to the people' and 'Selection before survey'. Somehow they scrounged a living for they were not paid for their parliamentary services.

In Victoria the squatters assembled a fund to protect themselves. It was used to pay the campaign expenses of any candidate who would support them. Very few of those were successful. So then they offered bribes to members who had been elected to go soft on land reform. Some members did take these bribes, among them radical land reformers, who needed the money most. Almost

59

certainly John Humffray of Ballarat accepted money. He told his
electors he had voted to give the squatters some protection in order
to get the squatters to agree to some measure of land reform. At the
next election he lost his seat.

In Victoria free selection before survey was not passed. Even if
the Assembly had agreed to it, the Legislative Council would have
rejected it. The Council watered down land reform proposals and
ensured there were plenty of loopholes in the law for the squatters.
So, under the new Victorian land law of 1860, land was resumed
from some of the squatters; it was surveyed; and then put on offer
to the selectors (as the new farmers were called).

In New South Wales free selection before survey was passed in
1861. The Legislative Council at first rejected it, but then the liberal
government showed that it was ready to swamp the nominated
Council with new members who would vote for the Land Bill. The
Council then gave way.

With the passing of the new land laws, the conservatives and
the squatters thought that democracy had brought disaster, as
they had always predicted. The poor had been given power and
they were going to destroy an industry from which they benefited.
The reformers said that farms would soon cover the squatters'
land, but the squatters knew that much of the land was not
suitable for farming. The squatters decided that, since the
politicians had gone mad, they would not obey the land laws that
they passed.

The laws gave any man who could pay the deposit the right to
select land. The squatters hired people to select land on their
behalf. These were called 'dummies'. The squatters gave them the
money to select the land and once they had acquired it they handed
it over to the squatter. In New South Wales the selector had to reside
on his land for three years and improve it before he could become
the owner. The squatter had to support his 'dummies' for all that
time. In Victoria, if the selector had the money, he could pay the
full price and become the owner straight away. The squatters
employed scores of dummies and within a week were the owners
of the land that they previously had leased.

Land reform did not establish small farms throughout the
country. This was not just because the squatters were determined
to get around the law. Until the railways arrived in the country, the
small farmer had no way of getting his wheat to market. No matter
what the reason for the failure, it harmed the reputation of the

new parliaments. Their laws had not worked, and they had encouraged fraud and corruption on a massive scale.

The parliaments themselves were now different places. Many of the new democratic representatives did not keep to the gentlemanly rules. They yelled insults at each other and the speaker struggled to keep order. We think of the nineteenth century as the time of strict 'Victorian morality'. It was—except for MPs. Parliamentarians survived deeds that today would wreck a political career. Henry Parkes was three times bankrupt, he kept a mistress and had children by her, and yet was five times premier of New South Wales. George Reiby was a very popular premier of Tasmania. He took office only a few years after a court case had revealed, in lurid detail, that he had attempted to seduce the wife of his best friend. At the time he was an archdeacon of the Church of England. The attorney-general of South Australia, Charles Kingston, son of George, was named in a divorce case for having sex with another man's wife; later as premier he was arrested for attempting to fight a duel.

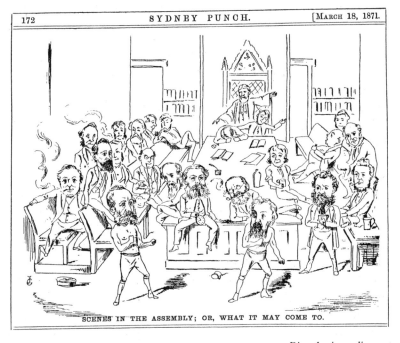

Disorder in parliament

Until the late nineteenth century only men voted. One of the arguments that women used to get the vote was that they would not support immoral MPs.

Constitutional crises

In New South Wales, after the Legislative Council agreed to pass selection before survey, political life became quieter. Only in Victoria did politics remain turbulent. To Victoria in the 1850s went most of the gold-diggers. They were better educated and more adventurous than the average migrant, and once the easy gold ran out they took a great interest in politics. Blocking the way to any radical changes was the Victorian Legislative Council, the most exclusive upper house in the country.

The Council had blocked bills for payment of members and for the separation of Church and State and had forced great changes in bills on land and electorates. By the 1860s the liberals (who were now more democratic) had decided that there could be no progress unless the upper house was reformed. This was hard to do. What pressure could be brought against it? You could not appeal to its electors to support change because they were owners of substantial property.

In 1865 a liberal government adopted a policy that it knew the Council would reject. It decided to raise customs duties to bring in more money, and to protect local factories and farms from outside competition. At this time, as now, the best economic advice was that to impose protective duties hindered economic growth. Industries should survive by being efficient, not by looking for government help. The liberals rejected this advice because they wanted to encourage new industry and to build a diverse economy; they did not want Victoria to be just an exporter of gold and wool.

The Council was made up of squatters and landowners, who grew wool for export, and merchants and bankers, who were involved in exporting and importing goods. Factories and farms were of no interest to them. Protection to them meant that the goods they bought in Victoria would cost more. They wanted to keep the policy of free trade.

The Council could amend any bill sent up by the Assembly except the annual budget. The liberal government of James McCulloch decided to tack their new tariff onto the budget—and then the Council could not interfere with it—unless it rejected the whole budget. That is what the Council did. If Councillors wanted to protect their power, they had to do that; otherwise anything could be tacked onto a budget and they would be forced to pass it. If a budget is not passed, a government has no authority to spend money: the public servants can't be paid; contractors who have done work for the government can't be paid; the whole business of government stops. Victoria was in crisis.

The government developed a shonky scheme to allow it to get money without parliamentary approval. It borrowed money from the one bank that supported the government. McCulloch, the premier, was a director. When the time to pay back the loan arrived, the government did not pay. The bank took the government to court and the court ordered the government to pay—and so funds were released from the treasury by court order instead of by parliamentary vote.

The Councillors and their supporters in the Assembly were outraged at this trick. It so clearly broke a central rule of the constitution. The liberals called their opponents conservatives; they called themselves constitutionalists. The liberals, of course, said their scheme was perfectly legal. They were driven to use it because they were sick of the undemocratic Council standing in their way. For the scheme to work, the documents had to be signed by the governor. Sir Charles Darling signed the papers because his ministers advised him to. During the crisis an election was held and the government and its supporters won easily. There was no doubt these ministers had the support of the people and the Assembly. The Colonial Office took a different view. It sacked the governor for going along with the scheme. That made the governor into a popular hero and led the Assembly to declare that Britain had threatened the colony's right to self-government.

The crisis was resolved by the Assembly withdrawing the tariff from the budget and the Council agreeing to pass both the budget and the tariff as separate measures. The Council had yielded, but all its powers were intact.

Ten years later there was a second crisis over the issue of payment of members. The Council had finally agreed to the payment of members of the Assembly in 1870, but only on a temporary basis. In 1877 a liberal government tacked payment onto the budget to show that this was to be a regular expenditure. The Council blocked the budget as before. The government responded

ELECTORS

OF

WEST BOURKE !

The Contest to be fought out to-day at the Ballot Box does not lie between Mr. Harper and Mr. Deakin, but between Conservatism and Liberalism; the former represents the Merchants, the Importers and the Squatters. The latter represents the Farmers, the Artisans and working men generally, (the bone and sinew, and the intelligence of the land.

Then like brave and true men

Rally Round the Standard

of your own independence, and prevent the power so hardly won from been wrested from your hands, by deep designing men:—Do not be cajoled,

VOTE FOR

Mr. Deakin,

VOTE FOR

Your Homes, Your Families, and Your Adopted Country!!

Printed at the "Chronicle Office," Romsey,

ALFRED DEAKIN;

Is the only LIBERAL and Ministerial Candidate in West Bourke. He is in favor of

The Ministerial Scheme of Constitutional Reform

Which does away with Deadlocks, obtains finality of Legislation, and places the

Supreme Power in the Hands of the People.

He is in favor of an

Equitable Land Tax,

of the existing

Education Act,

But with increased Powers to Boards of Advice; of

Protection to Native Industry,

To benefit the farmers by keeping a Market for them free from foreigners. In favor of the NEW LOAN, which will give a great impetus to all trade and business in the Colony; In favor of the

Great Railway Scheme

Of the present Government, which will connect all the districts with the interior of the Seaboard; and in favor of the

Exhibition Bill

Which will display to Strangers the vast resources of Victoria.

Vote for the People's Candidate
Vote for the Liberal Candidate
Vote for the Ministerial Candidate.

Do you want popular Legislation instead of Class legislation? Do you want Money brought into the Colony. Prosperity for the People, and Railways made to your Markets? Do you want Employment and Education for your children?

THEN VOTE FOR

ALFRED DEAKIN.

Printed at the "Chronicle Office," Romsey.

The election handbills of Alfred Deakin, later prime minister of Australia, who was first elected as a liberal to the Victorian Assembly in 1879, in the midst of the constitutional crisis

by sacking senior public servants, including judges and magistrates (who mostly supported the Council), because there was no money to pay for them. Even when the crisis ended, they never got their jobs back.

This time the liberals pushed harder to get the Legislative Council reformed. The Council finally agreed to lower the property qualifications for voting. The liberals had wanted more thorough reform—either to have a nominated Council as in New South Wales or a democratic solution to deadlock between the houses: the issue to be decided by the people at referendum.

The politics of development

In Victoria divisions between protection and free trade and liberals and constitutionalists lasted for decades. There were no divisions like this in the other colonies.

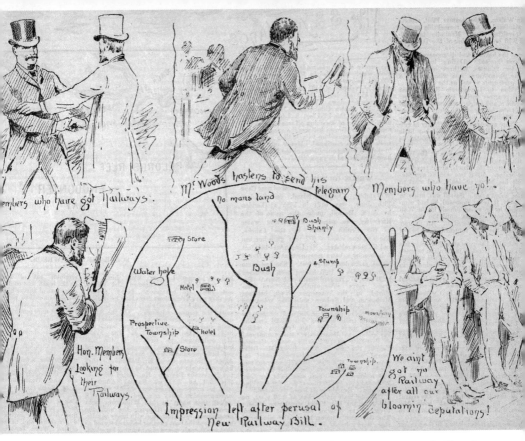

Getting a railway was the essential task of a member of parliament: responses to the Victorian government's 1890 Railway Bill

Nearly all the people elected to the Assemblies were liberals. They believed in an open society with no special privileges and that the government should provide opportunites for people to establish themselves and make money. They also supported progress and enlightenment by running schools and making sure that all children were educated.

The regular business of politics was the building of railways, ports, roads, post offices and telegraph lines. This was true too of Victoria. These public works would open up the country, help the settlers, encourage economic growth and give work to working men, who had the vote. How much work the government was offering and at what wages were important matters to them.

Even though most members were liberals, there was plenty of division among them. Each member wanted a railway for his electorate before any of the others, and members competed for the plum jobs of minister and premier. (Although members did

not get paid, ministers received a high salary.) There were no
organised parties, not even in Victoria; there were loose groupings
of members who came together to make ministries and give them
support. Quite often, men who had been fiercely opposed to each
other suddenly appeared together in a ministry. Ministries came
and went more rapidly than they do today. They did not change
only after an election.

The issue that could flare up into a colony-wide division was
religion. Church schools at first received government funding. Then
the parliaments decided to put all education funding into
government schools. So that all students could go to them, the
schools did not teach any religion, though ministers could teach
religion to the children from their church at set times. All churches
accepted this arrangement except the Catholic. It set about building
enough Catholic schools to take all Catholic children. This was a
huge task, and it kept asking for government help.

Three-quarters of the colonists were Protestant and highly
suspicious of the Catholic Church. When the Catholic Church was
trying to hold onto government funding or trying to get it back,
Protestants became alarmed and Protestant hard-liners whipped
up a panic.

Politicians sometimes used religious feeling to build up support,
but mostly they hoped that religious controversy would not break
out. Electorates were small, and Catholics and Protestants lived
amongst each other. There were other issues apart from religion.
If candidates were to get a majority, they needed to be able to
look for support in both groups. Henry Parkes was a great
Protestant champion, and sometimes he ran anti-Catholic
campaigns, but he was also willing to do secret deals to win Catholic
support.

Politics was highly local and personal. A member could know
all the people who voted for him; there might only be 500 or 600
of them. His close supporters would begin an election campaign
by meeting in a pub—with drinks paid for by the candidate—and
going through the list of voters to identify likely friends and
opponents. Then they would approach every elector and attempt
to get a promise of support from him. Free drinks, paid for by the
candidate, formed part of this process. On election day supporters
would arrange for cabs or buggies to bring their voters to the poll.
When they arrived, there would be refreshments provided by the
candidate. There was nothing to stop you taking a drink or getting

CATHOLICS AND CAMPAIGNING

Alfred Deakin, Australia's second prime minister, served for 20 years in the Victorian parliament. He was a liberal, a firm supporter of the state schools and opposed to helping Catholic schools. Here he reports on the education issue in his campaigns. At this time electorates returned two members. The second member with whom Deakin campaigned was attempting to get Catholic and Protestant support.

My strongest supporters were mainly Scotch, with a few Irish from the north of Ireland and an odd Catholic or two who dared to defy priest and neighbour. The English were rarely active, though staunch, and remained undemonstrative or were but quiet workers.

My opposition to the Catholic claims set almost the whole of the Irish of that denomination against me. However, in Bulla, a stronghold of the Catholics, I always polled well because there happened to be a deadly feud among them by which they were almost evenly divided.

My colleague was industriously trimming to catch the Catholic vote by an evasive dealing with the question of paying the priests' schools according to the results obtained. My own views were pronounced, but in order not to prejudice him I contented myself with a simple announcement of the fact and made no aggressive attacks upon them. Whenever we were addressing a meeting in a strongly Catholic neighbourhood, however, I used to amuse myself and torment him by frequently referring in the most unexpected way to the Education issue in some of its forms, occasionally with great apparent heat, until my unhappy colleague would almost slip from his chair with nervous anxiety lest I should break out in a declaration of war on behalf of the State Schools; thus making it inevitable for him either to support or oppose it. Then I would slip away to a new topic and just as he had regained his composure abruptly revert to the sore point and zigzag around it until his alarm became intolerable.

Nearly always he spoke first and had got his speech into good order after a few meetings, when one night at a small place where the risk might be safely taken I accepted his invitation to precede him, and without any warning delivered his speech for him leaving him to do the best he could with what was left of mine.

The Crisis in Victorian Politics, 1879–81, pp. 45, 48

GETTING DRINKS FROM THE CANDIDATE ON ELECTION DAY

Details of election campaigning were revealed when the results of elections were challenged on the grounds of bribery and corruption. 'Treating', though widely practised, was illegal.

You say you saw Mr Bennett at the 'Nugget and Woolpack'—just tell us what passed between you and him then?—He came and shook hands with me and asked me to walk into his committee room [from where supporters organised the campaign], I did so and he poured out some liquor there and said 'take some refreshment'.

He poured out what?—Spirits, and I soon got very tipsy.

How much spirits had you then?—I think I drank about a gill of 'Old Tom'.

Who gave it to you?—Mr Bennett poured it out and I took it off the table.

Did you see other persons drinking there at the same time?—Plenty. The room was full.

Did you see from whom they got the liquor?—I got tipsy very soon. I went in and gave my vote.

Did you get tipsy before you went in to give your vote?—I did not get so bad that I did not know what I was about.

Did you go back to the committee-room after you voted?—I did.

Did you see Mr Bennett in the committee-room after you came back?—Yes.

Did you get any more drink?—I did; I then got two or three more glasses.

Who gave you them?—There was a man or two there pouring out.

Was Mr Bennett there at that time?—He was there.

Did he see the liquor given you, do you know?—I do not know whether he did or not. I went in and sat down, and enjoyed myself.

Election Qualifications Committee, East Bourke, Victoria *Votes and Proceedings*, Vol. 2, 1856

---

a ride from one side and voting for another, but promises to vote a certain way were taken seriously.

'Treating'—giving voters drink and food—was meant to have stopped with the introduction of the secret ballot. It was not as extensive as it had been under open voting and it may not have influenced many voters, but voters expected that elections would

The candidate's committee meets (with tobacco and alcohol): the first stage in electioneering

still be a sort of carnival. A man wanting to get into parliament had to be willing to spend a bit on drink.

Candidates had to meet the expenses of an election themselves. There were no parties to pay them. As well as the drink, there were the costs of printing literature, ads in newspapers, and the hire of halls for public meetings. Costs went up if the electorate was large or the contest close. They were substantial. When payment of members was first introduced in Victoria, members got 300 pounds per year. A candidate would be lucky if his electoral expenses were less than half that amount. He might have to spend as much as four times his salary to get elected.

If a member was to be re-elected, he had to get roads or railways built, get a subsidy for the local hall or show society, help the selectors get the title to their land even if they hadn't met all the conditions, and find jobs in the public service for the friends and

Scenes in campaigning: 1 Questioning a candidate, 2 The paid canvasser, 3 Going to the poll, 4 Using persuasion

relations of his supporters. Members today still have to look after their electorate, but at that time, as the MP was not a member of a party, he was judged almost solely on what he could do for the electorate. And these local matters guided him in how he voted in parliament. We might think it corruption if members offered to vote for ministers in return for ministers promising a railway or a job in the public service, but this was standard practice.

It was very direct democracy. Members coming from small electorates could trade their support with ministers who were themselves in charge of the detail of administration. Ministers could let people out of jail early, set the freight rates on a railway, give a teacher a promotion or a transfer—things that boards and bureaucrats would control today. So there was plenty a local member could do for his constituents.

The governments borrowed huge amounts in London to build the public works. There was a lot of horse-trading over how this should be spent, but ministers and members did not siphon off

---

**A GOVERNMENT DOCTOR REPORTS ON THE EXAMINATION OF
YOUTH RECOMMENDED BY AN MP AS A POSTMAN**

An extract from the novel Jacob Shumate, *written by Henry Wrixon,
who was for many years a member of the Victorian parliament*

A tall young Irishman presents himself to pass the medical examination as letter-carrier, together with nomination signed by E.F.
Frankfort MP. All correct so far, my boy, thinks I. Chest measured
proper number of inches, height correct, limbs and trunk sound,
eyesight good, blew up the lung tester famously. 'Why, you'll do, as
far as I am concerned, Mr McGlumpy,' says I; 'just read over that
certificate and see if the particulars as to name, age, and so on are
correct. If so, I'll endorse it.' 'Read what, your Honour?' says he.
'Read that,' says I, putting the paper before him. 'I ax your Honour's
pardon,' says he, 'but I don't read or write.' 'Don't read or write!'
says I, dropping the paper as if it burnt me. 'Devil a bit!' says he.
'Devil a bit!' says I; 'and then how the—,' but I pulled myself up, as
I knew that strong language would be unbecoming from the
Government official, even in these novel circumstances, and only
addressed the young man in my blandest tones, and said: 'My
youthful friend, would you mind explaining to me how you propose
to deliver the letters at their proper destination, and to the people
named outside of them, when you are unable to read the address?'
'Quite aisy, your Honour. Won't the aunt there, the Postmistress,
put them down into me hand, and as I walk up the street the neighbours, all decent people, will just lay houldt on what belongs to
them, each of them.' 'Very well, Mr McGlumpy, as far as I am concerned, I can certify that you are physically competent to deliver a
twenty-four-volume encyclopedia; and perhaps you will permit me
too add that, on the whole, I am pleased that I do not reside in the
interesting town where you are to officiate.'

Henry Wrixon,
Jacob Shumate,
London, 1903,
Vol. 1, pp. 238–9

---

this public money to enrich themselves. There was no corruption
of this sort. Henry Parkes, five times premier, stayed a poor man.
Although ministers could appoint people to the public service, new
ministers did not sack existing office-holders when they came to
power in order to appoint their friends.

The politics of development in Queensland had an extra dimen-
sion. To provide labour for the sugar industry, the Queensland

Aboriginal prisoners in chains in Western Australia

government allowed the sugar planters to import workers from the Pacific Islands, who were known as Kanakas. They worked for low wages and did not have political rights. Sometimes they were virtually kidnapped from their homes. In Brisbane and in the southern colonies there was growing opposition to the use of Kanakas. People were afraid that a slave society was developing in the north.

In Queensland, where settlement occurred later than in the south, pastoralists were still expanding into Aboriginal territory. The Queensland government ran a special police force to punish Aborigines who got in their way. It was called the native police; the officers were Europeans, the troopers were Aborigines recruited from a district at a distance from where they served. The official word for what the native police did to the Aborigines was 'dispersion'. This was code for killing. There was little opposition to this in Australia. The British government was worried about it, but it could do little as it had let Queensland be self-governing.

The other colony where Aborigines stood in the way of pastoralists was Western Australia. Here the British government was in charge. In 1870 a partly elected Legislative Council was established, but the governor still ran the government. Aborigines who speared cattle were not shot by police. They were captured and taken in neck chains to court and then to prison. Photos of these prisoners survive to shame us. There are no photos of what happened on the Queensland frontier, where a democratic government was in charge.

Real democracy, 1880–1920

From the 1880s, in all the self-governing colonies, there was a movement for democracy. People believed in it, proclaimed it and worked for it. No longer did democrats have to proceed carefully and hide their true views. They boldly said that the people, both men and women, must rule; that the antidemocratic parts of the constitutions must be swept away and new ways found to put the people in charge. The people would really rule if there were referendums on all important issues.

Democrats saw their movement as the path of progress. All the world was heading towards democracy. Everywhere the people were becoming more prosperous and better educated. As power passed to their hands, a new era would dawn when governments for the first time ruled for the good of all. The idea that the people were dangerous and had to be checked and controlled was old-fashioned.

Democracy was no longer un-British. In 1867 the British parliament had given the vote to working men in the towns and in 1884 to working men in the country. They still had to be house-holders paying rent. The vote was not given to all men until 1918, but that was clearly the direction in which Britain was heading. Australia was now proud as a new country to be showing Britain the way.

The leading democrats were a new sort of liberal, the progressive liberals. Old-style liberals were not keen about full democracy and they had followers and supporters among the rich and better-off people. As liberalism became more progressive, the old-style liberals were becoming conservatives. They were in fact far more liberal than English conservatives. The Australian conservatives accepted manhood suffrage for the Assemblies, but were happy with the constitutions as they were. Progressive liberals wanted to press on to full democracy. (Democratic Socialism?)

Progressive liberals also believed that governments should do more for the people. The first stage of liberalism was to get rid of privilege and create an open society; new or progressive liberals believed that governments should provide all the people the opportunity to live a good life. So wages and working conditions should be controlled; government banks should offer cheap loans to farmers and home-owners; big business should be watched to see that it did not become too big and exploit the consumer; old people should get a government pension. *followed U.S. model*

In the two decades around 1900, progressive liberal governments adopted all these policies and put many of them into practice. New liberalism, like old liberalism, was a set of ideas that came from Britain, but it achieved more in Australia than in Britain. Australia was called a 'social laboratory', where ideas only talked of in other places were actually being tried. Social commentators from round the world came to visit Australia to see what the future would be like.

The progressive liberals were supported by a new political grouping, the Labor Party. It was keener about government action than the progressive liberals and keener to introduce full democracy. The Labor Party did amazingly well after its formation in 1891. This was made possible by the introduction of payment of members.

Payment of members

The Chartists in Britain in the 1830s had included payment of members as one of the six points in the people's charter. Democrats argued that the people did not get their full political rights if they could vote only for rich people—the only ones who could afford to go into politics. The opponents of payment said that payment

---

TWO VIEWS OF PAYMENT OF MEMBERS

EDWARD O'SULLIVAN
Democracy as laid down by Abraham Lincoln means this: Government of the people, by the people, and for the people. To achieve that end we have what is called manhood suffrage which is supposed to give us the opportunity of reflecting our sentiments and our ideas in Parliament. But how can manhood suffrage do that if our choice is limited to a certain number of conservative gentlemen? Why at the present time, I suppose the electors of New South Wales are confined in their selection of members to 350 or 400 gentlemen. Now, as a rule, these gentlemen are not democrats. Give the people payment of members, and every man of brains in the country—about 80,000 to 100,000 strong—is at the command of the electors. He may be a boundary rider, a navvy, a coalminer, a carpenter, or a blacksmith.

SAMUEL LEES
I hail with delight the statement of those who say that there are men in our ranks who are well qualified to take a seat here and legislate. I admit that is true; but on the other hand, I can see with as much clearness of vision that there are many others not so well qualified, who, if payment of members existed, would rush to secure the position. Politics would then become merely a profession, and the spirit of the delegate would take the place of the spirit of the representative.

NSW Assembly
Debates, 1889,
Vol. 37,
p. 494

would make politics into a trade or business like any other. Politicians would promise anything or do anything in order to keep their salary. In Britain politicians were still not paid, but in most other countries they were.

Payment of members of parliament operated in Victoria from 1870. None of the other colonies followed Victoria's example. Since politics there was so bitter and crisis-ridden, it was not regarded as a good model to follow.

In the 1880s Victorian politics became much calmer. The liberals and constitutionalists came together in a grand coalition. It was a boom time in the economy and the coalition governments pushed the boom along by borrowing huge sums in London and spending it on railways.

In the other colonies in the 1880s firmer divisions began to appear in parliaments that had previously been gatherings of independents. These colonies, unlike Victoria, were not booming. There were droughts and short-term recessions. Voters were no longer interested merely in getting roads and railways and government jobs in their electorate; they found they had interests in common with other people across the colony. They formed new organisations and parties to pursue them.

In Queensland the division came over how the colony should be developed. Thomas McIlwraith, who was premier from 1878 to 1883, was himself a businessman with huge confidence in the future of his colony. He owned pastoral properties, mines, and was director of a bank. He wanted to speed development by getting railways built across the colony by private companies, which would be paid by being given land along their routes. Land-grant railways were the way the American West had been developed. McIlwraith was also a firm supporter of bringing in Kanakas to work on the sugar plantations.

In 1883 McIlwraith was beaten in an election by Samuel Griffith, a clever, cold Brisbane lawyer. He was a new liberal who wanted to use the government not simply to promote development but to shape a society. He opposed the land-grant railways; he planned to replace the large sugar planters with small farmers who would not need Kanakas; and he supported better conditions for working people. For the rest of the 1880s there was a rough division in parliament between supporters of Griffith and McIlwraith. Griffith's followers were the Liberal Party, McIlwraith's the National Party.

In 1884 the Griffith government introduced a Bill for the payment of members. The premier said it was 'part of the programme of the democratic party all over the world'. In Queensland with its vast distances only rich men could afford to leave their homes for months on end to sit in parliament in Brisbane. Most members of the Queensland Assembly had no chance of going home for the weekend.

The Legislative Council rejected the Bill. It did the same to another payment Bill in the next year. Then Griffith simply put the money for payment in the budget and dared the Council to reject it. This was a 'tack', the method the Victorian liberals had used in their conflict with their Council. Neither side in Queensland wanted to see government brought to a halt, as had happened in Victoria. The Council agreed to pass the budget with

Thomas McIlwraith and Samuel Griffith: rival leaders in Queensland in the 1880s

payment included so long as the government agreed to ask the Privy Council in London (the court of appeal for the colonies) whether the Council could amend a budget or whether it could only accept or reject it.

Griffith argued that the Council should act like the House of Lords in England that had accepted that it should not amend the budget. The Queensland Council, like the Lords, was not an elected body; it was nominated by the governor. The Council argued that as the written constitution of Queensland did not put any limit on its power to amend Bills, it should be able to amend a budget (and so strike out the money for payment of members).

The Privy Council ruled in favour of the government and against the Council. It said that the Council should not amend a budget. As the government could establish payment by putting it in the budget each year, the Council now gave in. In 1886 it passed a Bill for payment of members.

In New South Wales the new force in politics was the protection movement. New South Wales followed a policy of free trade, which was the British policy. When Victoria adopted protection, New South Wales was more determined to keep to free trade. The two rival colonies followed opposite economic policies. Each boasted that its was the best.

In the 1880s wheat farming began to be better established in New South Wales. When the Selection Act was first passed it had done little to promote agriculture; the colony remained in the hands of the squatters, who ran sheep and cattle. Now the land law had been changed to give the farmer better protection from the squatter, and railways allowed the farmer to get his crop to market. But in Sydney the farmer faced competition from wheat shipped from South Australia and Victoria, where farming was better established and more efficient. This made the New South Wales farmers into protectionists. They wanted a duty put on the wheat from the other colonies. They had to fight Sydney businessmen, bankers and shipowners who wanted to keep trade flowing freely through Sydney's great port.

Some workers in Sydney were also turning to protection. They wanted duties on manufactured goods in order to create more jobs in Sydney factories. But the workers were not united on this issue. Protective duties put up prices. If a duty were put on wheat from the other colonies, bread would be dearer in Sydney. Many workers thought it was best to stick with free trade: this would keep Sydney as a great port, which created jobs, and it would keep the cost of living low.

So protection was chiefly a country movement. Apart from the question of customs duties, it collected support from country people who thought Sydney was too powerful and had too much money spent on it. It also got support from Catholics because the great free-trade leader was Henry Parkes, the Protestant champion, who had taken government money from Catholic schools.

More and more protectionists were being elected to parliament. In 1886 the protectionists organised a Protectionist Party, with branches and a central organisation. The free traders then did the same. Theirs was called the Liberal Party.

The protectionists were firm supporters of payment of members. In the country there was often no good local candidate willing to stand. Men from Sydney ran for country electorates and got elected. Some voters preferred them. When the issue was to get as much government spending in the electorate as possible, a Sydney man and established politician might be best. He was on the spot, always available to lobby ministers and departments, and he might get into a ministry. Henry Parkes in his long career had represented five different country electorates. But now the country was more resentful of Sydney. It wanted to send its own men to parliament. The protectionists included payment of members in their policy at the 1889 election.

Henry Parkes and the free traders won the election. Parkes was himself opposed to payment and so were most of his ministers. But Parkes let one of his ministers who was in favour introduce a Bill for payment. The Bill passed, and so the wily old premier robbed the protectionists of one of their weapons.

In South Australia wheat growing was a long-established export trade; its farmers were not looking for protection. However, the farmers in the north were hard hit by drought in the 1880s. They had taken up their land on time payment under the Selection Acts and now they struggled to pay interest and principal to the government. They formed a Farmers Association to get the government to reduce their payments. They made recommendations to their members on which candidates to support at elections and sometimes ran their own candidates. They did quite well and the government was forced to change the repayment rules.

The farmers also wanted a different sort of parliament, not one in which most members lived in Adelaide. The slogan of the secretary of their Association was 'Adelaide shall rule no more'. The farmers wanted to be represented by local men, and to make this possible they supported payment of members. They achieved that in 1887.

In Tasmania the large landowners and a few businessmen controlled the parliament, which was like a club for the best people. In the 1880s this began to change. Lawyers, doctors and other professional men got elected by appealing to the small farmers and city working men. Among them was the lawyer Andrew Inglis Clark, who was not only a democrat but a republican. He was a very short man—only 5 feet tall—and he did not speak well in public, but he was the teacher and leader of a group of young reformers. In the late 1880s and again in the mid-1890s he was the attorney-general in reforming governments. His name is honoured in the electoral system that he devised and which Tasmania still uses for its Assembly—the Hare–Clark system of proportional representation.

Tasmania had a lot of reforming to do if it were to catch up with the rest of eastern Australia. It still did not have manhood suffrage. Clark was of course in favour of it but it was not passed until 1900,

Andrew Inglis Clark:
the great democratic
reformer in Tasmania

when he had left politics to become a judge. He was successful in 1890 in getting parliament to agree to payment of members.

By 1890 payment of members operated in all the self-governing colonies. The chief pressure for it had come from the country. Once it was established, members of parliament in the country were nearly always local people. But the biggest change it brought was that it allowed working men to leave mines and workshops on one day and take their seats in parliament the next.

The Labor Party

In the 1880s trade unions became a stronger force. Previously only skilled men had formed unions, and these were usually small organisations operating in one city. Now unions were formed by unskilled and semi-skilled men—shearers, sailors, wharf labourers, carters—and they took in workers across a whole colony or across the colonies. A shearer could join the Australian Shearers Union in Ballarat before he left to go shearing in New South Wales.

81

The unions increased their strength by forming Trades and Labour Councils in the capital cities. If there was a strike, the council would make sure that workers in other unions helped the workers on strike. The councils met every few years in an Australia-wide conference.

Unions gained many improvements in pay and conditions—partly by negotiating with the bosses, partly by striking. The growth of unions was welcomed in the community at large and by some bosses. A worker paying his union subscription, learning to cooperate with his fellow workers and taking part in union affairs was a better man than the careless worker who spent his wages on drink. Unions did not attack all bosses. Often they were taking action to get the bad bosses to pay the same rates as the good bosses. However, bosses were becoming anxious about the growth of union power. They did not want to see all the workers in an industry belonging to a union and the union dictating to them how they should run their businesses. They began to form their own organisations to match the trade unions.

In the 1880s the unions were also taking more interest in politics. The Trades and Labour Councils lobbied ministers to get laws passed to improve working conditions. By the late 1880s they were recommending to unionists the candidates to vote for at elections and running a few candidates themselves. They did not make a great impact. Many workers were suspicious of unions getting too involved in politics. Workers were Protestants and Catholics, free traders and protectionists, drinkers and total abstainers; in politics they might lose the unity of being workers in the same industry.

The passing of payment of members encouraged union leaders to think more of politics. Previously when unions thought of sending working men to parliament they had to face the problem of how they would pay them.

In 1890 the trade unions blundered into a big intercolonial strike—the Maritime Strike—and were completely defeated. The bosses got non-union labour to work the ships and the wharves. They refused to compromise or even talk to the unions; they now had the chance to break their power. The governments stayed neutral but they did protect the non-union labourers and so helped to break the strike. They also enrolled special constables (ordinary citizens who volunteered to be police) and brought out the troops to preserve order.

'FIRE LOW AND LAY THEM OUT'

This was the instruction given by Colonel Tom Price to the men of Victoria's Mounted Rifles, citizen soldiers called out to preserve order during the Maritime Strike.

Men of the Mounted Rifles, one of your obligations imposes upon you the duty of resisting invasion by a foreign enemy, but you are also liable to be called upon to assist in preserving law and order in the colony. Should the necessity arise, I have no fear that you will do your duty like men and soldiers. I do not think your aid will be required, but if it is, let there be no half measures in what you do. Not to do your work faithfully would be a grave mistake. If it has to be, let it be done effectively. You will each be supplied with 40 rounds of ammunition, leaden bullets, and if the order is given to fire, don't dare let me see one rifle pointed up in the air. Fire low and lay them out. Lay the disturbers of law and order out, so that the duty will not have to be performed again. Let it be a lesson to them.

Silver Age,
Broken Hill,
26 September
1890

This was a shattering experience for unionists. They had thought they were moving steadily to better times, and suddenly bosses and governments had ganged up against them. There was no question now about the move into politics. They must get into parliament to control governments and get laws passed to improve pay and conditions. They had the vote; they must make that the new basis of their power.

After the strike came economic depression and bank crashes. Work dried up; unemployment rose. The bosses had no trouble cutting wages and getting non-union labour. In 1891 and 1894 the shearers struck, hoping to hold onto what they had gained in better times, and were beaten. The government in Queensland was no longer neutral; it jailed some of the strikers under an ancient English law that was no longer in force in England. The unions shrank and many disappeared altogether. Politics was now the only hope.

For the next elections in New South Wales, Victoria, Queensland and South Australia, the trade unions had their Labor Party ready. For the moment there was no attempt to form a Labor Party in

The police protect non-union labour in the Maritime Strike

Tasmania. The Labor candidates did very well, best in New South Wales, worst in Victoria. In New South Wales the party won 35 seats, a quarter of the total. These newcomers were instantly a power in the land. They held the balance of power between protectionists and free traders. Labor would determine which party would govern.

In Victoria there was a long-established party system. For decades workers had been voting liberal, the party of protection and reform. Many continued to do so, and Labor in Victoria was

John Oxley Library neg. no. 64845

The unionists who were gaoled in Queenland after the shearers' strike of 1891

a small group, not much more than a radical wing of the liberals. In South Australia Labor was a separate party and supported the progressive liberal government of Charles Kingston. In Queensland the existing parties came together to meet the dangers of strikes and depression and the Labor Party became the opposition. Samuel Griffith, now combined with his old enemy McIlwraith, decided that kanakas could continue to be imported.

The Labor parties had very little money—and didn't need money. The government paid the salaries of their parliamentary members. At elections they did not have to spend money on drink for committee members or on wages for canvassers and scrutineers.

A LABOR POLITICIAN TALKS OF HIS LIFE IN THE MINES, 1895

There were some remarkable men in that litle band of sixteen who composed the advanced guard of the Solidarity Labour Party in New South Wales. Amongst these, Alf Edden stands out in my memory. He was a powerfully built man in his fifties, of medium height, grey-haired, red-faced, bubbling with energy and goodwill to all mankind. He came from Staffordshire in England and had been a coal miner for over forty years before he was elected to represent Kahibah, one of the many mining areas on the Newcastle coal fields.

He had a natural eloquence that on occasions swept men away in floods of emotion. His speech on the Coal Mines Regulations Bill gained for the miners what neither argument nor threat of direct action could have done. In language simple and intensely moving, he told the House in rich Staffordshire dialect of the life and conditions of the miner in coal pits. He spoke of things which he knew from long and bitter experience: 'Ah were in the pit, Mr Sphaker, when Ah were a little laad of eight year old. Ah worked in t' pit for nigh on forty years.' As he went on, members hung on his words. All were strangely silent, deeply moved by his story. He told of poverty, child labour, and terrible disasters, and pleaded for better ventilation, improved conditions and higher wages. Towards the end of his speech George Reid, the premier, beckoned me, and when I came to his side he said, after wiping his eyes, 'Tell him, Hughes, that he can have anything he wants.' He wanted many things—and all he asked for he got.

W.M. Hughes, *Crusts and Crusades*, Sydney, 1947, pp. 123–4

All this work was done for nothing by party members. Thousands of men and women were devoted to Labor's cause. There had been nothing like this in politics before.

Nearly all the Labor members had been workers before they were elected. There were only a few from middle-class occupations (storekeepers, journalists and real-estate agents). The worker politicians took their duties very seriously. They were not like many of the other members who kept a business going or practised their profession while serving in the parliament (which they had to do before there was payment of members). The Labor men were full-time politicians. When parliament was not sitting, they travelled around the colony speaking for the party and founding new branches. As MPs they had a gold pass for the railways. Payment of members not only paid for Labor MPs; it paid for Labor organisers.

There had been poor men in parliament before, but they had been individualists living by their wits and the gift of the gab. The Labor men were more steady and responsible; they had been members and office holders in the unions where men learnt to work with each other for the good of all.

The Labor parties drew up platforms listing the policies they wanted adopted. Anyone wanting to be a Labor candidate promised to support the platform. Full democracy was a top priority, because until that existed the party could not hope to carry its other reforms. The platforms called for 'one man, one vote'. At this time large numbers of voters had more than one vote because they owned property in more than one electorate. Labor also wanted to abolish the rules that you had to be living in one place for three or six months to get on the electoral roll (which would enable shearers, drovers and sailors to vote). Labor's view was that there should be a properly democratic Legislative Assembly—and no upper house. The Legislative Councils should be abolished.

The rest of the platform listed changes that would bring benefits to workers. Mostly they were very practical and obvious benefits. The boilers of steam engines—which gave the motive power in factories—sometimes burst, killing and injuring workers. Labor wanted boilers to be regularly checked by government inspectors. They wanted standards set for shearers' huts and these too should be inspected. There should be government rules about safety in mines.

There was a great argument in the parties about whether the platforms should declare that Labor wanted society to be run in an entirely different way. Some of the party were socialists, who wanted all business and industry to be run by the government or the workers and not for the profit of individuals and companies. Why, asked the socialists, could people not cooperate and work together to produce what they needed? Why did human needs have to be met by a small group of people making money out of the rest?

The socialists were a minority. Many others in the party thought that socialism was an ideal that would eventually be reached but that Labor should not frighten people by committing itself to socialism now. Others thought that it was all pie in the sky, and

SOCIALISM

Manifesto of the Australian Socialist League to the People of Australia, October 1894

We live today in what is called the 'Capitalistic Era'. There are two great classes of Society—the one, the Capitalists, owns Land and Capital; the other, the workers, owns nothing except the power to labour. The modern wage earner receives only about one-third of the produce of his labour, the other two-thirds being taken by the capitalist who employs him or who employs his employer. In the capitalist era there is intense competition which is felt by the workers in the steady lowering of the standard wage-rate, and by the small business men in the fierceness of the struggle which they have to wage against the wealthy capitalists in their own lines of industry, and their steady disappearance as a class through their innumerable bankruptcies.

The cause of all these evils is the steady concentration of Land and Capital in the hands of the few, and the depriving of the workers of all ownership of them.

The only cure is the Socialisation of Land and Capital; that is, to let the State, as the representative of all, be the only Capitalist and Land-Owner, and consequently the only employer. Every citizen must have a share in the ownership of all the Land and all the Capital in the country.

Every citizen must have a right to employment on farms and stations, in workshops and warehouses, owned by the State or the local council, and controlled by administators elected by the people. If there is not room for everyone, working hours must be reduced all round, until there is. There must be work for all and overwork for none.

that Labor should concentrate on practical reforms. Most of the early platforms did not mention socialism. But it was socialism that gave to all the party members a sense that there was something wrong or rotten about how workers were treated under the existing system of capitalism. It was socialism too that gave Labor's opponents an easy target: they said Labor was heading towards socialism, which was a threat to private property and personal freedom.

AGAINST SOCIALISM

'Socialism', say the saviours of society with awful vehemence, 'will replace the system of private capital by a system of Collective Capital'. 'Collective Capital' seems very simple and pleases many, who seem to expect beer money will be supplied by passing the hat. But how are they to proceed? They are to create 'Collective Capital'—by confiscation and then by monopolising—they call it 'Nationalising'—all means of production and distribution—and this embraces all the activities of men. Further by closing all the avenues to private opportunities, they propose to extinguish the proud trait of individualism from among men—and that means life under universal monopoly, and that means the most oppressive of all despotisms.

It is our goods—that are to be confiscated; our individualism—to be crushed; our independence—to be destroyed, and our pride—to be humbled.

Colonel
G.W. Bell, in
*His Majesty
the Man*,
Sydney, 1902

In New South Wales the platform did not declare for free trade or protection because the workers were divided on this issue. The first Labor members elected in 1891 were split fifty-fifty between free traders and protectionists. Labor policy was to hold a referendum to decide the matter. But in parliament the Labor members could not avoid the matter. They had to decide whether to support a free-trade government or a protectionist government. If they could agree, and be responsible for keeping a government in power, then they could demand that the government implement some of Labor's policies. But the Labor members found it very hard to agree. The protectionists wanted to support a protectionist government and the free traders a free-trade government.

In 1892 a protectionist government headed by George Dibbs was in power. It prosecuted the leaders of a strike at Broken Hill and they were sent to jail. The Labor Party told its MPs that they must vote to bring this government down. But four protectionists refused. They said that a free-trade government would have treated the strikers no better, and they had promised their electors to support protection. The members were expelled and the party set about framing new rules to control its parliamentarians. The new

Socialism—an ideal for even the moderate Labor Party in Victoria

rules were that Labor members had to promise not only to support the platform but to vote as a majority of the members decided when the question was an important one, like the survival of a government. No candidate could give a promise to his electors on how he would vote on issues not mentioned in the platform. All he could say was that he would vote with the rest of his party, who would have the best interests of the party and its supporters in mind.

Most of the existing Labor members rejected this rule. They said it would lead to members voting against their conscience and the views of their electors. The party dumped them and began again with people who would support the rule. This was the 'solidarity' Labor Party.

The new rule did make the party more effective. After the next election in 1894 all the Labor members supported George Reid's free-trade government. It was a progressive government and passed laws on mining safety and taxing the rich that Labor welcomed. In 1899 a majority of Labor members thought they could get more reform from the protectionists, so in a body they voted Reid out and the protectionists in.

The rule worked out in New South Wales was adopted by all the Labor parties and is still the way the Labor Party is run. Members must vote as 'caucus' decides ('caucus' is the meeting of all the Labor MPs). From the time the rule was adopted, it has been criticised as undemocratic. The party puts itself between the people and the member they have elected. The party took a different view of democracy. It claimed that Labor helped the people to rule. It offered them a clear program; it made its parliamentarians, whatever their private views, support the program; when they were a majority the program would become law—so long as there was no interference from an undemocratic upper house.

The Labor Party boasted that it was the democratic party, the party of the people. But at first it thought of democracy as male. Women had to make their own claim to be citizens.

Votes for women

The Victorian Women's Suffrage Society, the first Australian organisation to demand votes for women, was launched in Melbourne in 1884. There were men present: their help would be

*Annie Lowe,
founder of the
Victorian Women's
Suffrage Society, the
first organisation
advocating votes
for women*

needed if women were to get the vote. One man, still unsure about the cause, asked whether even prostitutes were to get the vote. He could not say any more because the women shouted him down.

Henrietta Dugdale and Annie Lowe were the founders of this organisation. Dugdale was married at 14 and had a bad time with her husband. A few of the women in this campaign had experienced at first hand cruelty and abuse from men in marriage. Most were like Annie Lowe. She had been treated by her father as an equal of her brothers and took part in family conversations about politics. Then she discovered that the world outside did not treat her as an equal.

The old idea that girls and women were stupid and had to be controlled by men was on the way out, though it had not yet disappeared. Daughters and wives were being treated with more respect at home, but in legal and political rights they were still very much inferior to men. The women campaigners wanted equality for themselves, but even more for the women who were badly treated by their husbands. A cruel husband could make a woman's

Two Men on Women and Political Rights

Bartholomew Pumpkin, a fictional character

I consulted you about the schoolin' for the girls and gettin' married to you more'n fifty years ago. Consulted you about the trades for the boys. Consulted you about buyin' that there selecshun. I reckon I never did one thing that mounted to anything in life without consulting you, Sarah. And for my part I must say, if Parlyment ain't a fit place for my wife, it ain't a fit place for me.

Bessie Harrison Lee, *Mrs Pumpkin Goes to Town*, Melbourne, c.1890, p. 37

Henry Wrixon, a Victorian Legislative Councillor

How can you give women equal political rights with men, and, at the same time, preserve the unity of the home as we have known it? If you tell me the wife is to exercise her intelligence and independence as a voter, then you cannot have the unity of the home. If you tell me she will not thwart her husband, then I say the whole thing is a make-believe. It would be sad and strange if a woman, having given everything else to a man—having merged her life in his—could not trust him to express her political views, which, after-all, is only a small part of social life.

Victorian Legislative Council, *Debates*, 1898, Vol. 89, pp. 1442–2

life hell. There was little she could do about it. She was imprisoned with a tyrant.

There were no women's refuges. Divorce did exist, but it was hard to obtain and a divorced woman was looked down on. In divorce law there was great inequality. A wife who had an affair could be divorced by her husband. A husband who had an affair could not be divorced by his wife. The wife had to prove another offence in her husband, such as cruelty or neglect.

In Sydney, Louisa Lawson was the founder of the organisation demanding the vote for women. She was the mother of Henry Lawson, the poet and storyteller. Louisa hoped there would be a day when she was remembered for herself and not as the mother of her son. It took 100 years for this to happen. She is remembered now for running the first newspaper for women entirely produced

Temperance campaigners in Perth

by women. The men in the printers' union picketed her premises because she was not employing union labour—but they would not let the women printers join their union!

By the end of the 1880s there were small women's suffrage groups in Melbourne, Sydney, Adelaide and Brisbane. The real power in the movement came from another organisation, the Woman's Christian Temperance Union, which came to Australia from the United States. This had many more members and operated in all the colonies.

'Temperance' meant drinking alcohol in moderation. It was a misleading name because this organisation was opposed to alcohol altogether. Its members promised never to drink it and they wanted the government to ban it. They saw men who drank as the greatest threat to women's happiness. Men drank and hit their wives; men drank and left wives with no money to feed their children. The Woman's Christian Temperance Union wanted votes for women to increase the political force of the campaign against drink.

The Protestant churches had for some time been running successful campaigns against alcohol. In some colonies the electors in a suburb or a town could now decide how many pubs there would be—or decide to have none at all. The new organisation of temperance women was a great boost to the cause. The men from the churches supported them and their demand for the vote. However, men who liked a drink were suspicious of votes for women. It could not be a good thing if it was going to lead to the closing of pubs. Pub owners gave money to the opponents of woman's suffrage.

Women had to campaign for the vote in the way that men in Australia never had. The vote was not going to come to women automatically. Their chief strategy was to collect women's signatures on monster petitions. They needed to show that women did really want the vote. The politicians who opposed votes for women said no decent woman would want to take part in the rough-and-tumble of politics.

When this campaign began, no woman had the vote. So the women had to argue their case from first principles. They said they were humans and so had the same rights as men. They had to obey the laws and pay taxes and so had the same right as men to take part in the making of laws. These were claims based on the equality of men and women. Then the women went on to argue that since they were different from men they would make a valuable new contribution to politics. They were experts on children and caring for people and were more moral than men. They did not want the vote to become politicians, but to make sure politics was influenced by women and that the laws protected women and children. This line of argument reassured the male politicians. If women were still going to stay home and be wives and mothers, the world would not change too much if women had the vote.

WHY WOMEN SHOULD HAVE THE VOTE

Resolution passed by the 1890 Convention of the Woman's Christian Temperance Union

That as men and women are alike in having to obey the laws, this meeting declares its conviction that they should also be equal in electing those who make the laws; and, further, that the ballot in the hands of women would be a safeguard to the home, in which the interests of women are paramount, and as what is good for the home is also good for the State, the enfranchisement of women would be conducive to the highest national welfare.

WCTU of Victoria, *Annual Report*, 1890

95

In Britain and America, where the campaign for women's suffrage began, the women's demands were rather different. Many of the campaigners were well-educated, single women who were not going to find husbands as women outnumbered men. They wanted the vote—and the opportunity to move into men's world of work, even to move into politics. This really frightened the men. In Australia men outnumbered women, and nearly all women married. The women campaigners were going to stay at home. This is one reason why women secured the vote much earlier in Australia than in Britain and the United States.

Gains and losses

There was a long struggle to make the constitutions more democratic. The democrats had to argue their case again and again. Liberal progressive governments supported by Labor passed democratic measures through the Assemblies, but year after year they were defeated in the Legislative Councils, where big businessmen and large property owners held seats.

In Queensland, reform was delayed longest because in the 1890s conservative coalition governments ruled. The premier of Queensland would have liked to make the constitution even less democratic: he suggested that men who had saved 100 pounds should get two votes. It was not until the early twentieth century that progressive liberals and Labor formed a government in Queensland. In 1899 Labor had held office by itself—but only for one week.

Reform proceeded most rapidly in Western Australia. It acquired the right to self-government only in 1890, over 30 years after the eastern colonies. Its population had grown slowly and even in 1890 it amounted to only one-third of Tasmania's. The Western Australian constitution provided for a nominated Council, an Assembly elected on a rent and property franchise, no payment of members and no votes for women.

The first premier was John Forrest, who remained in office until 1900. He was a conservative, but also a great reformer. He did not want his colony to be lagging behind the rest. After 1893 men from the rest of Australia were flocking to his colony to dig for gold at Coolgardie and Kalgoorlie. They were unhappy with Forrest because the goldfields did not have many seats in parliament, but

John Forrest, first premier
of Western Australia
1890–1900, a reforming
conservative

Forrest was careful that they did not become too unhappy. In 1893 he introduced manhood suffrage and in 1900 payment of members.

In all the colonies plural voting was eliminated (New South Wales 1893, Victoria 1899, Tasmania 1900, Queensland 1905, Western Australia 1907). In South Australia it had never operated. Now possession or occupation of property had nothing to do with the right to vote for the Assemblies. When plural voting was removed Labor was ready to support votes for women. It did not want votes for women to happen first because then women with property in more than one electorate would get extra votes just as men did.

Getting on the electoral roll and getting to vote were made easier. Labor was very interested in these reforms. The rule that you had to reside in an electorate for a certain time before you could get on the roll was abolished. New South Wales introduced the system of 'elector's right' in 1893, but you did not have to pay for your right as in Victoria. Payment in Victoria was dropped in 1910.

Elections were shifted to Saturday and the polls stayed open longer. When they were held on weekdays, with polls closing at 4 or

5 pm, it was hard for workers to vote. They had to vote in their lunch break or take time off and perhaps be docked pay. Candidates sometimes gave workers money to vote because they would 'lose their time'.

Votes for women became law first in South Australia in 1894. The Legislative Council in this colony was the least exclusive of the elected Councils and for a few years the progressive liberals and Labor held a majority there. This allowed votes for women to pass. One Councillor thought he would stop the Bill passing by adding an amendment that women should be allowed to be members of parliament as well. He thought even supporters of votes for women would not come at that. But they did—and so the women got more than they asked for.

Western Australia in 1899 was the second colony to pass votes for women. Forrest was opposed to it, but he changed his mind

Mary Lee, the leader of the campaign for votes for women in South Australia

when he saw that it would help him out of his major difficulty. The goldfields deserved to have many more members of parliament, but Forrest did not want to give extra power to his enemies. However, if women were allowed to vote the goldfields would not have to be given so many seats. There were few women on the goldfields. Most women lived in the old, settled areas of the colony that supported Forrest's government.

Women's suffrage passed in New South Wales in 1902, in Tasmania in 1903, and in Queensland in 1904. Victoria was the last to make the change, in 1908, even though the movement for women's suffrage had begun there. This was because its elected Council was the most exclusive. One of its members was personally nasty to the women campaigners. When they came in a deputation to the Council, he said to two of the younger members, 'You girls— you don't want votes. You want [with a pause and a leer]— something else'.

The biggest task democrats faced was to reform the Legislative Councils. On this issue there was a division between progressive liberals and Labor. The liberals did not object to having a Council. They supported the argument that Councils could check governments that might be acting hastily or against the wishes of the people. But they did not want the Councils to be a block on progress. If the two houses came to a deadlock they wanted the will of the people to prevail. Their favourite scheme for settling deadlocks was to hold a referendum.

Labor wanted to abolish the Councils. It could see no point in having any check on the Assemblies. Labor's idea of democracy was that the people should elect Labor members committed to the Labor platform and the Assembly should vote the platform into law. They could not believe that a Labor government might do something wrong and need to be checked. Labor supported the schemes of the liberals to reform the Councils. But Labor might have made the Councils less willing to change by its threat to do away with them altogether.

The Councils that were elected were the hardest to reform (they operated in Victoria, South Australia, Tasmania and Western Australia, which shifted to an elected Council in 1893). The Councils gave way a little and allowed more people to vote for them, but never everyone. Charles Kingston, the fiery radical premier of South Australia, devoted himself to a campaign to reform the Council. He was not asking for adult suffrage but household suffrage, a vote to every head of a household. He held a referendum on the issue in 1899 and 52 per cent of the voters supported his plan. The Council refused to budge. It did not agree to household suffrage until 1913.

None of the elected Councils agreed that deadlocks should be resolved by a referendum. In Victoria in 1903, after a fierce campaign had been mounted against the Council, all it would agree to was this: if the Council rejected a measure, the Assembly could take the issue to the people at an election. If the Council again rejected the measure, there should be another election for both the Assembly and the Council. If the Council still rejected the measure, nothing more could be done.

In New South Wales and Queensland the Councils were nominated by the governor, on the advice of ministers. This made it easier to put them under pressure. In the 1890s in New South Wales, Premier George Reid twice got the governor to appoint new members to the Council when it was blocking his measures. The new members of course were men who would support the government. In Queensland in 1908 the Council, fearing that it would be swamped by new members, agreed that deadlocks could be settled by referendum.

Labor first came to power in New South Wales in 1910 and in Queensland in 1915 (the week in office in 1899 had not put them in power in Queensland). The party had a very simple scheme to fix the Councils. The Labor government should appoint lots of new members and they should then vote to abolish the Council. It was not so simple. It was not clear that the governor had to do exactly what his ministers said in this matter, and a governor might not want to make appointments when the aim was to do away with the Council.

In 1917 the Queensland Labor government held a referendum on the abolition of the Council—and lost. Sixty per cent voted to keep the Council. This did not change Labor's mind. In 1921 a former Labor minister was acting as governor. He did agree to appoint enough new members to vote for the abolition of the Council. A New South Wales Labor government tried the same thing in 1925, but once the new members were in the Council they refused to abolish themselves!

With the Council gone, was Queensland a pure democracy? Not quite. There were far fewer electors in country electorates than in city electorates. Labor got its best support in the country—from shearers, drovers, stockmen and cane-cutters—and so did not want to alter the electorates.

In other states the country also became overrepresented as capital cities grew. Here Labor did better in the capital cities and was a firm supporter of equal electorates. It was the other parties that were happy to leave electorates as they were. They said the country was entitled to extra representation because country people were more scattered and they provided most of Australia's wealth.

Some of the democrats had wanted the referendum to be a regular part of government, not just a way of solving deadlocks between the houses. A certain number of citizens should be able to get the parliament to put a proposal to the people (this was called 'the initiative and referendum'). This was not adopted. Labor was officially in favour of it, but when Labor governments came to power they did not really try to bring it into operation.

Referendums were held on particular issues where governments had trouble coming to a decision: whether religion should be taught in state schools (No); whether hotels should close at 6 pm (Yes).

So the basic system of government remained the same. The big change was the removal of the Council in Queensland. In the other states, laws were passed by two houses of parliament. The Assemblies were now much more democratic: members were paid; women voted; each elector had one vote. The undemocratic upper houses remained.

A democratic Commonwealth

The movement for the federation of the Australian colonies took place in the 1890s when the campaign for democracy was at its strongest. In the writing of the federal constitution, democrats had their greatest victories.

In 1889 Henry Parkes, aged 74 with white hair and long white beard, began a one-man campaign for federation. He managed to bring together delegates from all the colonies to form the first Constitutional Convention, which met in Sydney in 1891. Each colony sent seven delegates, who were elected by the colonial parliaments. In five weeks the delegates agreed on an Australian federal constitution. It was drafted by Samuel Griffith, the premier of Queensland.

WESTERN AUSTRALIA DEBATES DIRECT DEMOCRACY

In 1913 a Labor government introduced a Bill to provide for the initiative and referendum. It was opposed by the Liberals and rejected in the Legislative Council. Attorney-General Thomas Walker supported the Bill; James Mitchell, later a Liberal premier, opposed it.

For

Now what is this initiative that we are proposing? It means the granting to the people of the right directly to legislate.

There are those who think that it alters the most sacred principles of representative Government. In this Parliament the people elect representatives who are supposed to think for and frame laws for the people and on behalf of the people. But representative Government, even in its best form, in the form we understand it under the British flag, in British Parliaments, is only an expedient, only a convenience. It is no denial of the principle of direct legislation upon which it is founded. Originally all acts of the people of a legislative character were direct.

Against

Under such legislation, the Premier backed by the Trades Hall could become a dictator. With the 30,000 members who constitute the unions, the Premier will be able to do just as he pleases. If we take 15 per cent of the electors, a little over 22,000 signatures will be required to petition for a referendum. If we take a vote on other than an election day we will require very few more than 22,000 to constitute a majority of the people who will interest themselves sufficiently to go to the poll.

This Bill will place great power into the hands of people outside this Chamber. One could imagine the power which street-corner advocates will exercise under this measure.

Can we substitute this proposal for the existing methods?

We discuss every matter, the newspapers publish our discussions, they publish the intention of members and Ministers and the public know before our measures become law what we propose. After all, is not this parliament thoroughly representative of the people? Would we have trial by jury without a judge, without a special pleader, without a responsible advocate and without evidence? That is what we are asked to agree to now.

W.A. *Debates*,
9 December
1913, pp. 3416,
3508–9

Statue of Sir Henry Parkes, 'the father of federation', in Centennial Park, Sydney, where the Commonwealth was proclaimed in 1901

In a federation, power is shared by two levels of government. The colonial parliaments and governments were to remain, though in future the colonies would be called states. They would give up some of their powers to the new national government, which was to be called the Commonwealth of Australia.

The delegates borrowed heavily from the federal constitution of the United States. They used the same names for the two houses

103

of parliament, the House of Representatives and the Senate, and they were to be composed in the same way. In the Senate the states were to have an equal number of members. In the Representatives the people were to be represented, with the states having members according to their population. As in the United States, a court—the High Court—was to interpret the constitution. It would settle arguments between the Commonwealth and the states over their powers.

However, the Australians did not want to follow the Americans and elect a president. They wanted the government of the Commonwealth to be formed in the parliament and to be responsible to it. This was the Westminster system that they were used to in the colonies. Governments in this system are formed in the lower house and, as taxation and spending are at the centre of government, the lower house has to control these. If the government of the Commonwealth was to be formed in the House of Representatives, then some limitation would have to be placed on the Senate's powers over taxation and spending. But the small states wanted the Senate to be strong because only here would they have the numbers to outvote the large states. They wanted the Senate to have the same powers as the Representatives in everything.

The delegates compromised. The Senate was not to amend the annual budget or taxation measures but it could make suggestions. It kept the power to reject them outright—a power that would be used rarely, if at all.

There were progressive liberals at the 1891 Convention, but they were in a minority. They were not able to get democratic principles written into the constitution. The Senate was to be elected by the state parliaments, not the people, and its members were not to be paid. There was no provision to resolve deadlocks between the houses.

The political rights of the citizens of the Commonwealth were to be fixed according to the laws of the state they lived in. All the men of South Australia could vote in Commonwealth elections, but not all the men of Tasmania because manhood suffrage did not operate there. The big landlords of Melbourne, who had a vote in each electorate where they owned a house, would get multiple votes for the Commonwealth. Adelaide landlords would have only one vote because there was no plural voting in South Australia.

The constitution was not adopted. There was strong opposition to federation in New South Wales. Though Parkes was the leader of the federation movement, he found he would have to set federation aside if he was to remain premier. Members of his own free trade party did not like it because they thought the Commonwealth would adopt Victoria's policy of protection, which had been followed by the other colonies. Parkes now also needed the support of the new Labor Party, which was interested in wages and conditions and not in federation—certainly not in an undemocratic federation.

It was going to be hard to please the Labor Party, because it thought equal representation of the states in the Senate was undemocratic. But the small states would not join without equal representation in one house. They said that a federation had to recognise the equality of each of its member states. There was a clash between federal principles and democratic principles.

In 1893, the people living along the River Murray formed Federal Leagues to help revive interest in federation. They were very keen about it because federation would put an end to the customs duties they had to pay when they took goods and stock across the river. They decided to hold a conference at Corowa right on the river and to invite all people and groups interested in federation.

The people at the conference wanted federation, but they were uncertain about how to make it happen. They did not want just to talk about it: they wanted action. A lawyer from Bendigo, John Quick, came up with a plan. A new convention should be held elected by the people. It would draw up a constitution. The parliaments could not stall or argue about it; they would have to hold a referendum to see if the people agreed with it.

This was a new, democratic way to make a nation. The conference loved it. Quick took the plan to Sydney. New South Wales had a new premier, George Reid, who had taken over from Parkes as leader of the free trade party. He was fat, clever, talked in a slangy way and cracked crude jokes. Parkes thought he was not fit to be premier. He was in fact one of the great reforming premiers. Reid had been very critical of Parkes's undemocratic constitution of 1891. He liked the Quick plan and he persuaded the other premiers to put it to their parliaments for approval.

Four parliaments agreed with it—New South Wales, Victoria, South Australia and Tasmania. The Legislative Councils were opposed to democracy and yet they agreed to the people electing a convention and the people giving their verdict at a referendum—and that, in this voting, the principle of 'one man, one vote' was to apply. The Councillors had to agree to all of this if they wanted federation.

John Forrest of Western Australia was opposed to so much democracy and said he would have his parliament elect the delegates. The conservative government of Queensland was afraid of the democracy of the south and its opposition to Kanakas. Queensland did not send any delegates.

The new Convention, which met for three long sessions in 1897 and 1898, drew up a much more democratic constitution. This time the progressive liberals were in a majority. But even progressive liberals from the small states wanted a strong Senate and protection for small states.

The Senate was now to be elected by the people of the states and its members were to be paid. Its powers remained as they were and the states were still to have equal representation. The progressive liberals from the large states were willing to accept this so long as ultimately the people ruled. So now there were deadlock provisions. If the Senate twice rejected a measure from the Representatives, an election could be held for both houses (a double dissolution); after the election, if the Senate still would not pass the measure, the two houses would sit together. The progressive liberals wanted a simple majority to settle the issue, but the small states delegates made it three-fifths.

The constitution was to be altered by referendum—a very democratic method—but there had to be two majorities if a proposal were to be carried: a majority of the people and a majority of the states.

The progressive liberals led by Kingston demanded that the Commonwealth set its own voting rules and not rely on state law. Kingston wanted all men and women to be given the vote. The women campaigners sent petitions to the Convention, asking that the constitution set a new standard for the nation by creating a democracy of all the people and not just half.

At this stage female suffrage operated only in South Australia. Most delegates were in favour of it, but they did not want to endanger support for federation by pushing the issue too hard. They decided that for the first Commonwealth election state law should apply (so the women of South Australia would vote). Then

FEDERAL CONVENTION.
ADELAIDE, SOUTH AUSTRALIA, 1897.

McGann, Photo.

Leigh Street, Adelaide.

The elected federal convention of 1897–98 that wrote the constitution for the Commonweath of Australia

the Commonwealth parliament would decide who should have the vote in future. But the parliament was not to take away the vote from anyone who already had it. As the parliament would not be able to take the vote away from South Australian women, it would have to give the vote to all women.

The constitution now had to be put to the people. In mid-1898 four colonies voted on it—New South Wales, Victoria, South Australia and Tasmania.

George Reid, who had organised the second convention, was much happier with this constitution. But he still thought a free, progressive Australia should have a more democratic constitution. He set out all the good and bad points of the constitution in a great speech in the Sydney Town Hall and told the people to make up their own mind. He himself, despite his doubts, would vote Yes. He was given the nickname 'Yes-No Reid'.

Whether the constitution was democratic was one of the big

issues in the referendum campaigns. The Labor Party in New South Wales and Victoria campaigned for No because they still could not accept a strong Senate with equal representation. It was hard for democrats to agree to a new strong upper house when they were fighting to reduce the power of Legislative Councils.

Yes campaigners argued that the Senate was a different upper house—a states' house elected by all the people of the states, not a conservative house elected by property holders. Labor was not persuaded. It saw Tasmania and Western Australia as backward conservative states that would put a stop to progress through their equal representation in the Senate.

THE FEDERAL CONSTITUTION IS NOT DEMOCRATIC

This is a speech by H.B. Higgins at Geelong, 18 April 1898. Higgins was the only Victorian delegate to the Constitutional Convention to oppose the Bill.

To make a change in a single word of this constitution, there must not only be an absolute majority of both houses of the federal parliament; but the change has to be submitted to the electors in the several colonies; and unless there be a majority of the people, and also a majority of the States in favour of the change, the change cannot be made.

Suppose a change in the constitution is proposed, as to which the great bulk of the large populations of New South Wales and Victoria are agreed, but as to which opinion is nearly equally divided in the other three colonies. Suppose that in New South Wales 100,000 vote for the change and 10,000 against; in Victoria 90,000 vote for the change and 10,000 against; in South Australia 14,000 vote for the change and 15,000 against; in Tasmania 6,000 vote for the change and 7,000 against; in Western Australia 6,000 vote for the change and 7,000 against. Then you have 216,000 electors voting for the change, and 49,000 voting against it. You have more than four to one in favour of the change. Yet that change cannot be made. Public opinion is thwarted. And the Australian people have no remedy, for they have, in the words of the preamble, 'agreed to unite in one *indissoluble* federal commonwealth'.

I say nothing—nothing—nothing should be made so rigid, so absolutely unchangeable.

H.B. Higgins,
Essays and Addresses on The Australian Commonwealth Bill, Melbourne, 1900

To all those who did not like the constitution, the Yes campaigners said that the people could amend it. But Labor objected to the rule that a majority of the states as well as of the people was necessary for change. And what they disliked most would be impossible to change. No state could have its proportion of representation reduced unless it agreed.

The people of the four colonies voted Yes, but in New South Wales the number of Yes votes did not reach the minimum the parliament had set. Reid called all the premiers to a conference and they agreed on changes to the constitution. Some were to please New South Wales—such as that it should have the capital; two were to make the constitution more democratic. First, at a joint sitting of the two houses a majority vote would settle the issue. Second, a government could hold a referendum to change the constitution even if the Senate was opposed to it.

The constitution was carried in the four colonies in mid-1899 and later that year in Queensland. It was sent to London to be made legal in a British Act of Parliament. At the last minute Forrest put the constitution to the people of Western Australia and it was carried there as well. The six colonies came together in the Commonwealth on 1 January 1901.

IS THE FEDERAL CONSTITUTION DEMOCRATIC?

This constitution is not only the most democratic of any existing Federal Constitution, whether we compare it with that of Switzerland, Canada, the United States or Germany, but is infinitely more democratic than the Constitution of any Australian Colony. It contains almost every democratic principle for which the Democrats of Australia have been striving for the last forty years.

1. Abolition of plural voting for both Houses.
2. No property qualification for electors of the Senate.
3. No property qualification for members of the Senate.
4. Payment of members of the Senate.
5. Power to dissolve the Senate.
6. A remedy for deadlocks.

Handbill
Federal
Referendum,
1898

The inauguration of the Commonwealth and the swearing in of the first ministry, Centennial Park, Sydney, 1 January 1901

The first Commmonwealth elections were held soon after. The free traders and the protectionists fought over what the tariff policy of the new nation should be, and produced a dead heat. The balance of power would be held by the Labor Party, which was divided on the tariff issue. It decided to support the protectionists because they were the more progressive liberals.

This alliance produced the foundation laws of the Common-wealth. It was led for two years by Edmund Barton, the first prime minister. He was a protectionist from New South Wales who had been leader of the federal movement after the retirement of Parkes. In 1903 Alfred Deakin became prime minister and governed with Labor support in 1903–04 and 1905–08. He was a Victorian protectionist, a scholar and a dreamer, but also a most effective politician; he was handsome and spoke beautifully and powerfully, never pausing, never looking at notes.

Under Barton the White Australia policy was made law, the import of Kanakas was stopped and plans made to send them home, and a moderate protectionist tariff was established. Deakin cemented the alliance with Labor by offering protection to industries on condition that they pay fair and reasonable wages. That made the Labor Party into protectionists, and the tariff rates went up. An Arbitration Court was set up to settle disputes between workers and bosses and to fix wage rates.

In 1902 the parliament decided who should vote for the Commonwealth. Barton's government, as expected, planned to give the vote to all men and women. However, members and senators from Queensland and Western Australia objected to Aboriginal people having the vote. In their states only Aborigines who met the property qualification could vote (plural votes for property still operated). A few did own property; many were still tribal people with little knowledge of white affairs. Labor members were worried that if they got the vote the squatters would control how they voted. In the other four colonies, Aborigines as British subjects could vote.

The government gave in and agreed that Aborigines should be excluded. Those who already had the vote would keep it under the section that had been included to safeguard the rights of South

Edmund Barton and Alfred Deakin, first and second prime ministers

---

TWO VIEWS ON ABORIGINES AND THE VOTE, 1902

Sir Edward Braddon, former premier of Tasmania, in the House of Representatives

If anything could tend to make the concession of female suffrage worse than it is in the minds of some people, it would be the giving of it to any of the numerous gins of the blackfellow. It cannot be claimed that the Aboriginal native is a person of very high intelligence, who would cast his vote with a proper sense of the responsibility that rests upon him. And it can even less be claimed that the gins would give a vote which would be intelligible.

Commonwealth Debates, 1901–2, Vol. 9, p. 11977

Richard O'Connor, a minister in Barton's government, in the Senate

It would a monstrous thing, an unheard of piece of savagery on our part, to treat the Aboriginals, whose land we are occupying, in such a manner as to deprive them absolutely of any right to vote in their own country simply on the ground of their colour, and because they were Aboriginals. Although the Aboriginals in New South Wales, Victoria, Tasmania, and South Australia had the right to vote through all these years, now under the Commonwealth, with the liberal views we are supposed to hold, we are asked to take away from the sons of those people for ever the right to vote.

Commonwealth Debates, 1901–2, Vol. 9, p. 11584

Australian women. However, over time the people running the voting system kept Aborigines off the voting rolls.

Why did the objections from two states lead to total exclusion? The Commonwealth could not keep the property test of Queensland and Western Australia because its voting system was not to refer to property; it was to be one person, one vote. Aborigines had to be all in, or all out. The Commonwealth also wanted to make one rule for all Australia, so again it was all in or all out.

That the decision was 'all out' for the Aborigines is not surprising at a time when being white was becoming an ever more important part of the Australian identity. Australians thought of themselves as a progressive nation partly because they were racially

Women voting for the first time in Victoria at the Commonwealth elections, 1903

pure. They believed that the white race was the best, and their progress depended on remaining white. So immigrants from Asia had to be totally excluded and Aborigines within Australia seemed more of a threat. It was around this time that the states were beginning to pass laws that took away Aborigines' civil liberties. Governments took control of where they lived, whom they married, and whether they could keep their children.

Racial thinking helped the growth of democratic feeling because men and women of the one race saw each other as equals; they had something they took to be very important—their blood—in common. It also turned democrats into oppressors of those who did not share the blood.

Vote the party

The Labor Party was not the first political party in Australia, but it quickly developed an organisation and discipline like no other. It was not only that all its members of parliament voted together. If you wanted to be chosen as a candidate for parliament, you had to promise not to run if you were not selected. There was to be only one authorised Labor candidate, and all Labor people were to campaign for him and vote for him.

Having only one candidate was important because voting was 'first past the post'. If two men stood as Labor candidates, one official and one independent, they would split the Labor vote and make it easier for another party to win.

After 1900 Labor's vote went up in leaps and bounds. It threw all other parties into panic. How could Labor be stopped? The other parties criticised Labor's discipline, but wished they had some of it themselves. Their parties were more like movements of people with the same broad ideas; they did not control their members. They could not stop members running as independents or other members from supporting them.

Labor was no longer just a workers' party. It gained support from small farmers in the country and workers in the country who wanted to be farmers. Labor's policy for the country was to break up the large estates and help small men to get land.

Labor had support Australia-wide. In the federation debate Labor had feared that Tasmania and Western Australia would for a long time be backward and conservative. It sent its MPs to help the party get started in these states, and very soon they were electing as many Labor MPs as the rest.

Nearly all Catholics became Labor supporters. This was partly because most of them were workers. The church was opposed to socialism, but the Australian bishops declared that Labor was not a socialist party and encouraged their people to join it. They might have hoped that if the Labor Party received Catholic votes, it would support government money for Catholic schools. But the Labor Party did not want to buy into a religious fight. It had to keep Protestant and Catholic workers together. The socialists in the party would never agree to support church schools because they saw religion as a bar to progress.

After the 1906 federal election Labor had more members than Deakin's protectionists. It was now the second party, not the third. Its parliamentary leaders were still happy to support Deakin, but the party organisation was becoming restless. It had a Labor majority in its sights; it wanted no more alliances and to work for a Labor government that would turn all the Labor platform into law.

The largest party was the free traders led by George Reid. He realised now that free trade was a lost cause. At the election he had campaigned against socialism. That, he said, was the direction

Deakin and Labor were heading with their willingness to involve the government in more and more things. Reid himself had been a progressive liberal in New South Wales politics. He was now leading a group of conservative liberals.

ALFRED DEAKIN AND THE THREE PARTIES

In 1906, when Deakin was governing with the support of Labor, he gave this account at an election meeting in Adelaide of the three parties. His own party was called the Liberal Party. In 1909 he joined with what he calls here the anti-liberalism party to form the 'fusion' Liberal Party.

The Labor Party is an offshoot of the old Liberal Party. Before there was a labor organisation I had the honor of being associated with a party in my own State, which had placed upon its programme the great watchwords still echoing today. We sought and seek to unlock the lands, develop national industries, and to safeguard the rights of those engaged in them. [Cheers] Before there was a Labor Party those were Liberal aims, and they are Liberal aims today. Because the Labor Party has thought fit to separate itself for other purposes, it has not on this and many other subjects broken old ties.

The Labor Party is not divided from us in our use of the powers of the State; but it has associated with it those who desire to press on at once with an extension of the powers of the State which would threaten to absorb many of the great industrial functions of the community. They go farther and faster than we do, though the bulk of their party blends with our own. The wing of the party that holds extreme views is perfectly entitled to submit its case. There can be no objection to the men who believe that any monopoly can be better dealt with by the State than by individuals who are abusing its powers. In their antagonism to monopoly they have the whole Liberal Party with them. [Cheers]

Against the Liberals is ranked a party less easy to describe or define, because, as a rule, it had no positive programme of its own, adopting instead an attitude of denial and negation. This mixed body, which may fairly be termed the party of anti-liberalism, justifies its existence, not by proposing its own solution of problems, but by politically blocking all proposals of a progressive character, and putting the break on those it cannot block.

Federal Politics: The Liberal Party and its Liberal Programme, Adelaide, 1906

Some of Deakin's supporters said he must break the alliance with Labor, which was working to sideline him, and join with Reid in one anti-Labor party. Deakin refused. He hated Reid because he had been Yes-No on federation and he would not go along with Reid's scare about socialism; he was not afraid of government action. While Labor would support him, he would continue his work.

It was Labor that broke the alliance in November 1908. Then Deakin did agree to join with the other party so long as Reid did not remain as its leader. This is known as the fusion. The new combined party called itself the Liberal Party. 'Liberal' was an old name: it was used by those who fought the privileges of the squatters; by the independents who got roads and bridges for their electorates; by both free traders and protectionists; by those who had supported more government action and those who had opposed it.

How could it be all these things? Liberalism had two strands. It stood for an open society and personal freedom. It also stood for government action to allow individuals to live better lives and have more opportunity to shape their lives. The more conservative liberals stressed the first; the more progressive the second. There were tensions between them, but they also had much in common. They all believed in developing the resources of the country, which involved a lot of government activity. They were all opposed to

---

DEAKIN DENOUNCED

When Deakin joined with the group he himself had described as 'anti-liberalism', Billy Hughes of the Labor Party denounced him.

There is not a vested interest in this country now that does not acclaim him as their champion. Every reactionary in the Commonwealth is massed behind him.

What a career his has been! In his hands, at various times, have rested the banners of every party in this country. He has proclaimed them all, he has held them all, he has betrayed them all. The cause of Liberalism is hopelessly doomed when it depends upon the daily and hourly support of honorable members who have ever been its open and avowed enemies.

Commonwealth
Debates, 1909,
Vol. 49, p. 133

socialism as a threat to private property and personal freedom. They all disliked the tribal way Labor did politics. Deakin had worked happily with Labor in parliament to extend the role of government, but he hated the Labor organisation outside. He saw it as a threat to individual freedom and conscience. He could never join the Labor Party.

The supporters of the Liberal Party were big business, rich people, the better-off farmers, and middle-class people in the towns, those who did not work with their hands. They were nearly all Protestants. In state politics, at this time, the Protestant churches were at the peak of their influence in their campaign against drink. The brewers and pub owners naturally looked to the Labor Party to protect them. Respectable middle-class Protestants then had another reason to dislike Labor: it was the party of drink and the Roman Catholic Church.

The Liberal Party was a much looser organisation than the Labor Party. It existed to elect Liberals to parliament, but it did not aim to tell them what policies to follow. The membership fee was kept low so that more people would join. Most of the funds to run the party and pay for election campaigns came from a secret group of big businessmen, called the National Union. They did try to influence what the parliamentarians did and were sometimes very influential.

The local members of the Liberal Party insisted that they choose their candidate for elections and did not want any interference

LIBERAL UNION OF SOUTH AUSTRALIA: INCOME AND EXPENDITURE 1911–12 (IN POUNDS)

The Liberal Union was the name of the Liberal Party in South Australia.

Receipts		Expenditure	
Membership dues	1323	Organisers	1595
Business donations	5487	Central office	1033
Other	132	Elections	2892
		Other	1703
Total	**6942**		**7223**

Central Executive Minute Book, Secretary's report to 18 July 1913

CHOOSING A CANDIDATE

Billy Hughes describes how he was chosen in 1894 as a Labor candidate for the Lang Division of East Sydney. Voters had to produce their 'elector's rights' to show they were genuine local residents, a precaution that did not secure an honest ballot.

The place was packed at seven o'clock, when MacDermott—his hair cropped close, his great moustache yellow and curved like that of an ancient Viking—took the chair and called the assemblage to order in a voice that could be heard blocks away.

'Gentlemen, we're going to have everything fair and above board'. [Terrrific applause] Only electors of the Lang Division could vote, and in order to make sure that none others did, Mac looked round and observed in a casual way 'I notice a lot of our friends from the Rocks and Pyrmont here. We're glad to see them, but they can't vote because'—and here Mac smiled broadly—'every elector must produce his 'electric right'. [Loud, but not extravagantly loud, cheers]

And then the voting began. The trouble was not to get them to vote, but to induce them to leave off. They were so desperately in earnest that it was only by unwearing vigilance backed by *force majeure* that they were prevented from voting again and again. They would go out, refresh themselves with beer, rearrange their hats, turn up their collars of their coats, and jauntily re-enter and once more endeavour to record their vote. Baulked in one direction they tried another. Since they could not vote twice on the same 'electric right'—or vote at all unless they had one—they immediately set out in search of loose or unattended rights. Some sneaked furtively into their homes and lifted the old man's right while he was at tea. The tedium of those stretched on beds of sickness was relieved by numerous callers, who, oozing sympathy at every pore, sought to coax from the invalid 'the loan of your electric right'. And many a man dead these six month and more put in his little vote that night through the hand of one who had not forgotten him, or where his elector's right was to be found.

At nine o'clock MacDermott announced in thunderous tones that the ballot had closed, and that the result would be declared as soon as possible. The narrow street was crowded, an air of suppressed excitement prevailed. I waited near the door, trying to give a life-like imitation of a man supremely confident of victory. Then, suddenly, the end came! The crowd, which had been unnaturally quiet, sprang into life. A roar burst upon my ears. 'What is it?' I asked. 'Run for your life', said one of my friends, 'you have been selected'.

Crusts and Crusades, Sydney, 1947, pp. 114–15

from the central organisation. In the Labor Party the choice of candidates rested finally with the executive. In both parties 'branch stacking' occurred. A person who wanted to be chosen as a candidate would enrol his supporters in a branch just before it decided on candidates.

The Liberal Party still found it hard to have only one Liberal candidate running. To solve this problem it supported the replacement of first-past-the-post voting with preferential voting. (Under this system, two candidates can exchange preferences and they don't spoil each other's chances: each candidate tells his supporters to give the other candidate their second preference.)

At the federal elections in 1910, Labor had a great victory. It won a majority of seats in the House of Representatives and the Senate. It governed well and its prime minister Andrew Fisher was widely respected as a man of honesty and integrity. He was a goldminer from Queensland, who had started work at 9 years of age in a coalmine in Scotland. But now Labor experienced its first major setback. It wanted to make laws to control business and set wages and to take over monopolies, but the constitution had not given these powers to the federal parliament. The Fisher Labor government twice ran referendums to get these powers put in the constitution, and both times it was defeated.

The people had let Labor down. But Labor believed that the newspapers had misled the people. The daily newspapers were big businesses themselves and their papers were almost always anti-Labor. The party tried to overcome this handicap by running its own newspapers. Trade unionists and party members gave the money to get them started. They did not do well. The Sydney Labor paper survived longest because its racing tips were good.

By 1911 there were Labor governments in the Commonwealth and three of the states. The union leaders in the party organisation were very critical of them. They had not voted all the platform into law. The politicians faced great difficulties: in the states, the Legislative Councils; in the Commonwealth, the constitution; everywhere, the people who might not want all the platform passed into law. But the union leaders thought they could have done much better.

During World War I the party system was shaken up. After being out of office for 12 months, Labor returned to power in the Commonwealth in September 1914, just after the war had broken out. Andrew Fisher was again prime minister. In 1915 he retired

Billy Hughes, Labor and then Nationalist prime minister, speaks at a recruiting rally in Sydney during World War I

in favour of his deputy, Billy Hughes, a very different man. He was clever, quick and unscrupulous. In 1916 when he tried to introduce conscription for overseas service, the party organisation revolted. It had long been looking to bring the politicians under control, and it threatened any politician who supported conscription with expulsion. Hughes was not put off. He decided to hold a referendum on conscription. If the people were willing to accept it, the party would have to agree to it. The referendum was after all part of Labor policy. In the campaign before the referendum in October 1916, Labor people were fighting each other. All the Liberals were in favour of conscription. The result of the referendum was a narrow win for No.

The people themselves and not the politicians decided this very important question. The Labor organisation and its trade union leaders were overjoyed; it looked as if the people were willing to follow them and not the Labor politicians. Hughes and the Labor politicians who supported conscription formed their own

Labor Party. Hughes remained prime minister with the support of the Liberals. Soon Hughes and his followers joined with the Liberals to form a Nationalist Party. The party was called 'Nationalist' because it combined Liberal and Labor men dedicated to fighting the war. They were ashamed of the Australian people for voting against conscription. They thought they had let the British Empire down.

In May 1917 an election was held. Hughes campaigned on the slogan that only the Nationalists were committed to winning the war and standing by the Empire on which Australia's safety rested. He won a great victory. This was the first time there was a landslide against the Labor Party and never again did it look like an unstoppable force.

The finances for the Nationalist Party still came from big businessmen via the National Union. They wanted Hughes to remain leader to fight the war, but after the war they were less happy because he had not given up his Labor principles. He still believed in government-run enterprises and more power for the federal government.

In the war the government acquired all the farmers' crops and organised the selling of them. The farmers complained about how these schemes were run and began standing their own candidates for parliament. They had long felt that both the major parties were too concerned with the big cities. This was the beginning of the Country Party (which continues today as the National Party). The Country Party preferred the Nationalists to Labor, but in order to increase its influence it borrowed Labor's tight organisation.

There was a danger that Country Party candidates would split the non-Labor vote. The Nationalist Party government solved the problem by passing a law in 1918 for preferential voting. This system has operated in Commonwealth elections ever since. It allowed Nationalist and Country Party candidates to compete against each other in elections without giving the Labor Party an advantage.

After the pro-conscription politicians had been expelled from the Labor Party, the union leaders moved to take control. They planned to make it crystal clear to the politicians that they must obey the organisation. They rewrote the party rules to give much greater representation to the trade unions at party conferences. This meant that the union vote completely swamped the votes from the branches in the suburbs and country towns that the politicians had fostered in order to win elections.

HIS ONLY HOPE.

The Pastoral Review *1913 records country people's many grievances against city-based parties*

Union leaders also worked together to make sure that they controlled who was elected to the executive and other important committees in the party. They would agree on their candidates, and when the voting was held they would have to show their voting paper to each other to check that they were all voting the same way. By these means the party organisation, which was meant to be democratic, could be controlled by a few men. The organisation became a 'machine'.

In 1880 voters elected a person to parliament. After 1910 voters elected representatives of two parties, after 1920 of three parties.

A UNION VIEW OF LABOR MPS

This letter to an Adelaide newspaper in 1915 criticised Norman Makin, a Labor MP. It was sent by the the Australian Workers Union, whose officials came to dominate the Labor Party in several states.

The truth of the matter is that Mr Makin and other persons who masquerade under the name of the State Labor Party forget that they are servants, not leaders nor masters. The unions are the masters; the Labor politician is merely a necessary evil to enable the unions to register their decrees. When the industrial arm of the Labour movement does in reality direct and control the political arm, many of the so-called Labor MPs and Labor leaders will have to either radically alter their tune or get work.

Register,
25 February
1915

It was very rare for an independent to be elected. Working people mostly voted Labor; middle-class people Liberal, then Nationalist; farming people Country Party. Politics became more predictable, but more distant. Between the voter and parliament now stood the party organisations. Voters could of course participate in the parties, but if they did they would be competing with big money and big unions. The Country Party was the one in which ordinary members had most influence.

Electorates now had more people in them, and so it was less likely that voters would know their MP. When women got the vote the number of electors doubled overnight. After federation there was a huge outcry against the number of state MPs. People thought there should be fewer MPs, now that they had less to do. The numbers were reduced and so each MP represented more people. From the start federal MPS represented huge numbers.

Many of the supporters of women's suffrage hoped that women would not support the party system. They thought parties of men would not pass laws to protect women and children, and they did not like politics being reduced to a slanging match between two sides. But most women did vote the same way as their husbands and they helped to solidify the party system. Middle-class women, who had more spare time than working-class women, became great

123

The Bulletin *on women's position in the new Liberal Party led by Alfred Deakin*

volunteer workers for the Liberal Party. It could then match the volunteer workers of the Labor Party, who were mostly men. But the middle-class women did not join the Liberal Party or the Nationalist Party. They kept their independence and maintained their own organisation, the Australian Women's National League.

Threats to democracy, 1920–1970

When the United States entered World War I in 1917, President Woodrow Wilson said America would make the world safe for democracy.

The United States was one of the world's oldest democracies and until now had kept out of the battles between the countries and empires of Europe, most of which were not democratic. According to Wilson, this would be the first and last time America would have to fight in Europe. After the United States and its allies won the war, they would redraw the boundaries of Europe. The great empires would be broken up and the different peoples within them given the opportunity by referendum to decide which country they should belong to or whether they should rule themselves. Government by the people would replace emperors, kings and aristocracies. Secret deals and alliances between countries would cease. There would be a League of Nations to keep the peace.

The map was redrawn, but peace and democracy did not flourish. The peoples were so mixed that it was impossible to create unified countries. The war itself had created so much social division and bitterness and loss of hope that the new democracies struggled to survive. Germany was officially blamed for the war and its new democracy had to make heavy compensation payments to the allies that had defeated it. Punishing Germany stored up trouble for the future.

Even before the war ended a great new antidemocratic force emerged onto the world stage. In February 1917 the government of the Tsar in Russia collapsed under the strain of fighting Germany, and in October a small group of communist revolutionaries led by Lenin seized power.

Communists, like socialists, did not believe in private property or private businesses. They were different from socialists because they believed there was no peaceful or democratic way to socialism. They said that owners of properties and businesses would never agree to let the people or the government own them. Democracy, according to the communists, was a fraud. People were allowed to vote only so long as they did not interfere with private wealth and profit-making. To introduce socialism, the workers would have to use force, first to overthrow the government and then to take businesses and property away from their owners and give them to the people.

Communists claimed that owners of property and businesses had no rights. They were exploiters of the people who should simply be eliminated. The workers should rule as a dictatorship to rid society of private property and its owners. Then when all property and businesses were owned by the people, a new society of equals would emerge.

Communists believed that everything in the old order should be swept away because it was a part of a system that had denied economic justice to workers. This included religion, which they denounced as a collection of lies and tricks. Priests helped the bosses by telling workers not to use violence, to accept their position in society and to look forward to pleasures in heaven.

The communists promised to produce a new world by a ruthless destruction of the old. The communist government in Russia did modernise a backward country and raise the standard of living of ordinary people, but at huge cost. A government which had a licence to use violence very soon used violence on all its opponents, including workers and peasants. It brought not liberation but total control over every aspect of life.

Communists knew that it would be hard to establish communism in one country because the governments of capitalist countries would not want communism to succeed. The new communist government in Russia set about encouraging communist revolutions

*Marchers in Melbourne on May Day carry banners showing Marx and Engels,
the founders of communism*

in other countries which would make its own revolution safe. The
communist idea was that the workers of all countries should unite
to establish communism; to fight for your country was to fight for
the bosses who owned it.

The communist revolution in Russia produced a great surge of
support for communism around the world. Workers who wanted
to replace capitalism now had a model to follow. For the first time
in history there was a country where the workers were in charge.
Communist revolutionaries became a threatening force throughout
Europe. Just after the war the new democratic government in
Germany had to put down a communist uprising.

Communism encouraged the growth of another antidemocratic
force, fascism. The first fascist government was established in Italy
in 1922 under the dictator Mussolini. Fascists believed in a strong
nation; they hated communists for saying the workers should have
no love for their country and for always encouraging divisions
between workers and bosses to bring on their revolution. Fascists
also thought democracy was a weak and inefficient form of
government. The people needed a strong leader who knew what

the people wanted, who could get results and lead them to greatness—and put down the communists and any other group that threatened the unity and strength of the nation.

In 1933 Germany came under the control of the fascist Nazi party led by Adolf Hitler. This was a fascism more savage than Italy's. Hitler put all his opponents in concentration camps and planned to purify the German people by getting rid of the Jews. He was determined to have his revenge for the defeat of Germany in World War I.

Before World War I democrats believed that the whole world was moving to democracy. Now democracy was being rejected and new and terrible forms of tyranny were being established in once-civilised countries. This was also the time when democracy came under threat in Australia.

Dealing with revolutionaries

In Australia during World War I, small groups of radical unionists and socialists flew the red flag at their meetings. The red flag was the flag of the workers worldwide; those who flew it showed they were loyal first to all workers rather than to their country. Red was also the colour of revolution, the flag of blood.

The new communist government in Russia adopted the red flag and added to it the hammer and sickle: the hammer for town workers, and the sickle for country workers, the peasants, who used the sickle to harvest the grain.

To fly the red flag in the war was to show that you did not believe in the war. Socialists said that the war was a bosses' affair, fought over markets and territory; the workers should have nothing to do with it. As the war continued to slaughter millions of young men, the socialists became more convinced that they were right, and more people in the unions and the Labor Party listened to their message. The socialists became more radical and some of them became revolutionaries.

Most people, however, continued to support the war. They had sons or husbands or brothers fighting in it or already killed in it. They wanted the British Empire and its allies to beat Germany. They were proud of being British and they saw the Empire as the chief protector of Australia. Because they were committed to seeing this terrible war through to its end, they were enraged by those who declared that it was a worthless struggle. They hated the people who flew the red flag rather than the British Union Jack, which was then Australia's flag as well. The flying of the red flag was banned by the government, but it still appeared. When anti-war activists flew the red flag at their meetings in public parks, returned soldiers sometimes stormed the platforms, tore the flag down and beat up the speakers and their supporters.

At the end of the war, in 1918, a group of Russian revolutionaries was operating in Brisbane. They were workers who had come to Australia to escape the government of the Tsar. Now that there was a revolution in Russia they were waiting to go home. Meanwhile they teamed up with those who wanted Australia to have a workers' revolution like Russia's. They flew the red flag at their meetings and demonstrations.

The respectable loyal citizens of Brisbane organised a loyalty league to protest about the revolutionaries. They were upset not so much because they were the owners of properties and business which the revolutionaries wanted to take away; they were insulted and angry at the revolutionaries saying their society was worthless and should be destroyed. For them as loyal Australian Britons the Union Jack was the flag of political freedom and decency and equality before the law. Only a madman would tear this down for the red flag that stood for violence and destruction.

In March 1919, when the Russians and their friends paraded with red flags in Brisbane's streets, groups of returned soldiers launched an attack on them that lasted for three days and nights. The police tried to protect the Russians, but the soldiers destroyed their meeting hall and ransacked their homes. The *Courier Mail* praised the soldiers for their magnificent deeds in defending the honour of the flag for which they had fought. The president of the RSL said the local communists must be got rid of, in the same way that Australian troops treated German spies in the trenches.

Something new had happened in Australian politics. There were now people who wanted to overthrow democracy by force, and there were other people who did not mind violence being used against the revolutionaries. As in other countries, the war had led to bitter social divisions and extremism.

Until the military took it down in October 1918, the red flag flew over the Trades Hall in Brisbane, the headquarters of the trade unions. The unions and the Labor Party they supported became much more radical during the war. When they opposed conscription for overseas service in 1916 and 1917 they said they were in favour of the war; they wanted men to volunteer for it rather than being compelled to go. Even then there were many within the movement who were opposed to the war. By 1918 the Labor Party was close to declaring that the war was not worth fighting. This made it easy for the Nationalists, led by the old Labor man Billy Hughes, to denounce them as disloyalists, as betrayers of the Empire and Australia. They were defeated in the elections held during the war in May 1917 and remained out of office in the Commonwealth until 1929, just before the Great Depression.

Before the war the trade unions and the Labor Party were a positive, dynamic force in Australian life. They seemed to be on the verge of taking charge of Australia and making it into a more just society. After the war, unions and the party lived in a hostile environment; they were on the defensive, bitter, stroppy and resentful. The Labor Party became more radical and less likely to have the chance to put its program into effect. Unions fought long and bitter strikes in the 1920s and had very few wins. Some of the union leaders wanted strikes just to cause trouble and to bring on revolt against the bosses.

At its 1921 conference the Labor Party adopted socialism as its goal. It wanted banks, factories, large shops and businesses all to be owned by the government. This pleased the socialists in the party but it troubled the parliamentarians, who thought Labor could never get elected with this policy. So an extra sentence was added to say that any private business or property that was not being used to exploit workers could stay in private ownership.

Labor planned to reach socialism by using parliament and sticking to the constitution. Communists said this would never produce socialism. In 1920 in Sydney a small group of communists formed the Communist Party of Australia. Now an Australian organisation was officially linked to the worldwide communist movement that was run from Moscow and wanted to make workers' revolutions everywhere.

The Communist Party attracted more than its share of foreigners and misfits, but also over the years great numbers of talented and idealistic Australians. They cared deeply for those who suffered under capitalism—workers sacked because of an economic downturn, farmers losing their land to the banks, widows having to wash clothes or scrub offices to support their children. Communism came to them as a revelation: it explained why

*Revolution is proclaimed in
Australia*

peaceful reform had not worked and would not work, and it promised that a society of true equality could be established.

To reach the ideal society they were prepared to accept the discipline of the Communist Party, which was run like a machine: members were to suppress all their human feelings; they were to care only for the cause; and they had to obey the leadership without question. If the leaders decided that members had adopted dangerous views, they had to confess their faults publicly before they could be readmitted to membership. An individual could not be right and the party wrong. The party was a superhuman force carrying mankind to a new future; individuals did not count at all. So even in Australia members accepted the thinking which allowed the Russian government to kill and imprison millions of people to advance the cause of communism. The difference was that in Australia communists who could not stomach the party any longer

Noel Counihan. Australia 1913–1986
Katherine Susannah Pritchard. 1953
Oil on canvas 76.2 x 631 cm

Talented and idealistic Australians in the Communist Party:
The communist artist Noel Counihan paints the communist novelist Katherine Susannah Pritchard

could leave it and live, protected by the rights and freedoms which communists denounced as frauds.

The Australian Communist Party, like all others, received funding and instructions from Moscow. Communists around the world had to accept that the top priority was the protection and advancement of the Soviet Union, the first workers' state. Their first loyalty must be to Russia, not their own country.

Communists admired the new order in Russia and refused to believe that the revolution had gone wrong. However, taking orders from Moscow made it harder to be a communist and quite often damaged the local communist cause. Moscow for its own reasons and without warning would suddenly change tack and send out new orders. At one stage communists in Australia had to follow the policy of 'revolutionary defeatism', which meant that they had to tell the workers that they should not resist a foreign invasion because it might give the opportunity for revolution.

The communists were at first a tiny group, but in New South Wales they instantly became very influential. The leaders of several large unions joined the Communist Party and Jock Garden, the secretary of the Trades and Labor Council, became the leader of the party. In 1922 Garden went to Moscow to attend an international communist conference. He told the conference that communists in Australia led unions with 400 000 members and that they would come to power through controlling Labor Councils (as he did Sydney's).

Of course, Garden was big-noting himself. He and his friends controlled unions, but very few of their members were communists; they were supporters of the Labor Party. But it was a great victory for communism to have such persons of influence supporting the cause and promising a revolution in Australia. To opponents of communism (which was nearly everyone), this was very disturbing. Imagine what we would think today if the head of the ACTU announced that she was planning a workers' revolution to overthrow democracy, abolish private businesses and property, and close down the churches!

Some people have argued that the communists were no real threat: their numbers were small and the Australian people were too committed to democracy for communists to have a chance. They claim that there was no reason to fear communism or that fears were greatly exaggerated. However, by its methods of operation communism spread fear of communism, even when the number of communists was small. Lenin was in favour of a small, disciplined party. It should take advantage of chaos and confusion to seize power and impose its control on the country. (Once you abandon democracy you don't have to bother about majority support.) Nor did communists think they had to say openly what they were doing. They were perfectly happy to keep their communist identity secret. They could then infiltrate other organisations and, without their members realising, use them to advance the communist cause.

A small group, working in secret, creating division and conflict, and then hoping to grab power—this was the Communist Party. No wonder it aroused fear. Australian democracy had never had to deal with such an organisation.

In Australia there was no permanent army available to put down an attempted revolution. Full-time foot soldiers could be recruited only when there was a war. To fill this gap, large secret armies were formed by the owners of large businesses and professional men.

Their officers were men who had served as officers in the war and many of the ordinary members were ex-diggers. The armies never came together. They were a network of contacts that could bring men together if there was danger. Men knew who their section leader was, but nothing more about the organisation. These armies first came into existence during the war, when revolutionaries first became active. They did not have a permanent existence; organisation would lapse when things seemed calm. They became most active during the Great Depression of the 1930s.

Private armies are a threat to democracy. The only army should be the one controlled by the government, which is responsible to the people. These armies insisted that they were not a danger; they existed only to protect law and order and constitutional rule. Their plans were designed to beat the communists' plans for revolution. They knew the communists were a small group, but that a breakdown in essential services—caused, say, by strikes—might give the communists their chance. The first job of the secret army was to keep essential services going and help the authorities preserve law and order.

In 1923 Jock Garden and the other Red union leaders showed up at the New South Wales Labor Party Conference and asked that the Communist Party be allowed to join the Labor Party. He was acting under instructions from Moscow. Garden and his friends had joined the Communist Party because Labor was not radical enough for them, but Moscow now said that the revolutionary opportunities that had existed just after the war had passed. There was no chance of separate communist action succeeding. Communists should join the Labor Party and work to take it over and make it into a revolutionary party, ready to seize power at the next crisis.

The conference was evenly split on the admission of communists. Only on the casting vote of the chairman were the communists allowed in. At the next year's conference they were voted out 160 to 104. Only for one year did Labor ever give official recognition to the Communist Party. The debate over whether communists should be admitted was one of the most significant in the party's history, even though at the time the delegates gave more attention to whether the leader of the Australian Workers Union should be thrown out for using ballot boxes with sliding panels to rig party elections.

The case for admitting the communists was that they wanted

SHOULD COMMUNISTS BE ALLOWED TO JOIN THE LABOR PARTY?

Ten reasons against

- The Communists advocate revolution and armed violence. Labor stands for constitutional methods.
- Communists advocate wholesale confiscation of land, cottages, mines, money, factories etc.
- The Communists' iron dictatorship is the complete opposite of majority rule.
- The Communists aim at the destruction of Parliament and Local Governing Bodies.
- Communists cannot be loyal to the Labor Party because they must give undivided allegiance to the Communist Executive.
- The Communists owe allegiance to foreigners in Moscow.
- Communists preach the United Front as a matter of tactics to deceive the Trades Unions and Labor Leagues.
- The Communists aim at destroying the Trades Unions and the Labor Party and converting them into units for a mad revolution.
- The Communists' official attitude to religion is offensive to ninety-five per cent of Laborites and Trade Unionists.
- The admission of the Communist Party with the right to spread its views would destroy the solidarity of the Labor Party.

P.F. Loughlin (Deputy Leader of State Parliamentary Labor Party) *Ten Reasons Why Labor should continue to Exclude the Communist Party and Members of that Party from the ALP*, Sydney, 1925

Ten reasons for

- The Communist Party is a working-class organisation.
- The Ultimate Objectives of the Two Parties are the same—the Socialisation of Industry. The real difference lies in the means adopted: the Communist Party does not believe that the capitalist class will allow the workers to socialise industry by parliamentary action.
- The unity of the Working Class is essential to the Victory of Labor over Capitalism.
- The Affiliation of the Communist Party to the Labor Party will strengthen the Labor Party.
- Affiliation has been demanded by all Trade Union Conferences.
- The Communist Party is a fighting organisation in the trade unions and trade union support is the only power that the Labor Party can rely upon.
- The criticism of the Communist Party against the reactionary elements in the Labor Party will make for the advancement of Labor.
- The Labor Party at present is not a class party and therefore does not alone represent the working class.
- The Labor Party in its final fight for the complete overthrow of capitalism must have the support of all workers.
- The Communist Party, if rejected now, will continue its fight for affiliation and will in the end win.

The Communist Party and the Labor Party Central Executive, Communist Party of Australia, Sydney, 1924 the same thing as the Labor Party—socialism. They might differ in methods, but the workers would get nowhere unless they were united, and the communists were real stirrers who would help to keep the politicians on track. These were the views of the militant trade unionists.

The case against was that the difference in method was everything. Labor was and had to remain a constitutional party that would bring in its program only if the majority of the people supported it. Communism frightened and offended people by its attack on all property and on religion. These were the views of moderate union leaders, the delegates from the country, the Catholics—a large element in the party—and the politicians. The politicians most of all knew that an alliance with the communists would be electoral suicide. The Labor Party had taken a terrible hammering from the Nationalists and in the press for having allowed the communists in.

The second vote in favour of exclusion did not settle matters between Labor and communism. Communists who hid their identity could still be members of the Labor Party, as could communists who were not members of the Communist Party, and sympathisers with communism. Communists who gained control of unions would exercise an influence in the party whether or not they were allowed to be members of it. This was a real problem for the Labor Party. The unions were the most important part of the party, but the party could not control who joined or led the unions.

Communism became the central issue in federal politics in the 1920s. The Nationalist government led by Stanley Bruce won two elections by campaigning against communism.

Bruce had replaced Hughes as Nationalist leader in 1923. The son of a Melbourne businessman, he went to Cambridge University in England and then looked after the London office of the family firm. He returned to Australia after fighting in the war in the British army. He is the only businessman to have been prime minister. However, he did not see himself as governing for business; he was a Nationalist, the leader of a party that had brought together Liberal and Labor politicians to fight the war. He talked constantly of the need for national unity if Australia was to solve its problems and progress.

He talked about unity because in the workplace there was constant strife. Militant unions opposed to capitalism ran strikes against hard-headed bosses who wanted to keep costs down. Bruce

Prime Minister Stanley Melbourne Bruce with Rolls Royce

thought there should be no strikes. Australia had created an arbitration system to make strikes unnecessary, and workers should accept the rulings of the Arbitration Court. He considered—rightly—that communists were making industrial strife worse. His solution was to increase the penalties on unions for striking and defying the court and to deport foreign-born union leaders who gave trouble.

The most militant union leaders were often born outside Australia. Bruce was targeting in particular Tom Walsh and Jacob Johnson, the leaders of the Seamen's Union. Both were socialist revolutionaries. Johnson was born in the Netherlands. Walsh was born in Ireland and was thus a British subject. Bruce was himself a loyal Britisher and his party criticised Labor for not being loyal enough to Britain, but he was going to treat a union leader with British citizenship as a foreigner.

Many Labor politicians regarded the militant unionists as a menace, but the Labor Party in parliament opposed Bruce's plans as a general attack on unionism and on civil liberties. They criticised the method that was to be used to order deportation—a board of enquiry, not a court—and the inclusion of British subjects as foreigners.

137

"THIS LEGISLATION DRIVES US BACK TO THE DARK AGES OF CENTURIES AGO."—Labor member J. H. Scullin on the political clauses of the Crimes Act.

"A MEASURE WHICH IS A MENACE TO THE PEACE, ORDER AND GOOD GOVERNMENT OF THE COMMONWEALTH."—Labor member N. Makin on the Crimes Act.

The Communist Senate team — Sharkey, Thornton, Ross and Ogston—is pledged to fight for the repeal of this menace to freedom.

"I BELIEVE THE BILL HAS BEEN FRAMED WITH THE SOLE INTENTION OF SUPPRESSING TRADE UNIONISM."—Labor member W. H. Lambert on the Crimes Act.

"THIS BILL WILL REMAIN A BLOT ON THE FAIR ESCUTCHEON OF AUSTRALIA UNTIL A FUTURE PARLIAMENT WIPES IT OUT." — Labor member J. E. Fenton on the Commonwealth Crimes Act.

The communist criticism of Bruce's legislation directed against militant unionists

Bruce was confident that the people would support him. In September 1925 he called an election as the deportation board was examining the activities of Walsh and Johnson. Bruce declared that Australian democracy was in danger from the communists and that tough measures had to be taken against them. Labor could

TUESDAY, NOVEMBER 3, 1925.

ROUT OF COMMUNISTS.

HISTORIC DAY AT CAIRNS.

WORK RESUMED ON WHARVES.

FARMERS PROVIDE PROTECTION FOR LUMPERS.

Monday, November 2, will long be remembered as an historic day in the annals of Cairns and North Queensland, when the primary producers of the Tableland and the sugar districts delivered a most staggering blow to the Communistic forces who had sought to control the local waterside workers, and had held up the produce of this district, amounting to a total value of over £1,000,000, for the past eight weeks.

Early in the day 600 primary producers assembled in Cairns. An ultimatum was delivered to the waterside workers that, unless they commenced operations, they (the farmers) would undertake the duties themselves. Following meetings, about 20 lumpers commenced work, and the waterfront was picketed by the producers. Promptly at 2 o'clock, to the accompaniment of enthusiastic cheers, 80 waterside workers offered their services, and they started work, under the protection of the farmers.

Angered by the turn of events, extremists deliberately incited a crowd of waterside workers, who, however, were soon brought to their senses by the producers. It was a complete rout of the Communists, many of whom were forced to flee from the town, and others were afforded protection by being locked up in the police station.

Although at one stage there was a disturbance, in which 200 men formed a struggling mass, there was no bloodshed. The police, however, made several arrests. The farmers conducted themselves admirably, and aided the police in their duties.

The president of the Waterside Workers' Federation, who wildly exclaimed that if the "farmers wanted fight they could have it, tooth and nail," lost his bellicose attitude when the producers, their patience exhausted, pursued him. He sought the police station for protection, and afterwards tendered a written apology, and resigned his position as leader of the lumpers.

A report in Brisbane's Courier *during the 1925 federal election* not be trusted to deal with the menace; it was altogether too friendly with communists. The Labor Party said that Bruce was exaggerating the danger just to win an election. It attacked the Nationalists for taking away the ancient rights and liberties of British subjects. The Nationalists replied that the threat to liberty came from the communists.

The government had a great victory, increasing its majority. However, the High Court stopped its plan to deport Walsh and Johnson. The Commonwealth government has only limited powers. The government had based its law on deportation on its power over immigration. The Court ruled that Walsh and Johnson had been in the country so long that they could not be regarded as immigrants.

The government continued its anticommunist campaign. In the new parliament it added a section to the Crimes Act that declared revolutionary associations and their publications unlawful. Labor supported it. The law did not directly outlaw the Communist Party: the government would have to prove in court that the party was revolutionary; then its members could be jailed for up to a year and its property seized. The communists expected this and prepared to go underground. However, the government did no more than seize communist papers and literature coming from overseas and step up its spying on the communists.

Communism was an issue at the next election in 1928, which the government also won. It lost office at a special election in 1929 when the issue was the Arbitration Court. Bruce was a tidy-minded, efficient man. One of the difficulties of industrial relations was that both the states and the Commonwealth had power over them. In 1926 Bruce tried to change the constitution to get full power for the Commonwealth. He lost the referendum. Then he decided to abandon the Commonwealth Arbitration Court and leave industrial relations to the states. Some of his own party deserted him on this and he was forced to call an early election. This move against the Commonwealth Court that set the basic wage was very unpopular. The government was defeated and Bruce lost his own seat. A Labor government under James Scullin took office.

Economic collapse

The economic Depression of the 1930s was just the sort of crisis that communists hoped for. Capitalism around the world seemed close to collapse as millions of people were thrown out of work. Communists thought this was their chance to bring on the revolution. The instruction from Moscow was that communists were now to act independently. They were to denounce Labor and social democratic parties as enemies of the workers for helping to preserve the system that oppressed them.

The Depression was very severe in Australia. The prices for wheat and wool, the nation's chief exports, fell sharply. Governments had borrowed heavily overseas, and they now struggled to keep up the interest payments on the loans because they were collecting much less in taxes. They cut back on their spending, which threw more people out of work and made the Depression worse.

At the worst moment of the Depression, in mid-1932, 30 per cent of the workers were unemployed. Probably half the workers experienced unemployment at some point in the Depression. At first there was no government help for the unemployed. They had to rely on food parcels given out by charities. Because unemployment became so bad governments were forced to act— otherwise there might have been a revolt of the unemployed. Governments gradually provided food, a money dole and then work for the dole.

James Scullin, Labor prime minister 1929–32

The communists created an Unemployed Workers Movement to demand a better deal for the unemployed. They organised marches and demonstrations. When people were to be thrown out of their houses for not paying the rent, communists sometimes put together a little local guerilla band that fought off the police and the bailiffs. The Communist Party was itself still tiny, but communists, without revealing their identity, were now in charge of a large organisation. At its peak the Unemployed Workers Movement had 30 000 members. The authorities knew about the communist leadership of the unemployed so the police often broke up demonstrations and arrested their leaders. They were fined or jailed for offensive behaviour, unlawful assembly, meeting without a permit or vagrancy.

The Labor Party took office in the new capital, Canberra, just as the Depression began. The party tore itself apart, arguing about what it should do to get people back to work.

At this time economic experts said that governments should respond to depressions by making sure that their income and expenditure balanced. As governments were collecting less in taxes they must cut expenditure or raise taxes. Neither was easy to do when times were tough. But this was what 'sound finance' required, and unless governments followed this path confidence in the country would fall, people would not invest, and the economy would not grow again.

Most of the Labor members did not want to adopt the methods of 'sound finance'. They were elected to protect workers' wages and conditions and now they were being told by the Nationalists, the newspapers and economic experts that they had to pay government workers less and cut the old age and diggers' pensions. They would do anything but that. For a Labor government, to do that would be treachery.

What could they do instead? Some said that the government should get business moving again by making the banks provide easy finance or by printing more money. There were some economic experts who supported these schemes, but this was new and daring thinking and in most people's eyes dangerous and irresponsible. It was not 'sound finance', though it became so later. A few Labor members said that rather than cut wages and pensions they should stop paying interest on government loans. No experts supported this irresponsible policy. If governments stopped paying interest no-one would want to lend to Australia again, or only at very high interest rates.

THE REVOLUTIONARY WAY OUT OF THE CRISIS.

The Communist Party declares that capitalism is the cause of the crisis, and that the crisis will only be abolished when capitalism itself is abolished. The day-to-day fights of the workers with the capitalists must lead up to the seizure of power by the workers and the establishment of a Socialist order of society.

We point to the splendid example of Soviet Russia, where under Socialism there is no crisis, but complete security of employment, rapidly rising standards of living, and a universal 7-hour day with 6-hour day for heavy or dangerous trades, while the peasants organised in collective farms have reached a standard of living undreamt of before.

This was achieved through the setting up of Soviets (i.e., Councils democratically elected by all those performing useful work).

The Communist Party declares that only by setting up their own Soviets can the Australian workers and working farmers free themselves from capitalist exploitation and build Socialism in this country.

The first acts of these Soviets would be:—

1.—To take over without compensation all banks, insurance companies, large enterprises, railways and big department stores.

2.—To take over the big landed estates and Crown lands, cancel the debts of the working farmers and grant them a secure tenure.

3.—To cancel the debts which the workers and the middle class owe to the big capitalists and landlords. To cancel the public debt owed to Australian and overseas bondholders.

4.—To confiscate the houses and residences belonging to the rich and transfer them to those now under bad housing conditions.

5.—To confiscate all supplies of food and other necessities of life held by the State and big capitalists and place them at the disposal of the unemployed and those in need.

6.—To guarantee to all toilers full freedom of organisation, of assembly and of the press.

7.—To form an alliance with Soviet Russia and Soviet China and arm all toilers for the purpose of preventing all efforts of the capitalist class to restore its power.

8.—To plan all production, as in Soviet Russia, in the interests of the working population so as to abolish unemployment, raise living standards and reduce the working day.

The whole present situation compels us to make our choice between this revolutionary program on the one hand, and on the other hand the continuance of capitalism, greater crises, poverty, oppression, Fascism and War.

FOR A SOVIET AUSTRALIA
VOTE COMMUNIST 1

Authorised by A. S. Fisher, 182 Exhibition Street, Melbourne.

Printed by Starlight Press, 553 Elizabeth St., Melbourne.   F5375.

The communist solution to the Depression

A few Labor members believed in 'sound finance' and that for the good of the nation and the workers the party had to stick with it. Their strongest argument was that the government could not do anything else because it did not control the Senate, where the Nationalists had a majority, or the Commonwealth Bank, which had an independent board. Both the Nationalists and the bank board believed in 'sound finance' and were determined to stop Labor from adopting any 'funny money' schemes.

The leader of the 'sound finance' group in the Labor Party was Joseph (Joe) Lyons, an ex-school teacher from Tasmania where he had served as premier. The wild schemes he heard in the Labor caucus room in Canberra appalled him. While he was acting as Treasurer caucus told him to suspend repayment of a loan. He ignored them and appealed to the Australian people to lend money to the government so that it could repay the loan. The interest he offered was low; people invested their savings to help the country, not to make money. More money was offered than was needed. This great success made Lyons famous as a politician who had put his country before his party. A few months later, worried at the direction Labor was taking, he resigned as minister.

In New South Wales the Labor premier Jack Lang stopped paying interest on British loans. He declared: 'While there is a pinched and starving belly in Balmain, not a penny, not a penny, to the bloated bondholders in London'. The workers in Sydney loved him. Middle-class people in Sydney and around Australia hated him. They were ashamed and angry at what he was doing: he was ruining Australia's reputation in Britain, the country they admired, the country that they believed stood for honour and honesty, the country they still called 'home'.

To preserve Australia's reputation, the Commonwealth Labor government paid the interest that Lang had held back. The federal Labor Party expelled the Lang Labor Party and set up an 'official' Labor Party in opposition to his.

Lang had been a real estate agent in a Sydney suburb. He was a big man, a loner, with no real friends but plenty of henchmen to protect his position in the party. The New South Wales Labor organisation was a war zone; rival groups fought each other by standover tactics, fixing elections and rewriting the rules. Once Lang's followers were in charge, the party organisation ruled that Lang must be the parliamentary leader. Some of the Labor parliamentarians were critical of Lang, but they no longer had a

Jack Lang, Labor premier of New South Wales

voice in who should be leader. The party that had been so suspicious of politicians had now found one to whom it wanted to give all power.

Lang was a demagogue, someone who tells his followers what they want to hear and does things that look good but make no real difference—or make things worse. He was not as wild and radical as he made out to be. Within the party organisation were many socialists and a few secret communists who saw the Depression as the chance to implement Labor's ideal of socialism. Lang at first encouraged them, but then they produced a three-year plan outlining how Lang was to create a socialist society. The 1931 Labor conference adopted it—but for only 24 hours. Lang and his machine got to work on the delegates and the vote was overturned.

But to big business and middle-class people this was not very reassuring. For the moment Lang had beaten the socialists and revolutionaries, but he himself was steering to disaster. They feared that when disaster struck, the revolutionaries and wreckers would have their chance. The federal Labor government also seemed to be courting disaster by its failure to do anything and by playing with crazy remedies. Thousands of people were now convinced that

---

OATHS OF PRIVATE ARMIES

New Guard

I solemnly and sincerely affirm that I will by every means in my power and without regard for consequence do my utmost to establish in the state of New South Wales the high principles for which the New Guard stands. I will not consider my oath fulfilled until Communism has been completely crushed and until sane and honourable government has been established. I make this affirmation in the name of God and the King and in memory of my countrymen who lost their lives in defence of the same principles. So help me God.

Old Guard (White Army)

I pledge my services to assist constitutional authority in the maintenance of law and order, and on such other occasions as it may become necessary, of life and property. At such times I will implicitly obey the orders of my superior officers.

Quoted in Keith Amos, *The New Guard Movement*, Melbourne, 1976, p. 69

Quoted in Michael Cathcart, *Defending the National Tuckshop*, Melbourne, 1988, p. 178

---

something more than normal political methods would be needed to save Australia.

Big businessmen got the secret armies into shape and they now recruited large numbers. In New South Wales there were 5000 soldiers in the city and 25 000 in the country. In Victoria the army was a similar size. Together they were much larger than the official Australian army today. In northeast Victoria in March 1931 the message came that the revolutionary forces were on the move. In the country towns the army units came out of hiding, went on patrol and guarded strategic points. At Ouyen in the Mallee they dug a trench across the highway and waited. In the morning it was clear that it was a false alarm.

In New South Wales the secret army was called the Old Guard. In Sydney a new private army formed, the New Guard, which operated in the open. Its aim was to protect the 'decent' people of the state against Lang. It was run by small business and professional men, not very wealthy people like those at the top of the Old Guard. At its peak the New Guard had 50 000 members.

Lang as viewed by the
Constitutional Association of
New South Wales

They got into training by breaking up meetings of communists. The men of the New Guard would mingle in the crowd and start singing the National Anthem. They would then beat up the men who did not take off their hats. The New Guard thought the Old Guard was too passive, with its policy of not moving until there was a crisis. The New Guard was spoiling for a fight and hoped it would have the chance to remove Lang. The Old Guard thought the New Guard was a bunch of cowboys who might bring on the crisis that would give the revolutionaries their chance.

The New Guard was led by a solicitor and ex-army officer, Eric Campbell, who thought of himself as a strong leader in the fascist style. Members had to be loyal to him or they were thrown out. If the state faced a crisis, he said the New Guard would take over and install a few good men to run the country until democracy could be restored. That was the message he gave at a huge rally in the Sydney Town Hall that was broadcast on the new medium, radio.

Many minds turned at this time to the advantages of strong leadership. Some big businessmen and a few Nationalist politicians

Eric Campbell, leader of the New Guard, gives the fascist salute in the Sydney Town Hall

were sympathetic to what Mussolini had achieved in Italy. They were afraid that normal politics with its bickering and playing to the gallery was unable to cope with the collapse of the economy and the threat from socialists and communists. The man they most often thought of as the Australian dictator was John Monash, who had led the Australian troops in France in World War I. He always turned down these invitations. He was a much better democrat and a more loyal citizen than those who approached him.

The democratic response to Lang was the formation in Sydney of the All for Australia League. Again it was businessmen who started it, but it quickly became a mass movement. People of all sorts flocked to join it. Three weeks after its launch in February 1931, 30 000 had joined; after another week membership stood at 40 000; by June it was 130 000. No other political movement in Australia has grown so rapidly. Most members would have been Nationalist voters, but there were some moderate Labor people as well.

They called themselves 'All for Australia' because they thought politics promoted divisions between people: bosses and workers, city and country. They believed that people of goodwill could come together, put aside their divisions, and agree on a few simple

INVITING MONASH TO BE DICTATOR—AND HIS REPLY 1930

An invitation (by an Old Digger)

There is only one man who can save Australia, and that is John Monash. Put Australia under semi-military rule. Form camps for the starving women and children. Send the unemployed out to work for the farmers to grow food for the women and children. Put communists on some old ships and send them to the Antarctic with tools, six months food supply and each man a gun, and let them put into practice their political theories—with full power to use the guns. General Monash is one of the greatest organisers the world has ever seen, and with the advice of financiers, backed up by drumhead court martials, he would save Australia within three years.

Bulletin,
3 December
1930

Reply (to a group of Sydney businessmen)

What do you and your friends want me to do? To lead a movement to upset the Constitution, throw out the Parliament, and take over the government? If so I have no ambition to commit High Treason, which any such action would amount to.

What would you say if a similar proposal were made by the Communists and Socialists to seize political power for the benefit of the workers and the extinction of the middle-class, as they have done in Russia? Would you not call that Revolution and Treason to the Crown and Constitution?

The only hope for Australia is the ballot-box and an educated electorate. You and your people should get busy and form an organisation as efficient, as widespread, and as powerful as the Labor Party.

If it be true that many people in Sydney are prepared to trust to my leadership, they should be prepared also to trust my judgement.

Quoted in
Geoffrey Serle,
John Monash,
Melbourne,
1982, p. 520

principles to deal with the Depression. The principles were those of 'sound finance'. The League hoped that the sheer weight of numbers in its movement would force governments, federal and state, to do the right thing.

The League was a great revolt against political parties. These decent people felt that politics had become indecent; the party machines did not represent them; the parties were an immoral, alien force. They were disgusted with the New South Wales Labor machine, but they were critical of the Nationalists as well. They wanted to be rescued from Lang, but they did not want him to be replaced by the Nationalists. They wanted something better: they wanted the people to rule. The people's representatives should be free to vote as they wished, rather than being controlled by the parties, and the people should have a direct say through referendums.

The leaders of the Nationalist Party were upset at the formation of the All for Australia League. Why, they asked, did people who wanted to get rid of Lang not support them? In Melbourne the big-money men who bankrolled the Nationalists quickly saw that the All for Australia League would be a much more effective political force. They promoted the formation of a similar league in Melbourne. They also told Joe Lyons that they would install him as the leader of these new political forces if he left the Labor Party.

Lyons went home to Tasmania and consulted his wife Enid, who was a true partner in his political work and, some said, the brains of the outfit. She was for accepting the offer. He agonised for four weeks before he agreed.

Everything fell into place as the Melbourne money men had planned. The All for Australia League merged with what was left of the Nationalist Party. The leader of the Nationalists, John Latham, was pressured into giving up his position as leader of the Opposition in favour of Lyons. All the forces opposed to Labor were now united behind a man who a few months before had been a senior Labor minister. The new party was called the United Australia Movement. In New South Wales members of the All for Australia League cooperated with it, but took some time to join it. They had hoped for something different from the creation of another political party.

Lyons was already a political hero before the Melbourne money men took him up; that's why they took him up. He was a decent, homely man; he was not, as he said, a great speaker or a wizard at finance; he presented standard ideas in an ordinary way—and crowds flocked to hear him. Amid all the social and political upheaval he was a very reassuring figure, a sign that decency and honesty could beat the political system.

Lyons was a great political asset to Labor's opponents. As a

Joseph and Enid Lyons and children in the garden of the Prime Minister's Lodge, Canberra

former Labor man he could attract those Labor voters who, like him, did not want to make things worse by departing from 'sound finance'. He was also a Catholic, the father of 11 children. So he would attract some Catholic voters from Labor, the party Catholics traditionally supported. Lyons has been the only Catholic to lead the party opposed to Labor.

The Labor government's attempts to depart from 'sound finance' had all been rejected by the Senate and the Commonwealth Bank. Prime Minister Scullin then accepted that he would have to follow 'sound finance' more or less. He had been a socialist in his youth; now he recognised that he had no chance of implementing a distinctive Labor policy; his job was to find a consensus policy that would save the country from ruin. In June 1931 he and the state premiers (who came from both sides of politics) agreed on a plan for state and federal governments that cut wages and pensions and the interest paid on loans. Lyons and the United Australia Party supported it. Scullin needed their votes in the parliament because he allowed the Labor members a free vote on the Premiers' Plan. That meant that Labor men did not have to vote to cut wages and lower pensions.

The difficult part of the plan was the cutting of interest rates on loans. Lenders had contracts with governments that set down the interest rate. To break a contract was thought to be immoral and irresponsible—it was what Lang had done. But the principle of the Premiers' Plan was that the pain of government cutbacks should be equally spread. So lenders were asked to agree voluntarily to an interest cut. They nearly all did. Then by law the rest were made to follow, with exceptions allowed in case of hardship. The Melbourne money men were upset at this compulsion and wanted Lyons to oppose it. He refused.

The Scullin government lost office because the Labor members from New South Wales who were loyal to Lang voted against it. An election was held in December 1931. The Labor government that had chopped and changed so much was totally discredited. There was no sign of the Depression lifting. The result was a foregone conclusion. Lyons and the United Australia Party came in on a landslide.

Australia was now fully committed to 'sound finance', except for the government of Jack Lang. He had signed the Premiers' Plan and then ignored it. In February 1932 he again refused to pay interest on a loan.

In the early months of 1932 democratic government in New South Wales came very close to collapse. The government would not meet its financial obligations. There were three private armies. A Labor Army had been formed to fight the New Guard. The Old Guard was on standby. The state was physically breaking up because the Riverina and New England were on the point of declaring their independence. This was their way of escaping from Lang.

The New Guard had promised that Lang would not be allowed to open the Harbour Bridge, now nearing completion. It had plans to kidnap him and place him in the old Berrima Gaol. One Guardsman, Captain de Groot, was so concerned at these plans that he put forward a gentler alternative. He would ride with the lighthorsemen in the procession and cut the ribbon before Lang. The plan was accepted, and de Groot declared the bridge open 'in the name of the decent and respectable citizens of New South Wales'.

The Lyons government paid the interest that Lang was not paying. It then passed a law to recover this amount from New South

New Guardsman de Groot opens the Harbour Bridge before Lang

Wales. The Commonwealth government had the right to take what it was owed out of the bank account of the New South Wales government. To stop this happening Lang ordered that money collected in fees and taxes should not be paid into the bank. It was to be kept in the basement of the Treasury, which was guarded by members of the Timberworkers' Union. It seemed that the Commonwealth might have to use force against Lang.

There were two outside powers that could bring Lang down. He ruled a state within a federation, and so he might be controlled by the federal government. He held office as premier at the wish of the king's representative, and so he might be controlled by the governor.

The governor was an Englishman, Sir Philip Game. Acting according to the constitution, he had chosen and supported Lang as premier because he was the leader of the party with a majority in the Assembly. He had accepted Lang's advice to appoint new Labor members to the Legislative Council—and had been criticised by Lang's opponents for doing so. He had given the New Guard a very cold reception when they marched into

153

Government House grounds to present a petition asking him to dismiss Lang. But now Game decided that Lang was breaking the law in hiding money from the Commonwealth. He asked the premier to withdraw the order to keep money out of the bank. Lang refused. The governor then dismissed him. He made the leader of the Opposition premier and accepted his advice to hold an election.

The governor acted properly. Under the Westminster system the head of state—king, queen or governor—holds 'reserve powers' to be used in emergency to guarantee that the system runs properly. A government must itself obey the law. If a government persists in breaking the law, it can be dismissed. The one criticism made of Governor Game by some constitutional experts is that he should have waited until a court declared that Lang was acting illegally.

Lang went quietly. He knew he had run out of options. Force and the threat of force had become factors in the state's politics, but Lang made no attempt to use force to stay in power. Two hundred thousand people gathered in a Sydney park to support Lang after his dismissal, but this was an election rally, not the beginnings of people-power parade. The private armies melted away. A note of dismissal from a governor had brought peace. The respect for constitutional authority ran very deep.

Lang lost the election and was never premier again. The United Australia Party with Country Party support governed the state for the rest of the 1930s. The federal Labor Party knew it would never govern again while Lang retained his power base in New South Wales. The Lang machine was hard to break. Until 1936 the official Labor Party ran in opposition to Lang's. When the two agreed to combine, Lang remained leader. It was only in 1939, when Labor MPs regained the right to elect their leader, that Lang was removed.

In the Commonwealth too the United Australia Party with Lyons at its head remained in office throughout the 1930s. The Depression began to lift soon after Lyons became prime minister. His government did not perform so well after the crisis had passed. Lyons was much better at winning elections than at developing new ideas. He was the most popular prime minister the country had had.

Lyons had close contact with the big businessmen who backed the United Australia Party. He sought advice from them and they sometimes tried to influence government policy. They could not push Lyons too much; it was he, not they, who could win elections. He had his own firm views. His government was devoting more and more attention to preparing for war, but as an old Labor man he would not consider conscription, not even for training for home defence.

The parliamentary leader and the financial backers—the National Union—were the only links between the various state branches of the United Australia Party. Unlike the Labor Party it had no federal organisation. Each state body was independent, and local branches within the states did not want anyone to interfere with the choosing of candidates for election.

After winning three elections Lyons wanted to retire and let his deputy Robert Menzies take over. The National Union persuaded him to stay on because it did not think Menzies was a winner. He was a very clever lawyer, but not popular with the people or his colleagues. When Lyons died in 1939, Menzies took over. Soon afterwards World War II began, and Menzies had to try to mobilise the country for war and watch his back for attacks from his own party. After the 1940 election he relied on two independents to survive.

Robert Menzies, prime minister 1939–41, 1949–66, declares on radio that Australia is at war, September 1939

In October 1941 the independents decided that Labor could provide a stronger government to run the war. They switched their votes and without an election John Curtin and the Labor Party took over. There was never to be another United Australia Party government.

In the history books the party opposed to Labor is often called the non-Labor or the conservative party. This is not what it called itself. Between the wars it was the Nationalist Party and the United Australia Party. Against Labor's appeal to the workers, it claimed to rule in the interests of all. For more than half these years the party was led by former Labor men who did not give up all their Labor principles. Hughes, thrown out of the Labor Party for supporting conscription, committed the Nationalists to running government businesses. Lyons, having left the Labor Party because it would not support 'sound finance', refused to allow the United Australia Party to adopt conscription. There was a good bit of Labor in 'non-Labor'.

War and planning

In the 1930s communists became the leaders of several large unions: the miners, railway workers, ironworkers and waterside workers. In the early 1920s existing union leaders became communists, but these leaders made their way to the top as communists. They gained support by being tough with bosses and working hard for their members. Of course they wanted to use their union position to advance the cause of communism.

In the mid-1930s new instructions came from Moscow. Stalin was so worried about the growth of Hitler's power that he ordered communists around the world to cooperate with any group that would resist the fascist powers. The Lyons government, following Britain closely, was against being tough on Germany or Japan; it hoped that by giving these powers some of what they wanted, it could avoid another more terrible war. This was the policy of appeasement.

In 1938 the communist leader of the waterside workers at Port Kembla, Ted Roach, led his men in refusing to load pig iron for Japan. The strike threw thousands out of work, but local people kept up their support for the ban. The Lyons government insisted that the waterside workers would not decide Australia's foreign policy.

It threatened tough action against the workers; it tried to find other workers to load the ship and failed. Menzies, as attorney-general, went to Port Kembla to talk directly to the workers. There was a huge, hostile demonstration. Menzies said Australia alone of the nations could not start enforcing sanctions against Japan. Ted Roach replied that the Japanese would use the pig iron in a war machine that would destroy Australian cities, just as they were doing in China. There were many people in Australia who were happy to see Japan busy with its attack on China; that might stop her from turning south.

The pig iron did leave for Japan. The workers finally agreed to load it if the government withdrew its threats. From this incident

Some of the workers who tried to stop pig iron from being exported to Japan

Menzies got the nickname 'Pig Iron Bob', which was a reminder in the war and afterwards that he had been an appeaser. At the time, most political leaders in the Western democracies were appeasers. During the dispute, Menzies said that a Labor government would have acted as he did. In fact, Curtin the Labor leader did not give any support to the Port Kembla workers. The policy of the Labor Party was isolationist: not to take sides in overseas conflicts and to concentrate on defending Australia.

As the democracies continued to appease Hitler, Stalin feared that they would be happy to look the other way while Hitler conquered Russia and eliminated communism. So in 1939 Stalin made a pact with Hitler. The two countries agreed not to attack each other, which allowed Hitler to attack the democracies in the west without having to worry about an attack on his rear.

Communists around the world had to turn a somersault. They stopped attacking fascism. They said that the war between Hitler and the democracies was an ordinary war in which the workers had no interest. In Australia the communists in the unions hindered the war effort by go-slows and strikes. They placed members in the armed forces to spread their anti-war propaganda. In June 1940, as Holland and France fell into Hitler's hands, the Menzies government banned the Communist Party. It did not need a special law to do this. In war the federal government can do anything necessary to defend the country. Under the National Security Regulations the government could close down any organisation that hindered the war effort.

In June 1941 Hitler broke his pact with Stalin and attacked Russia. Communists did another somersault and became supporters of the war. In Australia they now opposed strikes and wanted all resources to be devoted to the war. The communists were enthusiastic about the war but not because they wanted to protect Australia: they wanted to protect communist Russia, which was now an ally of the democracies. In December 1942 Curtin's Labor government lifted the ban on the Communist Party, but made clear it was not a supporter of communism.

John Curtin was a very successful wartime leader. He came to power just two months before Japan entered the war and soon faced the terrifying responsibility of defending the country against invasion. He and his party rose to the occasion. They put aside their idea that Australia's safety depended simply on defending Australia, and they cooperated with Britain and the United States in the

THE GUARDIAN

Official Organ of the Communist Party of Australia

June 30, 1940

EDITORIAL

Fascism Comes to Australia

COMMUNIST PARTY FIGHTS ON

The Menzies Government has gone a step further in creating a fascist dictatorship in Australia. On the same day Menzies announced that the Communist Party had been banned, and that the government had assumed dictatorial powers over man-power.

In pushing the dictatorship decree through parliament last week Menzies refused to consider any amendment to safeguard wages and award conditions.

It is obvious that the government is setting out to attack the conditions of the workers in every way ; that is the reason for establishing a dictatorship and for suppressing the Communist Party.

Menzies knows that Curtin and other Labor party leaders are traitors to the workers, they support the employing class and the Menzies government in fascist attacks upon the workers.

Menzies also knows that the Communist Party is the only genuine working class party which fights for the true interests of the Australian workers ; that is why his government has declared the Communist Party an illegal organisation.

They are doing the same things that Hitler did in Germany ; the police are turning workers' homes upside down in the brutal way as Hitler's storm troopers do in Germany. They ask workers to pimp on one another, and children to pimp on their parents in the same way as the fascists do in Germany,

But they can never silence the Communist Party which will continue to organise and lead the workers in spite of all fascist suppression.

The Communist Party lives and fights !

Help this great fight for Peace, Liberty and Socialism !

A NATIONAL GOVERNMENT MEANS SELLING OUT THE WORKERS

Menzies wants the Labor Party leaders to join his government, and Curtin and his colleagues want to join the Menzies government.

The thing which so far has checked this further treachery of Mr. Curtin and company is the strong opposition of the organised workers to any kind of unity with Menzies, Cameron, Hughes and Thorby.

For the Labor Party leaders to join a National government would mean joining forces with the Australian fascists; it would mean uniting with those who bludgeoned the waterside workers into loading war materials for fascist Japan, introduced scabs into the coal mines, and threatened the miners with force if they did not obey the dictates of the bosses.

The war doesn't alter the fact that there are still two sides in Australia: the bosses' side and the worker's side.

The Menzies government is the bosses' government and will stand for the rich even if Mr. Curtin and others join it. The only difference will be that then the Labor Party leaders will do the bosses' dirty work as their fellow traitors do how in England

---

"ARGUS" TELLS WHY FRANCE CAPITULATED

Sometimes the daily press actually tells the truth ; only sometimes. Melbourne "Argus" on Monday, June 24, revealed that to defend Paris would have meant a Communist government and that President Lebrun chose rather to let France be overrun by the German fascists than let this occur

---

The Communist Party, though banned, continues to issue its newspaper

worldwide fight against Germany and Japan. Curtin, who had opposed conscription for overseas service in World War I, persuaded his party to accept it for this war.

Until the 1943 election the Labor government was kept in office by the vote of two independents. It went to the election as a united party behind Curtin, the trusted leader of the nation at war. The opposition to Labor was weak and divided. The United Australia Party was close to death. Several new parties had sprung up to replace it—Citizens, Liberal Democrats, National Unity, Middle Class—and there were many independents. Labor had a great victory, winning huge majorities in both Houses.

Running a war was not what the Labor Party was formed to do. Curtin left military matters to the generals. Taking control of business and making it work for the public good was what Labor had dreamed of. Like other governments involved in the war, the Labor government decided what would be made, who would work where, and the level of prices, wages and profits. All production was geared to the war effort. There was no unemployment.

This was a planned economy. In the 1930s many people thought governments should prevent another depression by using experts, chiefly economists, to plan the economy. The economists themselves had come around to thinking that governments should be concerned with far more than balancing their income and spending. They could direct an economy by controlling lending, interest rates, the amount of money in circulation and their own spending. Sometimes it would be better for governments to break the rules of 'sound finance' in order to stimulate the economy. Labor had wanted to do this in the Depression, but that was before the new thinking was accepted.

Curtin's Labor government wanted to continue planning after the war was over. It was determined that there would never again be mass unemployment. Full employment was its goal. Planning was the way a democratic government could give economic security to its citizens.

Around the world there was great support for planning—and opposition to it as a threat to democracy. The anti-planners argued that a planned economy meant a planned society, which was the opposite of freedom. Everyone would be under the orders of the government. Planning was meant to be the way that the people could control the economy; it would turn out that the planners would control the people.

John Curtin, prime minister 1941–45, and Ben Chifley, his treasurer, who succeeded him as prime minister, 1945–49

In Australia, the federal government in peacetime would not have the power to control the economy. In 1944 Curtin's government asked for a massive increase in Commonwealth power. It put to the people a referendum proposal to give the federal government fourteen new powers. This was a package: you had to accept or reject the lot. Menzies led the No campaign, which argued that

PLANNING: AGAINST AND FOR

P.H. Partridge, political scientist

This present-day tendency to look to the State to take the lead in solving our economic problems is a danger to democracy.

We are usually told that a much greater concentration of power in the hands of the State is at least more democratic than the only possible alternative—the concentration of power in the hands of 'big business' and high finance. But if the State were to take over supreme direction of economic life, the result may not at all be that the organisation and conduct of industry will become more democratic than it is now. It is far more likely that the State would assume the form of organisation typical of capitalistic business and industry. That form of organisation, as everyone knows, is not a democratic one.

The more the State takes responsibility for directing the economic and other affairs of the community, the more hostile it would grow to any serious opposition to itself. If we reach a stage where we are largely dependent upon the State for our work, for our education, for our medical services, for our leisure and cultural activities, the time for opposition is past. The State would have us where it wants us.

Democracy is something which, to a considerable extent, has to be maintained *against* the State.

ABC radio talk 1943, reprinted in *Prospects of Democracy* ed. W.H.C. Eddy, Sydney, 1944

Ben Chifley, Treasurer in Curtin's Labor government

In the Depression, in my electorate, I witnessed the freedom that was enjoyed by 2000 men who congregated outside the gates of a factory in an attempt to secure the one job that was offering. I was able to study the freedom to starve.

All this talk of freedom is sheer, utter hypocrisy. If regimentation be necessary in order to secure to everyone a decent standard of living, freedom from economic insecurity, proper housing and adequate food and clothing, I say quite frankly that I should prefer it to the economic individualism that we had under the old order.

Commonwealth *Debates*, 1944, Vol. 177, pp. 1287–8

if the powers were granted Canberra bureaucrats would take away Australians' freedom. Labor argued that with these powers it could guarantee the people full employment.

The No side had an easy win. This was the second time a popular Labor government had failed to convince the people to give it the constitutional power to implement its vision for Australia. The first attempt to give the Commonwealth power over the economy was made by the government of Andrew Fisher before World War I.

The defeat of the referendum was an important victory for Menzies. In 1941 his political career seemed to be over when he had to resign as prime minister because his colleagues would no longer support him. Now he was putting himself forward as the leader of a new party that would replace the United Australia Party and bring together all the new parties and movements opposed to Labor. He invited delegates from all these groups to a conference in Albury in December 1944, when they agreed to form the Liberal Party. The women of the Australian National League agreed to disband their organisation and join the new party on condition that they have equal representation on all committees.

Menzies planned the Liberal Party to be very different from its predecessors. The state branches would remain independent but there would be a national organisation to conduct research, develop policy and plan campaigns. The party would keep its distance from big business. It would accept donations but with no strings attached. It would do its own fundraising rather than relying on the National Union (which had tried to keep Menzies from becoming leader of the United Australia Party).

While he was in the political wilderness, Menzies thought deeply about government in democracies. He accepted that governments would now be more active in economic management and in the provision of social security. But he insisted that citizens must have a large measure of freedom to pursue their ambitions and develop their individual potential. A lively society and a dynamic economy cannot be produced by government direction. Governments instead should encourage self-reliance and develop the talents of the people. Menzies was the first national leader to insist that the government provide the best possible education for all clever children, no matter what their parents' backgrounds.

Menzies set out his ideas in a series of radio talks that were turned into a book, *The Forgotten People and Other Studies in Democracy*. His thinking shaped the policy drawn up for the new Liberal Party. The name 'Liberal' indicated the stress the new party put on freedom. It was adopted to declare a clear principle in opposition to Labor, which was committed to socialism and more recently to planning.

Communism and Catholics

The Communist Party reached its greatest strength in 1945, the year the war ended. The war helped the party because it turned communist Russia into an ally of the democracies. The newspapers switched from condemning atrocities in Russia to praising the Red Army. The dictator Stalin became 'Uncle Joe'. The courage and determination of the Russian soldiers and people seemed to show that communism had worked. Again, as in 1917, Russia was an inspiration to many activists who could not bear to think that the death of millions in war was to bring back a world of private profit and gross inequality. Writers, artists and students as well as workers joined the Communist Party.

In 1945 communists and their supporters had a clear majority at the national congress of the Australian Council of Trade Unions. The Labor Party was opposed to communism, but now communists controlled the institutions on which the party was based. Labor decided it must break the hold of the communists in the unions. It set up 'industrial groups' in the unions which were to organise workers to throw out the communist leaders.

There was already a secret organisation at work on the same task. It was called simply 'the movement'. The Catholic bishops had created it to organise Catholic workers in the unions against the communists. The movement was run by an extraordinary man, B.A. Santamaria, who was thinker, organiser and spymaster. When his cover was eventually blown, his name made him sound like an alien force. He was in fact born in Australia of Italian parents, who ran a greengrocer's shop in Melbourne's Brunswick. He went to Melbourne University on a scholarship.

Santamaria planned to beat the communists at their own game. He trained his activists well and put them in charge of a small group. Groups could later elect their leaders but only from the trained activists. The groups met secretly. The job of the members was to win others to their cause without revealing the organisation they belonged to. Then when the time for electing union leaders came around the whole network would be activated to elect a non-communist candidate. The movement merged easily into the industrial groups that had been set up by the Labor Party. The members of the movement were known as 'groupers'.

The first aim of the movement was to defeat the communists. Santamaria's long-term aim was to take over the Labor Party and use it to create a society in which the Catholic religion would flourish. Life in large cities, he believed, killed off religion. He wanted Australia to be a land of small farms and small towns, where most people would be property owners and where cooperatives and credit unions would replace private businesses and banks.

The Labor Party was in great danger. Within its ranks a civil war was hotting up: one side wanted to create a communist Australia; the other a Catholic Australia.

After the war communism was advancing worldwide. In the countries liberated from the Nazis by the Red Army, Stalin installed communist governments. Communist movements were becoming stronger in Asia. The communists were poised to take control of

B.A. Santamaria with Archbishop Romolo Carboni at a Catholic Rural Movement Convention 1956

China. It looked as if the democracies, having just defeated Nazism, might have to fight another war for survival against communism. Tension between the two sides mounted—not into a war, but into what was called the Cold War.

The communists in Australia thought they would advance their cause by showing up the Labor government as no friend of the workers. In the unions they controlled they organised many strikes and go-slows, pushing to get better wages than the Arbitration Court had awarded. Labor supported arbitration; the communists denounced it as a bosses' trick. In the winter of 1949 they organised a strike in the coalfields. Coal was a key commodity. Without it steam engines could not run, and gas and electricity could not be produced. As the strike continued, factories closed, many thousands were thrown out of work, and homes lost power for light and cooking. The communist strategy of creating a crisis was working.

The Labor government was now led by Ben Chifley, who had taken over when Curtin died just before the end of the war. Chifley had been an engine driver and had been involved in a great strike in New South Wales in 1917. He was devoted to improving the conditions of workers. He did not big-note himself as prime minister; as often as he could escape Canberra, he returned to his small home at Bathurst, the same one he had lived in when he was driving trains. Now his job was to break a strike. As prime minister he could not let the country grind to a halt, and he well knew that the communists were using this strike for their own purposes. The

---

LANCE SHARKEY, COMMUNIST PARTY LEADER, ON STRIKES, 1942

Strikes properly led and conducted, and properly timed, are a revolutionary weapon. Strikes develop the labour movement, organise and unite workers and win the intermediate social strata to the side of revolution.

Political strikes are a higher form of struggle than economic strikes. Such strikes challenge the Government, the State, and the rule of the capitalist class. One of our chief trade union tasks is the politicisation of strikes.

Menzies Papers, National Library, Box 436, Folder 3

security service, which had its spies in the party, was keeping the prime minister informed on the communists' plans. He hit back hard. He froze the funds of the union in the banks so that they could not pay money to the strikers, imprisoned the leaders of the strike, and sent in soldiers to cut coal. The miners soon agreed to go back to work. This was a great defeat for the communists.

Though he had to be a strike breaker, Chifley showed he was a true Labor man by his attempt to nationalise the banks. Labor people had a particular hatred for banks because in hard times banks thought of their profits, not the wellbeing of the community. They remembered, too, how the banks had refused to cooperate with the Labor government in the Depression.

Chifley had removed the independence of the Commonwealth Bank and brought it under the control of the government. Through the Commonwealth Bank the government could control the activities of the private banks. Big business did not like government interference in banking. It challenged one part of Chifley's law and the High Court held that it was unconstitutional. In August 1947 Chifley decided that before any other challenges were made he would settle the private banks once and for all. They would be abolished. There would be one bank, owned and run by the government. This was the way to secure control of the economy and full employment.

This was the biggest step Labor had ever made towards socialism. Labor people were delighted; here at last was a Labor government that took the Labor platform seriously. The nationalisation law passed through the parliament. Then the banks challenged it in the High Court, which ruled that it was un-constitutional because section 92 of the constitution declared that trade and commerce between the states was to be absolutely free. The government took the case to the Privy Council in London and lost again. So the private banks survived, but Labor's attempt to nationalise them was a central issue in the 1949 election.

The new Liberal Party denounced the Labor Party as a threat to freedom. Part of its case was that Labor was soft on communism. As Chifley had used troops to break the communist coal strike, this was not so convincing, though the strike showed that the communists were a threat. The Liberals promised to ban the Communist Party. It was Labor's own attempt to nationalise the banks that gave the Liberals the ammunition they needed for the election. How could Australians be free, they asked, if there was only one bank that

THIS ELECTION IS A REFERENDUM ON SOCIALISM

"The case against Socialism is a deadly one. It concerns the spiritual, mental and physical future of our families.

"Socialism must mean the reduction of human freedom.

"You cannot socialise the means of production without socialising men and women.

"The real freedoms are to worship, to think, to speak, to choose, to be ambitious, to be independent, to be industrious, to acquire skill, to seek reward."

REMEMBER : Every Labour candidate signs the Socialist pledge.

For Security and Progress
VOTE
1 LIBERAL

AND FOR THE SENATE :
1 SPOONER;   2 REID;   3 McCALLUM;   4 TATE

Authorised by: J. L. Carrick, 30 Ash Street, Sydney

William A. Cooney Pty. Ltd., Printers, 72 Liverpool Street, Sydney

Liberal Party handbill, 1949 election

could lend them money and look after their savings, and that bank was owned by the government? It was the first step towards the total control of society that socialists wanted.

The Liberals won the election and Menzies became prime minister again. He moved swiftly to bring in a law to ban the Communist Party.

The normal rule in a free society is that any group of people has the right to organise and put its viewpoint. Menzies himself had supported that position and had been opposed to banning the Communist Party. He said he had changed his mind because Australia and the other democracies would quite likely soon be at war with communism. This made the Communist Party in Australia a special danger. In a war with communism it would be working for Australia's enemies.

He gave other reasons why the normal rule should not apply to the communists: they were not a debating club trying to persuade people to their point of view. They were a secret organisation, receiving orders and funds from Moscow, with the aim of overthrowing democracy. If the communists were in charge they would stamp out freedom. Should they be allowed freedom to destroy freedom?

Chifley, as leader of the Labor Party, was in a very difficult position. The communist unions did not want Labor to support a ban. The Catholic 'groupers' were strong supporters of a ban. Chifley said Labor would support a ban but with safeguards for the civil liberties of people who might be accused of being communist. Menzies proposed that if the government declared a person to be a communist, that person had to prove that he or she was not a communist. The normal rule in British law is that you are innocent until proven guilty. Menzies said the onus of proof had to be changed, because if the government's secret agents had to appear in court to give evidence their cover would be blown.

Some people in the Liberal Party were worried about the switching of the onus of proof and some newspapers were opposed to it. On this issue Labor was in a strong position, and because it still had a majority in the Senate it was able to alter the Bill. Menzies accepted some changes but not the key one on onus of proof. Then the federal executive of the Labor Party told the Labor parliamentarians to let the Bill pass as Menzies wanted it. This showed that the 'grouper' influence in the party organisation was growing. The executive was also worried that if Menzies called an election on communism Labor might be defeated.

Chifley was very disappointed, but he accepted these outside orders calmly. This was how the Labor Party was run. No man, not even a prime minister, was bigger than the party. He believed that if Labor remained united, if its members maintained solidarity, the

169

Labor Party would eventually create a much better world for ordinary men and women.

As soon as the law banning the Communist Party came into force, the communist unions challenged it in the High Court. Chifley's deputy, Dr Bert Evatt, offered to be their lawyer. Evatt was a very clever lawyer—he was a doctor of laws—and a great defender of civil liberties. He was not of course defending communism in taking up this case, but the 'groupers' in his party and the Liberals attacked him as the friend of communists.

Evatt won the case. The High Court declared that in peace the federal government did not have the power to ban a party. The Commonwealth had tried to argue that banning the communists was necessary for the defence of the country as 'defence' is a clear Commonwealth power.

Menzies decided to hold a referendum to change the constitution so that the Commonwealth would have the power to ban the communists. Chifley died in June 1951, two months before the campaign began, and Evatt became leader of the Labor Party. He threw himself into the fight to win a No vote and was not put off by opinion polls showing that 80 per cent of the people supported the banning of the Communist Party. Evatt hammered the point that Menzies was attacking the principles of British justice. There were other ways of dealing with communism than by the public naming of people as communists who might or might not be communists, and leaving them to defend themselves. He accused Menzies of taking Australia down the road to a totalitarian state. The communists accused Menzies of being a fascist.

The No case won very narrowly. It was a great victory for civil liberties. But almost 50 per cent of Australians were worried enough about communism to support a ban. It is a great dilemma that antidemocratic movements present to democracies. Our bias must be in favour of allowing all parties to operate, but who will say that modern-day Germany is wrong to ban the Nazi party?

The fight in the unions between communists and Catholics continued. More and more unions were taken out of the communists' hands. Evatt did not handle this great conflict well. He did not have Chifley's solidity and patience or his concern for the party rather than himself. In 1954 Evatt launched a public attack on one side in this struggle—the Catholics. The general public heard for the first time about Santamaria and his movement. Evatt denounced them for wanting to take over the party.

The uncovering of a secret organisation of Catholics alarmed Protestants and those who wanted a strict division between Church and State. Of course Catholics could bring their Catholic outlook into politics, but was it right for Santamaria, supported by Archbishop Mannix, to organise a movement to take over one of the major political parties so that it would follow Catholic teaching?

Evatt drew on anti-Catholic feeling to strengthen his position in the party. He now opposed migration from the Catholic parts

---

SHOULD THE COMMUNIST PARTY BE BANNED? THE 1951 REFERENDUM

The Yes case

Communist activity in Australia has become a grave menace to our industrial peace, to production, to national security and defence.

Aggressive Communism follows the same technique all over the world. Its chief instrument is the local 'fifth column', small in numbers, who get into key places with the greatest capacity and opportunity for damage at the chosen time.

The Communist doctrine—which is the same the world over, and many advocates of which in Australia have actually been trained in Moscow—finds its fullest expression in the Soviet Union. There you will find no Opposition or Opposition Leader; no free or democratic Trades Unions; no free practice of religion; no free press. But outside the Soviet Union all these things are invoked by the Communists, falsely, for their own ends.

Do you really think that we must under all circumstances concede freedom of speech to the enemies of free speech?

The No case

Labor is utterly opposed to Communism. Labor has taken the only effective action to combat Communism in Australia.

The Question is not whether you are against Communism but whether you approve of the Menzies Government's referendum proposals, which are unnecessary, unjust and totalitarian and could threaten all minority groups.

Labor absolutely refuses to abandon British justice for the methods of the police state. In short, we are NOT going to end democracy.

Referendum to be taken on Saturday 22 September 1951...the Case FOR and AGAINST Canberra, 1951 of Europe, like Italy, because it was strengthening the Catholic Church in Australia.

The result of Evatt's attack was that the Labor Party split. About half the Catholic 'groupers' left, or were thrown out, and they formed a new party. It was called the Democratic Labor Party and was very strongly anticommunist. It had no hope of winning office,

Communist handbill, 1951 Referendum

but it was determined to keep the Labor Party out of government until it got rid of communists in the unions. It told its supporters at elections to give their second preference to the Liberal Party. In close elections it was these votes that kept the Liberals in power until 1972.

The Liberals now had an organised body of Catholic supporters in the Democratic Labor Party. Menzies in 1963 gave them what the Labor Party had always refused—state aid to Catholic and other private schools, which was resumed after being denied for 80 or more years. Though the Labor Party still had many Catholic parliamentarians and supporters, it was even more determined to keep to its old policy of opposing state aid rather than do what the Catholic Church wanted.

Communism continued to create difficulties for the Labor Party. In union elections Labor men sometimes ran on joint tickets with the communists in battles against the Catholic 'groupers'. The

CRISIS
IN
FEDERATION!
————:0:————

In Whose Interests shall the Teachers' Federation of N.S.W. be Controlled ?

In the Interests of the Teachers of N.S.W.
OR
in the Interests of Moscow ?

TWO FLAGS
Your school received a flag in honour of the Jubilee Year
It is an Australian flag

NOT
A Russian flag!
It consists of a combination of the Union Jack and the Southern Cross on a ground of BLUE

NOT
of a Hammer and Sickle on a ground of Red.
Hundreds of Teachers of N.S.W.

DIED
for the Australian Flag
Thousands FOUGHT for it!

YOU
And every teacher should work for it!

SERVE IT
by insisting on the application of the Democratic principles for which it stands, within the Teachers' Federation.

DEMAND
Election of all Senior Officers by secret ballot of all members.

The fight against communists in the unions continued in the 1950s: the anticommunists' campaign to gain control of the Teachers Federation

Stopping the communist threat from the north: an election advertisement of the Democratic Labor Party

IT'S YOUR CHOICE: WHERE DO YOU DRAW THE LINE AGAINST COMMUNIST AGGRESSION?

Labor Party instructed its members not to appear on 'unity tickets', but they continued to operate. This allowed the Liberals to attack Labor for being soft on communism.

In foreign affairs the Liberal government gave strong support to the fight against communism in Asia, in the 1950s in Malaya and in the 1960s in Vietnam. The Labor Party opposed these wars, which the Liberals said were important for Australia's security. In 1966 the Liberals under Harold Holt, the leader who followed Menzies, won a huge election victory on their policy of fighting in the Vietnam War.

After this defeat Labor chose a new leader, Gough Whitlam. He set out to make the Labor Party electable after its years in the wilderness. He got rid of 'unity tickets', and persuaded the party to give up its opposition to state aid and adopt a policy of giving aid to schools according to need. He got the party to change its rules so that the conference and the executive would no longer give orders to the parliamentary leaders. The leaders would always be members of these bodies.

In 1971 Whitlam visited communist China, a country Australia had not recognised. Whitlam promised that a Labor government would recognise it. The Liberal prime minister William McMahon attacked Whitlam for going to China. But it turned out that Richard Nixon, the United States president, had been talking to Chinese leaders and was himself planning to visit China! The United States had decided that different communist regimes posed different threats and that it would become friends with China as a way to control Russia.

McMahon was made to look silly. Communism as an issue in Australian politics was finally dead.

Rights and limits, 1960–2000

By the 1960s Australia was coming close to having a completely democratic political system.

The biggest blot on the system had been Legislative Councils elected by property holders. Now that everyone accepted democratic principles, it became harder and harder to defend special rights for property and finally they disappeared—in Victoria in 1950, Western Australia in 1964, Tasmania in 1968 and South Australia in 1973. All citizens in those states could then vote for both upper and lower houses of parliament. For the Commonwealth parliament they had been doing that since 1901. In New South Wales the upper house was elected, but not by the citizens. From 1932, instead of the governor nominating new members to the Legislative Council, the members of the Council and the Assembly voted for new members.

In most states the arrangement of electorates was also made fairer, so that country votes no longer counted for much more than city votes. The glaring exception was Queensland. It was the first and still the only state to have abolished its Legislative Council. It was the last to get rid of its very unequal electorates. These lasted until 1991.

By the standards of the democrats of 1900 the states now had democratic constitutions. But from the 1960s a new group of critics

and reformers said the system was far from democratic. The test
of democracy was not just elections and the make-up of parliaments.
A properly elected democratic government could be secretive,
heavy-handed, and a threat to the individual rights of citizens.
A democratic government, the critics said, had to be watched and
controlled like any other. Individual rights had to be better
protected and limits put on what governments could do. There was
the tyranny of kings, but there was also the tyranny of elected
governments.

Citizens versus governments

The new reformers of the 1960s and 70s were mostly middle-class
people, and generally from the professions rather than from
business. They were social workers, teachers and lawyers (especially
lawyers), not shopkeepers or bankers. The reform movement was
made up of many strands. There were some new organisations
formed to push for particular changes such as freedom of information; established organisations like the Councils for Civil Liberties
campaigned for new rights; some of the reformers were members
of the political parties and worked for the cause within their parties.
There were reforming lawyers in both the Liberal and Labor
parties.

The great democratic campaign around 1900 had drawn its
strength from working people. They wanted a more democratic
political system so they could get a fairer society economically. They
wanted better wages and working conditions and to tax the rich
and perhaps take over their enterprises. Now the strength of the
reform movement came from quite well-off people with a university
education. This was a new grouping in Australian politics. They
were concerned with social justice, which they thought would be
advanced by ensuring that all people possessed their rights and were
able to exercise them. To help the poor to exercise their rights,
they campaigned for legal aid to be provided by the government.
Young lawyers worked as volunteers in new community legal
centres.

Some of the changes the reformers worked for and achieved
were: police to have fewer powers to hassle people and complaints
against police to be properly examined; residents to have a greater
control over planning and development in their localities; people

Victorian Council for Civil Liberties Inc.

An Organisation for Civil Rights

'The price of liberty is eternal vigilance'

CIVIL RIGHTS CONCERN YOU

VICTORIAN COUNCIL FOR CIVIL LIBERTIES

AIMS AND OBJECTIVES

The Victorian Council for Civil Liberties is a voluntary organization concerned with the protection of individual rights and civil liberties. Aims and objectives of the Council are:

☐ To safeguard and develop civil liberties and respect for human rights and freedoms

☐ To be vigilant in matters affecting rights and liberties of individuals

☐ To collect information about threats to and abuse of individual rights and liberties

☐ To foster the study of legal and human rights

☐ To seek solutions to problems related to civil liberties

And, in furtherance of these aims —
☐ *To make submissions to Government, releases to the media, publish books and pamphlets, and organise lectures and radio programs.*

An important campaigner for human rights

on social security to have the right to appeal if their benefits were cut; tenants on housing commission estates to have rights so that they could not be ordered around or ordered off by the management; children at government schools to have a fair hearing before they were expelled. The aim was to make government at every level open and accountable.

The reformers proposed that a new permanent watchdog—an ombudsman—should be appointed to protect citizens against government. The idea of an ombudsman was first raised in

IS AN OMBUDSMAN NEEDED?

Mr Reynolds asked the Prime Minister:

1. In his recent address to the National Press Club did he state that the sphere of government has been, and was being, considerably extended?
2. Could this increase the chances of citizens being unjustly deprived of rights and entitlements through faulty administrative decisions?
3. What is the Government's attitude to the suggestion that an ombudsman or some equivalent be appointed to protect citizens' rights and entitlements as has been done in other countries?

Sir Robert Menzies: The answers to the honorable member's questions are as follows:

1. Yes

2 and 3. Citizens with administrative problems or individual grievances have ready access to their own senators or members of parliament who make many representations to Ministers and Departments and, in practice, secure many necessary adjustments. This is a democratic process. Parliament itself always had a watchful eye on the protection of civil liberties. I see no reason to create a special official or department.

House of Representatives, *Debates*, Vol. 44, 1964, p. 1875

Australia in the early 1960s. An ombudsman had operated in Sweden for over 100 years. He was a very powerful officer, able to intervene in the affairs of government to protect citizens. 'Ombudsman' in Swedish means commissioner. In 1955 Denmark set up an ombudsman but with not such wide powers. The Danish ombudsman wrote about his work in English and so the rest of the world first learnt about this officer with the strange name and the unusual job—a public servant checking up on other public servants.

In 1962 New Zealand became the first English-speaking country to appoint an ombudsman. In 1963 the New Zealand ombudsman visited Australia and explained his work. He could not give orders to public servants or ministers. He examined citizens' complaints against government departments and if he thought they had been treated unfairly, he asked the departments to change their decision. If a department refused, he had in reserve the power to make the matter public.

Governments in Australia at first resisted the idea that an ombudsman was necessary. They argued that citizens already had an ombudsman in their member of parliament. If any one was treated harshly they could tell their MP, who could raise the issue in parliament, which was the great protector of the people's liberties. The reformers said this was not sufficient protection. If that system had ever worked, it was no longer working. The MP had too many constituents and government had become larger and connected with the people in many more ways. Parliament was not a place where individual grievances could be raised; it was the place where governments pushed through their legislation and MPs voted along party lines.

The support for an ombudsman did not follow party lines. In the early 1960s the Labor government in New South Wales opposed the idea and the Liberal opposition supported it. In Victoria the Liberal government opposed the idea and the Labor opposition supported it. Governments were scared of having their decisions examined. Oppositions hoped to become popular by promising to allow an ombudsman to examine decisions. When oppositions became governments, the reformers had to watch them to make sure they kept their promise. In Victoria the Liberal premier Sir Henry Bolte continued to oppose an ombudsman even after his party organisation had voted in favour of it. Victoria got its ombudsman in 1973 after Bolte had retired. Western Australia was the first state to get an ombudsman—in 1971. South Australia acquired its ombudsman in 1972, Queensland and New South Wales in 1974, and Tasmania in 1978.

The ombudsmen worked well. They made it easy for people to lodge complaints. The rules said that complaints had to be in writing, but they accepted complaints over the phone as an informal first step and were sometimes able to settle them with a few phone calls. South Australia's first ombudsman believed in bringing government officials and citizens together face to face. He settled one dispute in a farmer's paddock and another on a street corner.

The ombudsmen worked cooperatively with government departments. The only power they had was to make a public report if departments were ignoring them—but this was enough and few reports were made. The ombudsmen's work went on in private behind the scenes.

Ombudsmen did not deal only with individual cases. They looked at how government departments interacted with citizens and encouraged them to set up their own complaints offices. If they became aware of any major shortcoming in government administration, they could start their own enquiry.

The ombudsmen worked so well that governments gave them more reponsibilities, for example examining complaints against police. The number of people working in the office of the ombudsman grew. The danger was that, with success, the office of the ombudsman would grow too large and become another bureaucracy.

Aborigines become citizens

In the 1960s the Council for Civil Liberties in New South Wales was chiefly concerned with police corruption and the banning of films and books. In 1963 it was asked to support the protest of the Aborigines at Mapoon in Queensland, who were being compulsorily moved to another site to make way for mining. The council had not considered that Aboriginal affairs were part of its business. It started to take an interest in the position of Aborigines in its own state. A body concerned with civil liberties had overlooked the worst abuse of civil liberties: a whole people had been denied their liberty on the grounds of race.

In colonial times, after the frontier violence was over, Aborigines were not subject to any special control. They possessed the civil and political rights of British subjects, except that their right to drink alcohol was removed. There were reserves and missions, but Aborigines were not made to stay on them. They came and went, taking work in the countryside and then returning to their homes.

The attack on their civil liberties occurred in the late nineteenth and early twentieth centuries when Australia was defining itself as a white society. This was when the ideas of breeding out the Aboriginal blood and keeping Aborigines separate from the rest of society took hold. Under state laws, Aborigines could be told where they were to live; they had to seek permission to marry; and their children could be taken away from them. The managers of Aboriginal reserves became like mini-dictators.

After World War II state governments changed their Aboriginal policy. Instead of Aborigines living separately, governments wanted them to move into the rest of the community and become assimilated. It was now clear that the Aborigines were not going to die out. But it was also clear that they could not be treated forever as

Aboriginal workers in the southwest of Western Australia, before closer settlement and before the loss of civil rights

second-class citizens. Since racism in Nazi Germany had led to the destruction of seven million Jews, racism was now recognised as a terrible evil. The new world body, the United Nations, had declared against it and had published its declaration of human rights. Australia's treatment of Aborigines was beginning to be noticed overseas.

Slowly governments began to restore civil rights to the Aborigines. Some restrictions were dropped, but not others. In some states full rights were given to Aborigines who could show that they were not mixing with tribal people and that they were 'respectable' individuals living in the European way. They received what was called an 'exemption certificate' to show that the special laws controlling Aborigines did not apply to them. Aborigines called the certificates 'dog licences'.

In the 1950s and 60s new organisations were formed to campaign for the return of rights to Aborigines. They were made up of Aborigines and white Australians, with the white Australians at first usually being the leaders. Help for the Aboriginal cause came from church people, women's groups and trade unions, especially radical and communist unions. Because communists wanted to unite all working people round the world, they had always been opposed to racism and in favour of Aborigines being treated as equals.

Some of those helping the Aborigines thought that they would eventually blend in with the wider population and disappear. This was the plan of the governments. It was not how most Aborigines thought of their future. They wanted equality and government assistance, but they wanted to remain Aboriginal.

By the end of the 1960s most Aborigines had regained their civil rights. Only in Queensland did the government still keep a tight control on Aboriginal reserves. Aborigines also regained their political rights—for Commonwealth elections in 1962, Western Australia in 1962, Queensland in 1965. In the other states they had not lost their political rights, though it had not been easy to exercise them. Because their names did not appear on the Commonwealth roll, officials assumed they did not have the vote for state elections.

When Aborigines regained their civil and political rights it did not mean that they were treated equally. In some outback towns in New South Wales they still could not sit upstairs in the best seats at the cinema or swim in the council pool. In 1965 a group of students at Sydney University, including the future Aboriginal leader Charles Perkins, decided to highlight these injustices. They were inspired by the civil rights movement in America, which was working to bring equality to black people. The students travelled west in a 'Freedom Ride' bus.

At Walgett and Moree the students stood beside local Aborigines and demanded they all be let into the pool and into the good seats at the cinema. There were angry confrontations as the townspeople resisted this outside interference in their colour bar. The media were present to carry the story all round Australia. The colour bars were dropped, but white townspeople became more hostile to the Aborigines.

The greatest victory for the Aboriginal cause in the 1960s was the changes made in the Commonwealth constitution. Aboriginal people and their supporters had thought for a long time that only the Commonwealth government could establish a new deal for Aborigines. The constitution gave the Commonwealth power to pass laws for a particular race—except for Aborigines. The Aborigines were left as a state matter. The reason for this was that New Zealand, which was involved in the early discussions on federation, did not want Australia to take control of the Maoris. New Zealanders were proud of treating the Maoris much better than Australians treated the Aborigines. The only other reference to the Aborigines in the constitution was that they should not be counted in the census. This was to exclude them from calculations about state finances, but it suggested that Aborigines were not real people.

WHY VOTE YES, 1967

The official Yes case supported by all political parties

The purposes of these proposed amendments to the Commonwealth Constitution are to remove any ground for the belief that, as at present worded, the Constitution discriminates in some ways against the people of the Aboriginal race.

The changes will make it possible for the Commonwealth Parliament to make special laws for the people of the Aboriginal race, wherever they may live, if the Commonwealth Parliament considers this desirable or necessary.

Referendums to be held on Saturday, 27th May 1967, Canberra, 1967

They will also remove the prohibition on Aborigines being counted in the census. Our personal sense of justice, our common-sense, and our international reputation in a world in which racial issues are being highlighted every day, require that we get rid of this out-moded provision.

Chicka Dixon's case for Yes

There's a simple reason why I want a huge 'Yes' vote. *I want to be accepted by white Australians as a person.*

I have not thought through what would be my reaction—and the reaction of my people—to a No vote. It would be a crushing rejection. It would create disastrous bitterness. And it could mean bad blood between black and white for the foreseeable future.

But I find it difficult to believe that Australians would do this. Yet we fear this result. We fear that apathy, ignorance, a complicated ballot paper* and racial hatred—in that order—could defeat us.

Sun Herald, Sydney, 21 May, 1967

* There was another referendum on the number of politicians being held on the same day.

Will THEY have equal opportunities?
WRITE "YES" ON MAY 27.

Advertisement for the Yes case 1967

The Aboriginal organisations wanted the constitution changed so that the Commonwealth could make laws for the Aborigines and so that they would be officially counted in the census.

In the early 1960s a group of Aborigines and their supporters went to Canberra to ask Prime Minister Menzies to put these changes to the people. He listened sympathetically. After the meeting he offered the Aborigines a drink. One of them told him that if they were in Queensland he would be breaking the law. He was taken aback for a moment—he probably did not know about the Queensland laws—but then he said 'I'm the boss here'.

Menzies did not want the Commonwealth to become involved in Aboriginal affairs. Nor did Harold Holt, the Liberal prime minister who took over from him in 1966. But Holt was more concerned about Australia's image in the world and he wanted to show that he was sympathetic to the Aboriginal cause. As these were the changes Aborigines and their supporters wanted, he would put them to the people. He thought that even if the Commonwealth got the power to make laws for Aborigines, it did not have to use it.

Black and white campaigners celebrate the success of the 1967 referendum

In 1967 the constitutional referendum on Aborigines was easily carried. The Yes vote was nearly 90 per cent, by far the highest ever for constitutional change. Many people think that Aborigines became citizens and acquired the vote as a result of this referendum. They did not. For most Aborigines those changes had already happened.

But the referendum stood for much more than the changes it made to the constitution. Aboriginal people were looking to the Australian people to vote Yes to show that after years of cruelty and discrimination they were now fully accepted in the nation and were truly to be equal citizens. The Australian people did not let them down. Later, when Aborigines asked to be treated differently because they were Aborigines, the Australian people were not so ready to agree.

Protests in the streets

The issues at an election were never clearer than at the Commonwealth election of 1966. The Holt Liberal government was a supporter of the war in Vietnam and a supporter of sending conscripts to fight in it. The Labor Party under Arthur Calwell was opposed to the war and to the sending of conscripts to fight overseas.

The Liberals declared that it was important for Australia's security to stop communist North Vietnam from taking over South Vietnam. It was even more important to show support for the United States, whose war it was. The Liberals claimed that Labor's policy of withdrawing from the war would threaten the alliance with the United States.

The Holt government won in a landslide. The Australian people had voted for the war. But that did not settle the matter as far as some young men were concerned. They refused to register for conscription. If you were a pacifist, opposed to fighting in all wars, the law allowed you to avoid army service. But these men were opposed just to the war in Vietnam. They went to gaol or they went into hiding.

By the late 1960s opposition to the war was growing in the United States. This encouraged the anti-war movement in Australia. The movement was made up of peace organisations and radical unions, in both of which communists were prominent. They were joined by a group of mothers who called themselves 'Save Our Sons' and by university students. Among the students were communists of a new sort. They said that Russia was not a real communist state and they criticised the old communists in Australia for being too cautious and respectable. The student communists wanted to stir things up, to attack the police and break the law, to make the government use force against them, which would show that democracy was a fraud—just a front to protect capitalism and imperialism.

The anti-war movement wanted peace in Vietnam and it believed in peaceful demonstrations. It always faced the problem that some of its keenest supporters believed in force. A peaceful demonstration would be organised and then the radical students would show up, raise the Viet Cong flag (the flag of the enemy) and throw fire crackers at the police horses. Everyone said violence was bad, but violence got you on TV, which was becoming the chief source of news.

In 1970 the anti-war movement planned moratoriums in Australia's leading cities. This was an idea copied from the anti-war movement in America. Moratorium means a stopping of activity.

The aim was to bring the life of the city to a halt, for workers to go on strike and demonstrators to occupy the city streets. As people stopped going about their normal business, they were to think about the terrible things that were being done in their name in Vietnam.

Liberal leaders who supported the war opposed the moratorium. They said people had a right to meet and protest but not to stop the city's life and inconvenience everyone else. In huge crowds there was always the risk of violence, and some of these

---

TWO VIEWS OF THE MORATORIUM, 1970

Billy Snedden, Liberal Minister for Labour and National Service

The government had to oppose the moratorium and the demonstrators. I feared that if you took political decisions in the street, you were creating an enticement to take all political decisions in the streets. It would subtract from people's confidence in the elective process and the democratic system. Some people were being seduced into a form of political expression which they would not have contemplated otherwise and others, without realising it, were being manoeuvred by people who objected to the system of government we have adopted in Australia into a larger protest against that system.

An Unlikely Liberal, Melbourne, 1990, p. 110

I described these moratorium organisers as 'political bikies packraping democracy' because they were not prepared to allow democratic decisions to be taken democratically.

Ian Turner, Labor activist and historian

The Moratorium was the young saying, on the streets: to hell with the Protestant ethic, and petit-bourgeois morality, and conformity, and with the way you oldies are running the world.

A culture and a sensibility are being transformed before our eyes. Representative democracy, as run by the old bureaucrats of the tribe, will no longer do. Politics takes on new dimensions: the young no longer see themselves as apprentices to the old power structures; they demand policies and institutions which are responsive to their needs. Happily they are as little given to wielding authority as they are to being on the receiving end; they are likely to transform democracy rather than to supersede it.

Meanjin, No. 2, 1970, p. 244

demonstrators were looking to make trouble. Democracy depended on the maintenance of law and order. Billy Snedden, a Liberal minister, said the organisers of the moratorium were 'political bikies pack-raping democracy'.

The Labor Party too was wary of the movement. Its new leader Gough Whitlam was trying to regain ground by not opposing the war altogether, and he did not want his party associated with violence in the streets.

The organisers of the moratorium argued that the streets were closed for Anzac Day and Christmas pageants. Why should they not be closed for something far more important—citizens exercising their democratic right to protest? But they were told the whole community supported Anzac Day, whereas they wanted to close the streets to make a political point on an issue that bitterly divided the community. The organisers were upset that there was not a clear right to demonstrate in the streets. It was an offence to block the free flow of traffic. You could seek permission to demonstrate or you could let the police know your plans. But many anti-war people did not want to do either of these things. Bombs were raining down on Vietnamese peasants and young men were being forced to fight—and they had to get *permission* to protest!

In Melbourne the organisers decided not to seek permission or talk to the police. But the police decided to talk to the organisers. The leader of the movement in Melbourne and throughout Australia was Jim Cairns, a radical Labor politician, a man of principle and a responsible leader who did not want violence. It so happened that he was also an ex-policeman. When the police approached him, he agreed to talk. The arrangement was that the demonstrators would move down Bourke Street, the chief shopping centre of the city; they would sit down for 15 minutes, and then move off to the city square.

Up until the day of the moratorium, 8 May 1970, the Victorian premier Sir Henry Bolte and the Melbourne newspapers condemned it and warned of the dangers of violence. Police reinforcements were brought in from the country. But the police kept well back from Bourke Street. They were leaving Jim Cairns and his appointed marshals to control the crowd. There were 70 000 demonstrators. When they sat down they filled Bourke Street, from side to side, block after block. There was no violence; no arrests. After it was over, everyone was proud that Australia could have such a huge demonstration without violence.

Moratorium in Bourke Street, Melbourne, May 1970

In September there was a second round of moratoriums, not so well attended as the first. In Melbourne the government was determined to stop the marchers entering the main thoroughfare of Swanston Street. Police blocked the marchers' way. Cairns was in the front row. He and the policeman in charge talked, and then Cairns gave the order to take another route. Some of the students booed him. They called 'Oink Oink' to the police and threw fire crackers at their horses. Cairns called on them to stop, but some raced through the police lines. Four were arrested.

In Adelaide the organisers told police their route and that they would occupy one intersection for as long as possible, but they would not tell them which one. The police tried to guess which one, but got it wrong. The marchers stopped at the first major intersection they came to: King William Street and North Terrace. The police plan was to move them on. They looked for the leaders of the demonstration, but they were in the centre of the crowd where street theatre was being performed. The police found a deputy

Police break up moratorium march in Adelaide, September 1970

leader, but he refused to cooperate. The police then gave orders to the demonstrators to move on and, when these were ignored, they started arresting the demonstrators. On some they used violence. Overall, 130 people were arrested before the intersection was cleared.

South Australia had a Labor government led by Don Dunstan. The Labor Party had been involved in the planning of the moratorium, but withdrew at the last minute when it was clear that there was going to be trouble. Dunstan ordered a royal commission into the demonstration. The commission recommended that the law make clear that there was a right to demonstrate, but that as demonstrations inconvenience other people, organisers should apply for a permit beforehand so the police could make plans. If the permit was granted, demonstrators could not be arrested for obstructing traffic or any other street offences. If the permit was refused, organisers should be able to appeal to a court. The government passed a law along these lines in 1972.

This law would not have prevented trouble in Adelaide in September 1970 because the organisers of the moratorium did not

---

BANNERS CARRIED IN MORATORIUM

Adelaide, 18 September 1970

End Conscription Now
How Many Mai Lais Have There Been?
Smash US Imperialism
Smash Capital
Stop the Country to Stop the War
The Enemy is Imperialism
Stop Australia from its Disgrace
Resist the Draft
End Conscription
Withdraw All Troops Now
Peace in Vietnam
Save Our Sons
Christians for Peace
Peace Now

South Australia, Royal Commission on the September Moratorium Demonstration 1970, p. 64

want to cooperate with the authorities. Actually they were divided on this matter. Opinion swung to and fro from meeting to meeting. Like many other protest organisations, this one had decided to run open meetings. Meetings were not limited to delegates from the various organisations cooperating in the moratorium; anyone interested in the cause could turn up to a meeting. So those who did not want to cooperate with the police could get their way by bringing their friends along to meetings.

The anti-war movement in Australia was part of a wider movement which was against doing things in the usual way and obeying the rules and going through the proper channels. This movement for freedom and liberation was strong throughout the Western world. Young people were at the forefront of the revolution, and the Beatles gave them their beat. The young men let their hair grow long and wore jeans, the young women wore kaftans and sandals; they were true to their slogan 'Make love, not war'.

In politics this revolution was a revolt against the formal structures of government, of electing committees or parliaments and letting them decide things. It wanted a more open and inclusive politics. This was when organisations called themselves a 'collective' to show that all members were equal; and leaders were called convenors to show that that they just called the meetings and did not run the organisation; and if there was a committee elected

RUNNING A COLLECTIVE

The Rape Crisis Centre in Adelaide is run on a collective basis, which means that all workers, paid and volunteer, have equal power and responsibility for the way the Centre is run ... Every woman here can initiate and change things with of course the approval of the rest of the collective. For the most part women working at the Rape Crisis Centre agree on important political and philosophical questions and we put a lot of time and effort into sorting out differences. We try very hard to come to consensus decisions, to please everyone without being wishy-washy. We think it's really important that everyone in the collective knows what's going on and takes an active part in making decisions.

Julie Bannister, in *Women's Movement, South Australia*, Adelaide, 1980 to run things, any member could turn up to its meetings to listen and speak.

Of course all members cannot participate equally in an organisation, and organisations do need leaders. The hopes of these reformers could not be realised. But from these times survives the idea that any governing body should consult with the people affected by its decisions. Local councils and governments do this regularly—and not just because they think it right. If they don't consult, they may find a demonstration with banners and TV cameras outside their doors.

The opponents of democracy used to say that interests had to be represented in government, not mere numbers of people. Democrats opposed this view, but modern democracies have to some extent returned to it. When making decisions, governments consult all those who have an interest in the matter—the stakeholders, as they are called. The danger in this approach is that the general interest of the citizens might be ignored.

The removal of Whitlam

The Labor Party captured the mood of the 1960s in its election campaign of 1972, with its slogan 'It's Time'. The Liberals had been in power for 23 years, and Gough Whitlam said it was time for a change, time for a fresh beginning, time to do things differently.

Whitlam's government was in tune with the times because it was committed to protecting human rights, to setting up an ombudsman and to running an open government where there would be freedom of information. But in one thing Whitlam was old-fashioned: he believed in the original Labor idea of democracy. The party drew up its platform, the leader took the platform to the people, and if the party won the election the parliament should pass the platform into law.

The platform was very much the one Whitlam wanted. He had persuaded the party to revise it so that it was more appealing to middle-class people. In his opening campaign speech, he made many detailed promises, all drawn from the platform. Everyone knew what Gough Whitlam would do if he won the election.

He did not win the election by a large margin. It would take some time before all the results were known. In the Labor Party the parliamentarians elect the ministers, so the ministers could not be chosen until the election results were finalised. But Whitlam did not want to delay. He wanted to start governing immediately. He told the governor-general to appoint himself and his deputy Lance Barnard as a two-man ministry. Whitlam took charge of 13 departments and Barnard 14. They began putting the platform into practice. No new laws could be passed because parliament was not yet assembled, but there were many actions the government could take on its own, and many changes could be made by altering regulations, not laws.

The two-man government stopped conscription; it freed seven young men who had been jailed for defying the conscription law; it began negotiations to recognise communist China; it took the sales tax off the contraceptive pill; it asked the Arbitration Commission to reopen the case on equal pay for women; it set up a commission to classify schools so that they could be funded according to need.

A new batch of decisions was announced every day. Never did a change of government make so much difference so quickly. Thousands of old Labor men had gone to their graves without ever seeing a Labor government like this one: it believed in the platform and was in a hurry to implement it.

However, when it came to passing new laws Whitlam met the barrier of the Senate. There had been no Senate election in 1972. Labor did not have the numbers there to pass its laws. The Liberals, the Country Party and the Democratic (anticommunist) Labor Party could together outvote Labor. Whitlam said he had the authority of the people—a mandate—to pass his platform. The opposition parties in the Senate said they too were elected by the people and they had the right to change and reject the Bills Whitlam sent to them. The Senate was a very strong upper house. The one limit on its power was that it could not amend the budget and tax Bills; it could, though, reject them outright.

The Labor Party thought all upper houses were antidemocratic, and its platform called for the Senate to be abolished. It was strange, then, that in 1970 the leader of the Labor Party in the Senate, Lionel Murphy, had introduced a plan, not to get rid of the Senate but to strengthen it. He organised with the other parties to set up a system of committees that were to look closely at the Bills sent to the Senate. Committees would include members of all parties and each would specialise in one area of government. This made the Senate a much better house of review.

But Whitlam did not want his Bills reviewed; he wanted them passed. The Senate in fact passed many of his Bills, but by early 1974 six important ones had been rejected twice. When the two houses are deadlocked, the government can call a double dissolution election, which allows the people to elect a whole new parliament: the House of Representatives and all the Senate. Whitlam called such an election in May 1974. His government was returned with a reduced majority in the House of Representatives and it just missed out on controlling the Senate. At this election the senators from the Democratic Labor Party all lost their seats, which brought the history of that party to an end.

The deadlock provision in the constitution now allowed Whitlam to call a joint sitting of both houses of parliament to vote on the six Bills that the Senate had twice rejected. With members and senators voting together, Labor had a majority and it passed its six Bills. They included Bills to establish the first universal health system, the forerunner to Medicare; to allow the territories to elect two senators; and to keep the difference in population of electorates to no more than 10 per cent (instead of 20 per cent). This is the only time a joint sitting has been held.

The first duty of a government, even a reforming government, is to govern well. The Whitlam government was a blundering, poorly disciplined government. Whitlam himself was so committed to the platform and his mandate that he refused to change course when Australia, along with the rest of the world, entered an economic recession in 1974. He continued to spend big money on his reform programs when he should have been cutting back on spending.

The government's biggest blunder was to enter a dodgy scheme to raise a huge loan overseas so that the State could become the owner of mineral and gas resources. The government pretended that this was a loan for 'temporary purposes' so that it did not have to tell anyone about it, and it used as go-between a shady character from Pakistan, Tirath Khemlani, who said he had access to big money in the Middle East. No loan money ever showed up and when all this became public, the government was in very deep trouble. It promised that it had abandoned the whole scheme— but the minister responsible secretly kept up his contact with Khemlani. When this became known, the Liberal leader Malcolm

Fraser said that this government was so bad and so damaging to Australia that he would force it to go to the people.

He planned to do this by having the Senate block the government's budget. Without money a government cannot carry on. The Senate had the power to block the budget, but it had never used it. The founders of the constitution had given it that power thinking that it would be used very rarely, if at all. If a government ever introduced a budget in which all the money was to be spent in the big states, then the small states wanted the Senate to be able to reject it. But now the opposition parties in the Senate were blocking a budget not because they disagreed with it—they simply wanted to starve the government of money and force it to an election.

Whitlam said this action threatened the system of responsible government. Governments were made in the House of Representatives; it was not for the Senate to tell a government that its time was up and that it must face the people. The opposition parties said that as the power was in the constitution, it must be alright for them to use it. But Whitlam replied that they were breaking a convention, an unwritten rule, which had to be upheld if the system of responsible government was to work with a strong Senate.

Whitlam declared he would never give in and hold an election. He would make Fraser back down. He would break the power of the Senate for good. He would establish that only the House of Representatives, the people's house, controlled the fate of governments.

Whitlam's government was now very unpopular—which is why the opposition parties were keen to have an election. But polls showed that the people did not like what the opposition parties were doing. A few Liberal senators were not happy with the breaking of the convention, though they went along with it. They told Fraser that it would be much better to wait for the normal time of an election, when he would be sure to be elected without all the controversy over whether it was right to block the budget.

The government began to think of ways it could get money when its funds ran out. In the nineteenth century in Victoria, governments had found ways of holding on when the Legislative Council blocked their budgets. That had required the cooperation of the governor. Governor-General Sir John Kerr was certainly not going to support any dodgy schemes. He was naturally very worried that the two political leaders were bringing the system of government to breaking point.

197

DEADLOCK IN THE PARLIAMENT, 1975

The Senate will defer a vote on the budget until the Government calls an election because of:

- the continuing incompetence, evasion, deceit and duplicity of the Prime Minister and his Ministers as exemplified in the overseas loan scandal which was an attempt by the Government to subvert the Constitution, to by-pass Parliament and to evade its responsibilities to the States and the Loan Council;
- the Prime Minister's failure to maintain proper control over the activities of his Ministers and Government to the detriment of the Australian nation and people;
- the continuing mismanagement of the Australian economy by the Prime Minister and this Government with policies which have caused a lack of confidence in this nation's potential and created inflation and unemployment not experienced for 40 years.

Senate *Debates*, 1975, Vol. 66, p. 1221

The House of Representatives responds:

- This House affirms that the Constitution and the conventions of the Constitution vest in this House the control of the supply of moneys to the elected Government.
- This House asserts the basic principle that a Government that continues to have a majority in the House of Representatives has a right to expect that it will be able to govern.
- This House condemns the threatened action of the Senate as being reprehensible and a constituting a grave threat to the principles of responsible government and of parliamentary democracy in Australia.

House of Representatives, *Debates*, 1975, Vol. 97, p. 2199

Whitlam said again and again in public that the governor-general could act only on his advice. In normal times that was true. But in times of crisis a governor-general does have special powers—reserve powers. Kerr began to think he would have to use them. He should have warned Whitlam that he was worried about a government trying to govern without money and that he might have to act. But he was put off by Whitlam's bullying style; he was afraid that if he told Whitlam that he might have to use his powers, Whitlam would ask the Queen to dismiss him.

So Kerr acted secretly. Without any warning, on 11 November 1975, he dismissed Whitlam as prime minister, installed Fraser as caretaker prime minister, and on his advice called an election for both houses of parliament.

On 11 November the money had not run out. Some constitutional experts say that Kerr should not have acted until the money had run out. If the government had then tried to spend money not voted by parliament, it would have been acting illegally and a governor-general would certainly have been right to dismiss it.

Kerr said that he had not acted too soon. He explained that the rule of our system is that a government denied money has either to resign or call an election. Everyone agrees that that is the rule if the government is denied money by the lower house. There is no agreement that this rule applies when it is the upper house denying the money. However, Kerr had the support of Chief Justice Barwick in his interpretation of the constitution. After Kerr had made up his mind to sack Whitlam, he checked with Sir Garfield

The governor-general's secretary reads the notice dissolving parliament 11 November 1975, with Gough Whitlam, the sacked prime minister, looking on

Barwick to see whether he was doing the right thing. Barwick said he was: as the Senate can deny a government money, the government is ultimately responsible to two houses, not one.

The Labor Party and its supporters could not accept this view. They hated Sir John Kerr and what he had done. They felt they were no longer living in a democracy. They said to each other: we come to power after 23 years with a clear program of reform, and what happens? The Opposition in the Senate blocks important parts of the program; then it cuts off the government's money; then the governor-general dismisses the government and installs the leader of the opposition as prime minister. What's the point of trying to win elections if that's how we are treated?

The Liberal Party said the holding of an election could not be against democracy. The system of government had come to a stalemate and the governor-general let the people decide who should rule. Fraser won the election in a landslide. The people had not liked his tactics, but when they had a chance to pass judgement on Whitlam, they took it.

For the Labor Party and all who supported and sympathised with it, constitutional reform became a top priority. The Senate's

Malcolm Fraser, the Liberal leader, at a rally during the 1975 constitutional crisis

A call for continuing citizen activity

Fellow Australians,

We believe that Australian political institutions are at present facing a danger which has serious implications for all Australians and all political parties. This is the use of an undemocratic constitution as an anti-democratic weapon.

We therefore urge all Australians to take part in a broad national movement that will work towards a People's Convention framing a new Constitution that will have as its guidelines:

- *All public power emanates from the Australian people.*
- *Australian democracy is founded on freedom of opinion and information and on a universal and equal voting system fairly reflecting the political wishes of all Australians.*
- *Governments are chosen by and can only be dismissed by the Australian people.*

- *The inclusion of a Bill of Rights guaranteeing the liberties and rights of all Australians.*

In the meantime we deplore any suggestion to make our Constitution even more undemocratic.

Further, we believe, that with no proper constitutional safeguards, one of the few ways to prevent further erosion of the rights and liberties of all Australians is by continuing public outcry at the events of last November 11 and their consequences.

Accordingly, we urge all citizens who share our concern to organise and take part in activities that will mark this November 11 as a Day of Peaceful Protest.

Donations welcome, payable to Citizens for Democracy, P.O. Box K2, Haymarket 2000.

James Calomeris	Jack O'Toole	Dennis Altman	Roderick Shaw	Pat O'Shane	Bernard Smith	Allan Ashbolt
Patrick White	Sarah Sheehan	Dorothy Isaksen	R. C. Taylor	Gillian Bottomley	W. T. Smale	Barry Egan
Jack Mundey	E. L. Wheelwright	Edmund Campion	Christina Stead	John Coburn	Ted Binder	Antonio Bamonte
Russel Ward	John B. Healy	Barbara Murphy	Max Taylor	J. Tzannes	Leo MacLeay	Dick Diamond
John Ducker	Marea Gazzard	Les Murray	Rupert Lockwood	Tas Bull	D. R. Burns	Donato Di Giacomo
Faith Bandler	Graham Richardson	David Boyd	Hermia Boyd	Barry Manefield	Craig McGregor	Sergio De Mari
Geoffrey Dutton	Donald Horne	Evan Phillips	Bob Goote	Michael Hourihan	Pat Bishop	John McCarthy
James McClelland	John Gaden	Tony Gentile	Elaine Thompson	Eva Isaacs	Joan Evatt	Greg Symons
Louis James	L. Carmichael	Colin Simpson	Jack O'Toole	Donald Gazzard	Gianfranco Creciani	
Jack Garland	Dinah Forden	J. Cambourn	Franca Arena	Van Davey	James A. Baird	
Frank Hardy	George Dreyfus	Maurice Isaacs	R. T. Scott	Peter Upward	Dorothy Buckland	

November 11. Rally. Sydney Town Hall Square. 5.15 p.m.

Authorised for Citizens for Democracy by Greg Woodburne.

Printed by Hyland Offset, 69 Dickson Avenue, Artarmon 2064.

Citizens for Democracy advertise their rally on the first anniversary of the Whitlam dismissal power to block a budget must be removed. The power of the governor-general must be curbed. A movement called Citizens for Democracy held huge rallies in Sydney and Melbourne. Many books were written on the constitution and how it might be changed. But the constitution remained the same.

After only seven years Labor returned to power. With Bob Hawke and then Paul Keating as prime minister, the Labor government lasted for 13 years (1983–96), the longest period ever for a federal Labor government. This government was not as radical as Whitlam's and it was much better run. It never controlled the Senate, but it achieved most of what it wanted. There was never any suggestion that its budgets would be blocked. The anger of 1975 began to ebb away.

During the time of this Labor government, the balance of power in the Senate was held by a new party, the Australian Democrats. The party was formed in 1977 by Don Chipp, a progressive Liberal who thought Malcolm Fraser's Liberal government was too conservative. The Democrats' policy was somewhere between that of the Labor and Liberal parties. One of its aims was to make sure that the government, whichever it was, kept to its promises—its slogan was 'Keep the Bastards Honest'. But knowing how much bitterness flowed from the dismissal of Whitlam, it promised that it would never block a government's budget.

Small parties like the Democrats can gain seats in the Senate only because it is elected by proportional representation. The whole state votes as one and parties get seats in proportion to their overall vote. A party that gains only 10 or 15 per cent of the vote never wins a seat in the lower house, but that's enough to win a Senate seat.

Proportional voting for the Senate is not set down in the constitution. It was introduced by parliament in 1949. And it can be abolished by parliament. The Liberal and Labor parties are sometimes annoyed by the influence of the small parties in the Senate, but they would be very unpopular if they tried to change the system of voting. More and more people think it is a good thing that the major parties do not control the Senate. Thousands of people at elections vote for a major party, Liberal or Labor, and then vote for a small party in the Senate.

Because neither of the major parties is likely to control the Senate, the Senate acts as a true house of review. In the Senate a government has to argue its case and accept amendments. The

Senate committee system set up in 1970 works only because the government has to listen to what the Senate says.

The Labor Party no longer argues that upper houses should be abolished. In three states Labor governments were responsible for giving upper houses new life.

In 1961 a Labor government in New South Wales made the last attempt to abolish the upper house. A referendum on the issue was lost. In 1978 another Labor government made the upper house into a body elected by the whole state with proportional voting— something like the Senate. A Labor government introduced a similar system to South Australia in 1974. In Western Australia in 1987 a Labor government divided the state into six regions for Legislative Council elections. By proportional voting two regions elected seven councillors and four regions elected five councillors. In these upper houses, as in the Senate, small parties and independents have a good chance of being elected. Governments are not likely to control them.

Once an upper house checking an elected government seemed to many people undemocratic; more people now think an upper house not controlled by the government is a proper part of a democracy.

Revealing government secrets

Gough Whitlam had plans to give the people more power, as against their governments. There was to be a Commonwealth ombudsman, a new court where people could challenge what ministers and public servants did in administering the law, and a freedom of information law. None of these came into force in Whitlam's three years as prime minister. His government had so many plans and was so often in crisis that many things did not get done.

The Liberals were not opposed to this part of Labor's program. The Fraser government set up an Administrative Appeals Tribunal in 1976 and a Commonwealth ombudsman in 1977. Freedom of information came later—in 1982—and after a long struggle.

The campaigners for freedom of information said governments gained a huge power by collecting information and being able to keep it secret. Governments told people only what they wanted them to know. If the people were to control their governments, instead of being controlled by them, they must have access to the

---

THE DEBATE ON FREEDOM OF INFORMATION

The advantages of freedom of information

- Easier access to useful information, such as statistics, held by Government.
- Increased participation by the public in policy-making. Knowledge is power. If the public is not informed, it cannot take part in the political process with any real effect.
- Making government more objective and accountable in dealing with the public.
- Improving the quality of decision-making.
- Improving the collection, storage and retrieval of Government information.
- Giving citizens the right to obtain and if necessary to correct personal information held by Government.

The disadvantages of freedom of information

- The cost of the hours spent by civil servants responding to requests.
- Government processes are made more complex and Government is distracted from its main task.
- Civil servants will be less honest and frank in their written advice to ministers.
- Some information may be released that is personally or commercially sensitive. People and companies will be more cautious in dealing with government.
- Law enforcement may be hindered if law-breakers can find out what information the government holds on them.

Queensland Electoral and Administrative Review Commission *Freedom of Information: Issues Paper*, 1990, pp. 4–8

---

information governments possessed. Freedom of information was a truly democratic cause because it would enable more citizens to participate in government.

Campaigners for some other causes were very interested in freedom of information. Environmentalists wanted to get access to government reports on new developments and their impact on the environment. Those interested in consumer protection wanted to see government reports on the safety of products. Those who were opposed to large government spending wanted to know in detail how much governments were spending and on what.

The opponents of freedom of information were the top public servants. They argued that freedom of information would damage the Westminster system of government. Cabinet members met in secret and argued over policies, but when a decision was made they all supported it in public. Clearly what a minister really thought and what had happened in the cabinet room had to be kept secret. And public servants helped ministers to reach decisions by preparing papers that contained a number of options and suggestions. If these working papers were to be made public, public servants would be more careful in what they wrote and ministers would not get such good advice.

The freedom of information campaigners agreed that cabinet papers and proceedings should remain secret and also some working documents. Good, thought the top public servants, we can call many things a cabinet paper and a working document. The public servant at the head of the Treasury thought he would be able to stop nearly every document in his department from being released.

The ordinary public servants took a different attitude. The head of their union was a firm supporter of freedom of information. Public servants were put in a difficult position. They saw all the government information, but they were not allowed to talk about it and certainly not allowed to release documents to the public. They might know that governments were not telling the truth, but they had to keep quiet. Their job would be much easier if government information could become public information.

When the Fraser government decided to go ahead with freedom of information, it asked the top public servants to draw up a plan. This was normal procedure but in this case the wreckers were in charge of the planning. They produced a very limited proposal. All existing documents were to remain secret. Many categories of new documents were to be exempt. A minister or top public servant could block the release of any document—and there was to be no appeal from their decision.

The Fraser government accepted the plan of its public servants and put it to parliament. It passed in the House of Representatives. The Senate referred it to its standing committee on constitutional and legal affairs, which had representatives from the Liberal and Labor parties. Its chairman was a Liberal from Victoria, Senator

Alan Missen. To help it conduct its enquiry and draw up its report, the committee hired a radical young lawyer, John McMillan. Missen and McMillan already knew each other. They were the two leading campaigners for freedom of information in Australia.

Alan Missen had always been a great supporter of civil liberties; he was a man of principle often at odds with his own party. When Menzies was campaigning to ban the Communist Party in the 1951 referendum, he wrote a newspaper article opposing the banning of the communists. At that time he was deputy president of the Young Liberals at Melbourne University. He was suspended from his office and was lucky not to be expelled from the party. In the 1960s he annoyed the premier Sir Henry Bolte by leading the campaign in the Liberal Party for the appointment of an ombudsman. He entered the Senate in 1974. In the 1975 constitutional crisis he was one of the Liberals who were not happy with Fraser's actions.

John McMillan studied law at the Australian National University. In his fourth year, he wanted to write his honours thesis on government secrecy. He was told that he would not find out much about secrecy because it was secret! That did not faze him. He was interested in establishing ways to defeat secrecy, particularly by freedom of information, which had been adopted in the United States in 1966. When he became a law lecturer, he visited the United States and worked with the great consumer advocate Ralph Nader. In Australia he became the leading figure in the organisations formed to advocate freedom of information.

McMillan knew how to use the media effectively. He would write off to government departments asking for information and then publicise the reasons they gave for turning him down. After many knockbacks, he asked the Bureau of Statistics how much it spent on indoor plants. The public servants found it hard to think of a reason why he should not be told, so they asked him why he wanted to know. They had fallen into his trap. This was the attitude he wanted to expose. Citizens should be able to know what governments were doing without having to give a reason—after all, it was their government.

McMillan was a typical reformer of this time: a professional person—a lawyer—who criticised governments and was hired to work within government. Twice he worked on government enquiries into the public service and wrote the section of their reports dealing with freedom of information. On the Senate committee enquiry on freedom of information, he helped Senator

Missen write a report very critical of Fraser's proposal. Then, in the newsletters produced by the freedom of information campaigners, he praised the committee's work and urged the Fraser government to accept its recommendations.

The Liberal and Labor members on the Senate committee were unanimous in recommending a much more open system for the release of information than the Fraser government was proposing. Missen and several other Liberals in the Senate crossed the floor and voted with the Labor Party to force the Fraser government to accept changes. Documents of the past five years were to be available; if a minister or public servant blocked the release of a document, an appeal could be made to the Administrative Appeals Tribunal; and individuals were to have access to their personal records. The Freedom of Information Act 1982 was the greatest achievement of the rebellious Senator Missen.

When freedom of information came into force, there was not as much use made of it as had been expected. Newspapers had been great supporters of it, but getting information takes time and journalists usually want information they can use today. Opposition politicians made use of it to get damaging information about governments. The most regular use was individuals asking to see the files held on them by Social Security or Veterans Affairs. Requesters had to pay a fee to help cover costs. This meant you had to be well off or backed by an organisation to ask for large amounts of information.

Governments of all sorts did not like freedom of information. In opposition the Labor Party had criticised Fraser for introducing a very limited measure. But then in office the Hawke Labor government put up the fees because it was worried at the cost of answering requests. Senator Missen led the move in the Senate that forced them to back off. The Cain Labor government in Victoria was the first to introduce freedom of information at state level, in 1982. But the Opposition then found such damaging information about the government that the government tightened up the rules.

The government's power to control information had been lessened by freedom of information. But at the same time governments of both parties were spending more of taxpayers' money on getting the stories they wanted in the media. Ministers employed press secretaries and governments media units to plant stories and ensure that journalists put the right spin on stories. Public information campaigns were sometimes close to being propaganda for

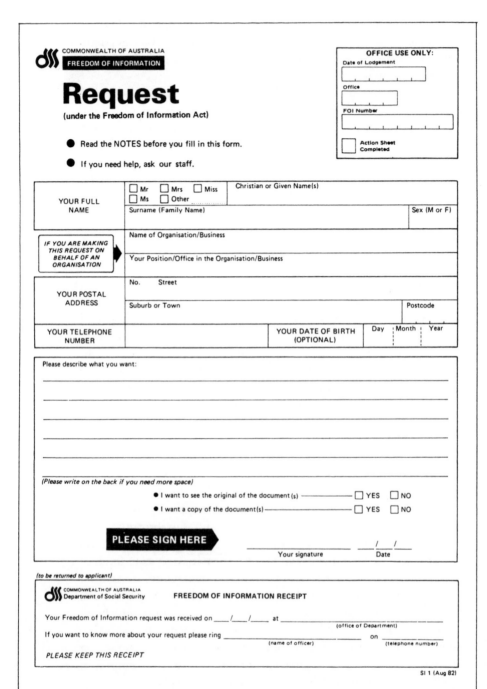

the government. This was another way of governments controlling information.

Freedom of information allows for an individual citizen, on payment of a fee, to have access to government documents some time after they are produced. It is not perhaps the best way to encourage wider participation in government. The best effect of freedom of information is that it has encouraged governments to be more open in their decision making. Without anyone asking, they publish a report on some issue and invite individuals and organisations to make comments on it. Then the government makes its decision. All who are interested have learnt what the issues are, seen the conflicting views being put to the government, and are better able to judge what government decides.

Exposing government corruption

The government of Queensland ignored the demand that government should be more open and accountable. For 20 years from 1968 the premier was Joh Bjelke-Petersen, a peanut farmer—a tough leader who quashed opposition and made himself popular by promoting Queensland and attacking the government in Canberra.

He was the leader of the National Party, the former Country Party. He did not have to be very popular to remain as premier because of the unbalanced electoral system. His support was strongest in the country, which had many more seats than it was entitled to. The Liberal Party and the National Party cooperated in government, as they did in the rest of Australia, but in Queensland the National Party was the bigger party.

Bjelke-Petersen changed the law so that protestors had to get permission to march from the police rather than a court. Then he told the police to refuse permission to protestors he did not like, such as environmentalists. He passed very harsh laws against strikes. He kept the laws controlling Aborigines after they had been removed in the rest of Australia.

Queensland became a battle ground for civil liberties. But the premier banned demonstrations in favour of civil liberties. Many people did march and were arrested.

The premier and the National Party were in favour of Christian and family values. There were laws against casinos and prostitution.

Police in Brisbane drawn up to stop a march

Such laws are always difficult to enforce. Many people who are not criminals want to gamble and pay for sex. Casinos and brothels will operate even though they are banned. In theory the police should try to close them down. But it is hard for the police to get evidence when all the people involved in an activity are happy about it. And in the eyes of the police brothels and casinos are not causing much harm. So instead of closing them down police may allow them to operate in return for bribes.

In Queensland there was a regular system of bribing. The owners of brothels paid police so that they could operate without interference. But they had to agree to the police charging one of their girls every so often. In court the girl had to plead guilty. Then it would look as if the police were enforcing the law.

Within the police force it was well known who was making a lot of money from bribes. The government promoted one of them, Terry Lewis, to the position of assistant commissioner ahead of 100 men who were senior to him. The police commissioner resigned in protest. The government then appointed Lewis commissioner. A corrupt cop was now running the force.

Phil Dickie, a journalist working for Brisbane's newspaper, the *Courier Mail,* spent months investigating the illegal brothels and casinos. In 1987 he published stories asking why they were able to operate so openly under the noses of the police. He knew the answer. Then the ABC's national current affairs program, *Four Corners,* exposed the corruption. People talked on camera of making payments to the police. The government would find it hard to ignore this.

At the time Bjelke-Petersen was absent from the state. The acting

On September 4th, 1977, the Queensland premier announced there would be no more political street marches.

"The day of the political street march is over. Anybody who holds a street march spontaneous or otherwise, will know they are acting illegally.. Don't bother to apply for a permit – you won't get one. That's government policy now."

smash the march ban
defend the right to organise

DEMONSTRATE

SUPPORT THE STRUGGLE IN QLD

Qld Govt Tourist Bureau
king st., city

SAT. MARCH 4   10:30 am

Since the ban was introduced over 1,000 people have been arrested and now face 2,000 charges.

The Civil Liberties Co-ordinating Committee (C.L.C.C.) has been organising against the ban since September, 1977. The organisation is made up of anti-uranium activists, unionists, students, left groups, and people from Civil Liberties and Church groups. Several marches have been held. The CLCC is organising its next mobilisation on Saturday March 4th.

Money is urgently needed for bail and defence funds.
Donations Can Be Sent To:

Queensland Solidarity Group	or	Civil Liberties Co-ordinating C'tee
Box 9, 232 Castlereagh St.,		46 Birley St.,
Sydney......2000		Spring Hill.......4001

In Sydney, the Queensland Solidarity Group meets regularly building support for the struggle in Queensland. Contact QSC on 827-3857 or 692-0284.

The campaign for civil rights in Queensland was Australia-wide: a Sydney protest premier was Bill Gunn, the police minister. He ordered a royal commission into police corruption. Bjelke-Petersen warned him of the dangers of an enquiry—you never know where it'll end up. Gunn told the premier that if he tried to stop it, he would resign.

The enquiry headed by Tony Fitzgerald uncovered the police corruption going right to the top. Commissioner Lewis went to gaol. Fitzgerald followed up every lead; as the premier had feared, this enquiry did not stop with the police: Fitzgerald found that several ministers had taken money for themselves from their ministerial allowances. They went to gaol. He revealed a government that was rotten at the core. Government contracts were awarded to those who had made donations to the National Party. Bjelke-Petersen involved his friend Commissioner Lewis in decisions that had nothing to do with the police. If ministers were caught speeding, Lewis would organise for charges to be dropped.

The premier himself was questioned by Fitzgerald. He had no understanding of the need for checks and limits on the use of

---

WHAT IS GOOD GOVERNMENT?

The Fitzgerald Commission, Queensland, 1989

Quoted in Phil Dickie, *The Road to Fitzgerald and Beyond*, Brisbane, 1988, p. 287

Good government is more likely to result if opposition, criticism and rational debate are allowed to take place, appropriate checks and balances are placed on the use of power and the administration is open to new ideas, opposing points of view and public scrutiny.

Queensland Treasurer Keith De Lacy, 1993, on the Fitzgerald reforms

We have freedom of information, judicial review, public financial standards, a public accounts committee, the Criminal Justice Commission, the Electoral and Administrative Review Commission and ombudsman requirements, but in solving one set of problems we have created another. In making it difficult to steal the public's money, we have made it virtually impossible to manage the public's money.

Courier Mail, 14 April 1993

OH YOU CAN'T MARCH

You can march your flamin' feet off in Victoria,
You can march from Back O' Bourke to Wollongong!
But once you cross the Tweed
You're another race and breed
And should you in any way think things are wrong:

> Refrain: Oh you can't march,
> No you can't march
> If you live in the Sunshine State!

You can march your ankles off in South Australia,
You can march from Darwin down to Esperance Bay!
But should you venture forth
Into our dark Deep North
There's one small thing may cause you some dismay:

> Refrain: Oh you can't march,
> No you can't march
> If you live in the Sunshine State!

You can march from Timbucktoo to Copenhagen,
You can march the length and breadth of U.S.A.!
But in the State we're in
It's a special kind of sin
To demonstrate in this old-fashioned way:

> Refrain: Oh you can't march,
> No you can't march
> If you live in the Sunshine State!

Oh, we've got the greatest *beaches* in Australia,
And we've got the greatest *peanut* of them all!
And we've got (you name it, mate!)
A hundred things that're great
But *democracy* is getting rather small . . .

> Refrain: Because you can't march,
> No you can't march
> If you live in the Sunshine State!

— Bruce Dawe

Queensland poet Bruce Dawe makes his contribution to the civil rights campaign

power—government was to get things done and to keep him and his party on top.

Fitzgerald thought that if corruption was to be prevented, more checks would have to be placed on government. There should be freedom of information, a public register of the private interests of ministers and members, and a parliamentary committee to examine all government spending. These checks were already standard in other states and the Commonwealth. There should also be two new permanent bodies: a Criminal Justice Commission to search out corruption and an Electoral Commission to plan a fair system of electorates. These bodies should not be under the control of the government. They were to be supervised by a parliamentary committee with members from all parties.

Before the Fitzgerald commission made its report the National Party had dumped Bjelke-Petersen, who was lucky to stay out of gaol. The new premier set about putting Fitzgerald's recommendations into law. But this did not prevent the National Party from being thrown out at the next election. In 1989 the Labor Party formed a government for the first time in over 30 years. It promised to continue with the Fitzgerald reforms.

A few years later Western Australia was having enquiries into government corruption and setting up a new body to try to stop it. The government in the spotlight here was led by Brian Burke of the Labor Party.

In the 1960s and 70s Western Australia helped to make Australia rich with its oil and minerals, but Sydney and Melbourne remained the key economic centres. Burke wanted Perth to have its own banks and investment houses, which would use the state's wealth to develop new industries. His plan was to use government money to kickstart this process.

The old Labor Party believed that the government should run businesses. When Burke came to power in 1983 a few of these survived, such as a brickworks and an engineering repair shop. To the dismay of the old Labor men, Burke sold these off. He took the government into partnership with private business to create new modern industries. Once the industry was established, the government would sell its share and put its funds into another project.

The government did its deals with the businessmen in secret, and usually it was the same group of businessmen who were in on the deals. They were not from old established firms but were new, flashy millionaires, who gave generously to the Labor Party.

All might have been well except for the stock exchange crash of 1987. The bank run by Laurie Connell, one of the new millionaires, was about to go broke. The government decided it

ICAC INDEPENDENT COMMISSION AGAINST CORRUPTION

CORRUPTION

SOME IMPORTANT INFORMATION FOR THE PEOPLE OF NSW

The Independent Commission Against Corruption is a new State body set up to fight corruption in the public sector of NSW — that includes all departments and agencies of State and local government.

Why does corruption matter?

State and local government and other public authorities exist to serve the public. Corruption involves breaching public trust — your trust. It means that a public servant or official, who has agreed to serve the public honestly and with integrity, has broken that agreement. Corruption produces frustration and inequality, wastes resources and public money, and leads to inefficiency and despair. It is unfair to all good citizens.

What is corruption?

Corruption is any dishonest abuse of position by a public official. For the ICAC to become involved, the corruption must involve criminal offences or conduct serious enough to warrant dismissal or disciplinary action.

Corruption can have many specific forms — taking or offering bribes, officials dishonestly using their influence, blackmail, fraud, election bribery, illegal gambling.

For example:

- A company wants to do business with the Government and pays an official to choose that company for the job.

- A council town planner accepts money, or just a bottle of good whisky, to promote a development application.

- A driver is 'over the limit' but the police let him go because he is a sporting hero.

- An official uses public resources for private purposes.

New South Wales acquired its anti-corruption commission in 1988 should save the bank because so many people and businesses had money in it. Twice it supplied the bank with funds, but it still went under. The government did not give the money directly. It announced that it was investing in a new petrochemical industry, part-owned by Connell. The government money went into the 'industry' (which was not off the drawing board) and straight out again into Connell's bank.

With the collapse of the bank, the enquiries began and eventually, as in Queensland, a royal commission was set up to examine all the government's record. Burke and his deputy went to gaol. The Labor government after Burke stopped investing in business.

The royal commission criticised the Burke government for all its secret deals with business. It wanted government to be more open and accountable. Western Australia, unlike Queensland, had an upper house. The commission thought it would be a better watchdog if no government ministers sat in it. Ministers should all be in the lower house. The commission recommended more freedom of information, a register of members' interests, and an anti-corruption commission. Western Australia got its anti-corruption commission in 1996.

Though governments set up these commissions, they don't like it when the commissions uncover government corruption or corruption in the political party that supports them. People concerned with civil liberties worry about the large powers the commissions possess. They can compel people to give evidence. It may be that they will not become a permanent part of government.

Under the Westminster system, parliament is meant to be the watchdog over governments. New watchdogs like anti-corruption commissions have been introduced because parliaments are less able to control governments. This is chiefly because governments can rely on the loyalty of their party followers to keep them in office.

Parties: the great survivors

Parties begin at a particular point in time. If they want to remain powerful, they need to change with the times. They keep the same name, but they may end up with different followers and different ideas from those they started with.

The Labor Party was in the beginning a workers' party. But to become a party that could form governments it had to look for support from lower-middle-class people and small farmers. That meant some changes to its policies, which upset some of the workers. From the 1960s the Labor Party faced a bigger challenge. The working class, its key group of supporters, began to shrink. The new jobs were for middle-class people in the professions and service industries. The party would have to look for new supporters.

Gough Whitlam made the party more acceptable to middle-class people, particularly professional people employed by governments: teachers, nurses, social workers. He campaigned on education, the quality of city life, support for the arts, assistance to Aborigines—not things that the Labor Party had been much interested in before. He was himself from the middle class, a lawyer whose father had been a lawyer and public servant. A few of his ministers had been workers, but most of them, like the prime minister, had not worked with their hands.

Whitlam was not interested in nationalising existing private businesses. Chifley had tried that with the banks and had been stopped by the courts, which ruled it unconstitutional. Whitlam was interested in starting new government businesses. He planned a government insurance scheme that would have taken business from the private insurance companies. The overseas loan scheme that brought him down was to give the government the funds to invest in oil and minerals.

The Liberal Party was formed in the 1940s, when Labor was still talking of nationalising private businesses. The Liberals stood for private enterprise. However, when the Liberals came to power under Menzies, they kept the chief government-owned businesses, Qantas and the Commonwealth Bank. They did oppose Whitlam's attempts to start new government businesses.

In the 1980s the Liberals decided that they should be truer to their principles of free enterprise. Government businesses should be privatised: that is, sold off to private business. Government itself should be kept small and efficient. As much government work as possible should be contracted out to private business. Wages should not be set at the same rate for all industries by the Arbitration Court. Workers and bosses should bargain directly and reach agreements suitable to their industry and circumstances.

The Liberals also turned against protection for local industry, which had been supported by both major parties since 1910. They accepted the argument that protection meant the propping up of inefficient industries which became a drag on the whole economy.

These new policies were called the 'deregulation' or the 'liberalising' of the economy; the most common term used in Australia (similar policies were being followed in the United States and Britain) was 'economic rationalism'.

The Country Party, when it was founded, was opposed to protection of local industries because buying higher-priced goods made in Australia put up the costs of farming. It soon discovered that it could not get rid of protection. So it decided to join the club and get protection for farming in the form of subsidies and marketing schemes.

In the 1980s the Country Party (now the National Party) moved with the Liberals against protection and government involvement in the economy. In joining this movement it might get rid of protection for Australian industry, but it would also have to give up the marketing schemes and subsidies. That upset many of its traditional rural supporters.

The Liberals and the Nationals made these changes to their policies while they were in opposition. From 1983 until 1996 the

Bob Hawke, prime minister 1983–91, and his treasurer, Paul Keating, who succeeded him as prime minister, 1991–96

Labor Party was in power under Bob Hawke and Paul Keating. The Labor Party was in favour of government-owned businesses, of wages set by the Arbitration Court and protection of Australian industry. At elections it attacked the Liberals for supporting economic rationalism. But when elections were over the Labor government adopted economic rationalism—it lowered protection for Australian industry, sold off Qantas and the Commonwealth Bank, and began to encourage workplace agreements.

The Labor Party had changed its policies before. Whitlam had changed policy, but he had done it first by persuading the party, then placing the new policies before the people and then putting them in practice when he became prime minister. These changes were made by a Labor government; they were put to the party for approval, sometimes after the decisions had been made; the party never put them to the people. The Liberal Party put them to the people and lost. When Labor introduced these changes in parliament the Liberals supported them. This was how they passed through the Senate, where the government did not have a majority.

The adoption of economic rationalism by both parties was the greatest change in government policy since the early days of the Commonwealth. The Australian people never voted to make this change. Insofar as economic rationalism had been an issue at elections, the people had voted against it. The economic rationalists in both parties argued that these changes had to be made if Australia was to remain prosperous in a changing world. They might have been right. But the way the change happened made it look as if the Australian democracy was not controlled by the people. It looked as if the parties had ganged up on the people.

Labor lost office in 1996. At this election a majority of workers for the first time voted for the Liberal Party. Having changed its policy so drastically, the Labor Party lost many of its traditional supporters.

Parties still have a firm hold on the system of government, but their hold on the people is much weaker. There is a decline in the number of people who always vote for the same party. Supporting a party is not so strongly a way of declaring who you are—a worker or a respectable middle-class person. People are shopping around more and looking for new options. Support for independents and minor parties is growing. The two major parties got a large shock when One Nation, a new party formed in 1997, attracted strong support. It was opposed to policies supported by both the major parties—economic rationalism, special assistance to Aborigines, and migration from Asia.

The major parties have trouble attracting and keeping members. There are more members of conservation groups than of the political parties. The parties now have less need of members. There are no longer local meetings to be organised at election time. Campaigning is organised by the central office, with the aim of getting the prime minister or the leader of the Opposition on the evening TV news. Voters are reached individually, not by personal visits but by letters mailed from the central office.

Party branches still have a role in selecting candidates. In fact, in many places it is only when candidates are being discussed that members take any interest in branch affairs. That's when people wanting to be candidates sometimes 'stack' the branches with new members who will vote for them.

Parties no longer depend wholly on subscriptions and donations for their finance. Since 1983 the government pays them money to help run their campaigns. Once citizens supported parties to campaign for government; now government supports the parties by taxing the citizens. When individuals and companies give large donations to parties there is a danger that the givers will expect some special favour if the party wins office. This danger is reduced by the government funding of the parties. But it also helps old parties beat off newcomers.

The Democrats, the oldest of the minor parties, set out to be a party that was controlled by its members. All policy is decided by members voting by post. Members elect the parliamentary leader of the party. This should be the party for all those people who complain that the big parties fix things without consulting the people. But the Democrats have attracted only a very small membership. And most of the members don't bother to vote on policy!

An old idea for making the people the real rulers has been revived. This is 'the initiative and referendum' which allows people to propose laws and vote on them. This used to be put forward by radicals; now it is conservative groups who want it. They say that the people are opposed to large immigration and in favour of capital punishment, but the parties ignore their wishes. The initiative and referendum exists in several states in the USA. The operation of the system shows that it does not simply put the people in charge. Big business and rich people can organise to have proposals put to referendum and can spend heavily on advertising during referendum campaigns.

Talkback radio is a new way for ordinary people to participate in politics. They can pick up the phone and thousands of other people will hear what they think. They don't have to join anything or write down their views or make a speech. Governments take notice of talkback. It has made them take a tougher approach to the punishment of crime. The phone lines run hot if someone who has committed a horrible crime gets a light sentence.

But talkback is not the pure voice of the people. The parties listen to the shows and organise their supporters to phone in. The producers of the shows choose the calls they allow to go to air. The hosts have their own views. For a long time the most popular talkback host joined his callers in attacking the banks for charging high fees and closing branches. Then the banks paid him money and he switched his views.

The parties can seem like a barrier between the people and their representatives. But it is not possible for the people themselves to rule directly. The parties are still organisations that anyone can join, and they support candidates who could not run for parliament if they had to pay their own campaign costs.

Human rights

From the 1960s society went through a series of great changes. Women demanded equality in all spheres of life. Australia accepted immigrants from all over the world and they fought against discrimination. Handicapped people no longer accepted that they could be locked away, and wanted access to all facilities. Homosexuals 'came out' of their secret lives and campaigned for acceptance and the abolition of the laws that made them criminals.

All these people got changes made by calling for their human rights to be upheld. The protection of human rights was one of the great issues of politics. It was part of a worldwide campaign. The United Nations began its life in 1945 with a Declaration of Human Rights, and it has added to this other declarations about the rights of women, handicapped people and children, and against racial discrimination.

In the constitution the Commonwealth government was not given power over human rights. It has gained this power through its power over external affairs. The High Court has decided that signing a UN declaration is an 'external affair', and so the Commonwealth can pass laws to put the declaration into practice.

The Whitlam government passed the Racial Discrimination Act in 1975 and the Hawke government passed the Sex Discrimination Act in 1984. The Fraser government set up a Human Rights Commission in 1981. In 1986 this body became the Human Rights and Equal Opportunity Commission.

This Commission is a watchdog for all human rights and a protector against discrimination of all sorts. People can lodge a complaint with the Commission if they think their rights have been denied or they have been discriminated against. The Commission examines the matter and tries to get the people involved to agree on a settlement of the dispute. Anyone who doesn't like what the Commission has decided can appeal to the courts. The Commission can itself go to court if a case comes up in which human rights are involved. The Commission educates the community on human rights and makes reports on human rights issues. It has made reports on such matters as the rights of homeless children and the rights of those suffering from epilepsy.

The campaigners for human rights were not satisfied with these changes. They want Australia to have a Bill of Rights. This is a document that sets down the rights of citizens that all governments have to accept and which no law can overrule. The most famous Bill of Rights is the one included in the US constitution. The courts ensure that the Bill of Rights is upheld. Individuals denied their rights can appeal to the court. If their rights have been denied by a law passed by parliament, the court declares the law, or part of it, invalid.

Labor governments tried to introduce a Bill of Rights in 1973 and 1985. They caused great controversy. Some people were upset that the right to own property was excluded; others wanted the right to life to include the right to life of unborn children; others were worried that children were given rights. Some state governments did not want their laws brought into question by a Commonwealth Bill of Rights.

One argument against a Bill of Rights is that it sets rights in stone and does not allow for changes in values and beliefs. But these Bills were not to be part of the constitution as in the United States;

A BILL OF RIGHTS

The case against

This formed part of a lecture given by Sir Robert Menzies in the United States after he had retired as Liberal prime minister.

I am glad that the draftsmen of the Australian Constitution, though they gave close and learned study to the American Constitution and its amendments, made little or no attempt to define individual liberties. They knew that, with legal definition, words can become more important than ideas. They knew that to define human rights is either to limit them—for in the long run words must be given some meaning—or to express them so broadly that the discipline which is inherent in all government and ordered society becomes impossible.

Responsible government in a democracy is regarded by us as the ultimate guarantee of justice and individual rights. Except for our inheritance of British institutions and the principles of the Common Law, we have not felt the need of formality and definition.

Should a Minister do something which is thought to violate fundamental human freedom he can be promptly brought to account in Parliament. If his Government supports him, the Government may be attacked, and if necessary defeated.

I would say, without hesitation, that the rights of individuals in Australia are as adequately protected as they are in any other country in the world.

In America, as Ministers are not directly answerable to Congress, where they do not sit, it has been thought necessary to impose constitutional limits upon them, with the Supreme Court as the interpreter of those limits. And as the interpretation of such provisions will be largely affected by political and social concepts, the judgments of the Supreme Court of the United States tend to possess a political flavour which is notably absent from the judgments of the High Court of Australia.

Sir Robert Menzies, *Central Power in the Australian Commonwealth*, London, 1967, pp. 52, 54

they were to be ordinary laws and so could be changed by the parliament. Another argument against a Bill of Rights is that for the good of society individual rights have to be limited. But these Bills allowed that rights could be limited to the extent allowable in a free and democratic society.

However, the government decided not to press on against this opposition. Those who want a Bill of Rights have not given up. They argue that human rights are not safe if they are not firmly laid down and if governments are not prevented from overriding them.

The opponents of a Bill of Rights argue that it is undemocratic to hand over to unelected judges the difficult business of balancing rights against each other and weighing up claims of individual

A BILL OF RIGHTS

The case for

Lionel Murphy was Attorney General in the Whitlam Government and responsible for introducing a Bill of Rights.

We are legislating now for the protection of human rights because too often in the past our courts and our parliaments have let us down. The legislators have told us to look to the common law for our protection, the judges have excused themselves by pointing to the enactments of 'responsible legislatures', and between the two of them a series of grave injustices has been perpetrated, mainly on those groups in the community who lack the power or the popularity to answer back.

The common law, because it can be over-ruled by parliamentary law, is often powerless to protect rights and freedoms. The common law does not say we have freedom of speech; it says we may speak as we wish, so long as what we say is not unlawful. The common law does not say we have the right to freedom of assembly; it says that people may not be prevented from meeting together unless the law forbids that meeting.

The common law and our system of responsible government do not stop any Australian government, that feels so inclined, discriminating against whomsoever it pleases. Ask Aborigines, particularly in Queensland, and many women what equality before the law and the equal protection of the law means to them.

And whatever Sir Robert Menzies may think of the capacity and wisdom of our founding fathers, they rejected a Bill of Rights not just because of their faith in parliamentary democracy, but because of their fear that an 'equal protection' guarantee would rule out discriminatory legislation against Chinese. This is the legacy we must now try to live down.

Lionel Murphy, *Why Australia Needs a Bill of Rights*, Canberra, 1974 rights against the common good. They want politicians as representatives of the people to do this. But politicians are the enemy, say those who want a Bill of Rights; they are the threat to liberty. Most Australians agree with them in not trusting politicians. A recent poll showed that 70 per cent of the people wanted a Bill of Rights and wanted judges to be the protectors of their rights.

The balance of this argument has shifted, as Australians no longer think of themselves as British. This change too began in the 1960s. Britain ceased to be the centre of Australia's world: the place whose standards Australia accepted; the place it looked to for experts and high-quality performance; the place that Australians were proud to call the mother country.

Britain had been among the first countries in the world to protect the freedom of its citizens and curb the power of kings. Australians had been proud of this part of their heritage. Most of those who had worked to extend political rights in Australia were very respectful of what had been achieved in Britain, and in Britain they found heroes and models to inspire them. It was by appealing to the principles of British law that Evatt had beaten Menzies' plan to ban the Communist Party.

The British system of government and law was not written down in a constitution and a code of laws. Some of it was defined in laws passed by parliament, but much of it rested on convention and the rulings of the judges that made up the common law. For instance, in theory the British monarch was still sovereign and in charge of the government; it was only by convention that the monarch acted on the advice of ministers responsible to parliament. British people—in Britain and in Australia—were proud that not everything was written down. It showed that they had freedom in their bones. They were rather scornful of people who had to rely on written constitutions for their freedom—bits of paper that often turned out to be no protection at all.

When Australians no longer thought of themselves as British, they lost touch with their British political heritage. They had a British-type system of government but they no longer judged it by British standards and in the light of British history. More and more Australians who cared about politics thought that the gaps in what was written down were dangerous holes. They did not want a constitution that relied for its working on convention, and they wanted their rights to be clearly spelled out. The United Nations declarations and the US constitution became their models.

Read and Pass On

Sane Democracy

A Common Sense Journal for Common Sense People

VOL. 1. NO. 12.   JULY, 1933.   PRICE 3D.

WE ARE BRITISH !

It is fashionable nowadays to say that our society must accept either one of two alternatives — Fascism or Socialism.

We do not believe that that is true. It is not consistent with British tradition.

Here are some inspiring reminders from the pen of Lieut.-Col. Graham Seton Hutchison, D.S.O., M.C., author of " Footslogger," " Warrior," etc.

WE, to whom fair dealing as between man and man implies a moral integrity beyond the penal code ;

WE, who inspired the freedom of mankind from slavery, and will not endure its imposition on ourselves ;

WE, whose spirit responds to the profound and eternal truths traditional in the British character ;

WE, who cherish the ideals for which, in good times and bad, Great Britain has stood ;

WE, summoning courage from the heart of our land, in which it is vested ;

WE declare that we stand unmoved for the ideals which have inspired our race, and will go forward renewed, regenerated, united, towards the great destiny which an unerring history contributes as our right.

GOD SAVE THE KING.

Speakers' Notes

"Defend Democracy - Vote NO!"

Issued by the Australian Labor Party New South Wales Branch, Trades Hall, Sydney

...to be held on the 22nd September, 1951, the Menzies/Fadden Coalition Government is making an outrageous attempt to write fascism into the Australian Constitution.

● The powers being sought by the Government constitute a frontal attack upon all the established principles of British justice.
● Fundamental liberties and rights are under attack.
● Trial by jury is set aside.
● The established principle of British law that the onus of proof rests on the prosecution. is to be seriously weakened.
● Confiscation of property would take place without there being any investigation or appeal to the courts of the land.
● The right of appeal, the recognised and established principle of law, is to be broken down.
● The Federal Government is seeking powers which are contrary to any recognised constitutional precedent.
● The amendment is contrary to the whole spirit of the Constitution.
● The amendment involves the sacrifice of Magna Carta and the rule of law.

When Britain set the standard—for the Labor Party and the anti-Labor organisation,
Sane Democracy

Actually, the Commonwealth constitution is a mixture of the British and American constitutions. The British element is a government formed in the parliament and responsible to it, and the leaving of important matters to convention. The American elements are a strong Senate; the sharing of power between federal and state governments; a High Court able to cancel federal laws if parliament exceeds its powers.

For the first 70 years of the Commonwealth the Labor Party fought against the American elements. It had too often been blocked by the High Court and the Senate. It wanted a true British system: one parliament for Australia and no limit on the laws it could pass.

Labor has now given up its opposition and has come to accept the constitution, partly because the High Court has been more ready to expand the Commonwealth's powers. Constitutional experts now look at the constitution as a genuine mixture and not just as a British system slightly altered. More and more it is the American elements that people value: the Senate and the High Court. They would be happy for the High Court to be the interpreter of a Bill of Rights.

In the 1980s and the early 1990s the High Court became a very active force in political life. While debate over a Bill of Rights continued, the Court found some rights did already exist in the constitution. Because the constitution set up a system of representative government, it ruled that there must be a right to freedom of expression, though there is no mention of freedom of expression in the document. In 1992 it decided in the Mabo case that native title to land existed in the common law of Australia. Since the 1960s Aboriginal people had been campaigning for land rights; they had been granted in the Northern Territory and some of the states, but there was no national policy on the subject. The Hawke Labor government had intended to pass national legislation, but backed down in the face of strong opposition. So it was the judges and not the politicians who overturned the doctrine of *terra nullius*, with which European settlement in Australia had begun.

Democracy and society II

Comparisons

Democratic countries have their democracy in common, but how democracy works and what it means to the people differ from country to country. The society in which democracy operates is different in each country, and each country has its own history of democracy—how it came about and what came before it.

France became a democracy suddenly when a movement to reform the royal government turned into a revolution in 1789. The first democratic parliament was elected in 1792. It supported a dictatorial government that kept itself in power by executing thousands of its opponents. Ten years after the revolution began, a military dictator, Napoleon Bonaparte, took charge. In 1815 the royal governments of Europe, having defeated Napoleon, put a king back on the throne.

From then on France was regularly in turmoil. Kings, republican democracies, and another dictator ruled in turn. Democracy frightened upper-class and middle-class people because the first democracy had been so bloody. The divisions went deep into French society. A town did not have one chess club; there would be a royalist chess club and a republican chess club. Because the Church supported the kings, the democratic republicans were fiercely opposed to the Church. A republican mayor would take pleasure in building a public toilet against the wall of a church.

Britain became a democracy very slowly and peacefully. The violence in England took place in the seventeenth century, when the parliament made itself supreme over the king. That parliament was elected and controlled by landowners. The franchise was first widened 150 years later in 1832, but it took 100 years to establish full democracy. As there was no payment of members until 1911, the rich landowners, their friends and relations continued for a long time to be the largest group elected to parliament.

In 1776 the United States became a separate country by rebelling against Britain. The rebels proclaimed that all men were created equal and set up a new republican form of government. To belong to this new nation was to believe in certain political principles. At first the United States was not democratic. It became so quite soon and without violence. Democracy became identified with America, the natural result of the principles of equality with which the nation had begun.

The Australian colonies became democracies suddenly (like France), peacefully (like Britain), and while remaining colonies (unlike the United States). These three circumstances, as we shall see, had a great effect on what sort of democracy it was and how the people related to it.

The democracies established in the Australian states are now almost 150 years old. The central democracy, the Commonwealth of Australia, is over 100 years old. They are among the oldest and most stable democracies in the world.

This should be one of the things Australians are proud about, but Australians do not think of their political record when they think of what sort of people they are. Society itself in Australia is very democratic, but Australians have little regard for their democratic government. How this strange gap came about, and how government works well despite it, are the questions we will now try to answer.

Society

The European settlers of Australia were very diverse. There were people from three nations—the English, Scots and Irish; and they followed two faiths—Catholic and Protestant.

The people of the three nations were traditional enemies. Scotland had been a separate country, had fought England to keep its independence, but in 1707 had agreed to join it. Ireland had been conquered by England and from 1801 was ruled direct from London. The Irish had not accepted their English masters.

The English and the Scots were Protestants. They believed that their liberty depended on their Protestantism; they associated Catholicism with absolute monarchy and tyranny. They were even more suspicious of Irish Catholics, for they were generally poor and not well educated and so more likely to be under the sway of their priests.

There was a variety of Protestants. The Scots were Presbyterians, which was the official church in Scotland; the English belonged to the Church of England, which was the official church in England— although not all Protestants belonged to it. Methodists, Baptists and Congregationalists were allowed to practise their faith in England, but they did not enjoy full civil and political rights.

Most of the Irish were Catholic. The English had tried to force them to become Protestants. They had passed laws against Catholic

233

worship and Catholic schools and made the Irish pay for the Protestant Church of Ireland, which most of them did not attend. The Irish Catholics associated Protestantism with cruelty and tyranny.

Taking people from the three nations, Australia inherited their history of suspicion, prejudice and bitterness. The English made up roughly 60 per cent of the colonial population, the Irish 25 per cent, the Scots 15 per cent. Every colony received people from the three nations, though the proportions varied. South Australia had fewer Irish; Victoria had more Scots.

From the first the different people lived among each other. Unlike North America, Australia had no localities that were solely Scottish or solely Catholic. In the United States the Irish came late to a settled society and crowded into ghettos in the cities. In Australia the Irish were part of the founding population, and settled throughout the country with everyone else.

When different people live in their own areas and maintain their own culture and faith, it is hard for them to agree to belong to the one country. They need some idea or principle or feeling to bind them together. If this does not happen the country might split up.

In Australia the people of the three nations and two faiths were thrown together from the beginning. The oddity of Australia for the new settlers was not simply the physical environment: it was having so many half-foreigners as neighbours. They all had to make their lives in this new, strange mixture. They created a harmonious society by setting their differences aside and being good neighbours, or workmates or committee men. Australian society was integrated from the bottom up rather than from the top down. It did not need politics to unite it; sometimes politics was a destructive force.

From the earliest times there was a widespread determination to stop Old-World hatreds from taking root here. Of course there were some who wanted to keep them alive. The ministers of the churches and their closest followers believed their faith was the true one and were ready to denounce the others as false. But even people who took their own religion seriously might not want to join in open warfare with others—unless something happened to reignite the old fears they usually kept under control. Fortunately for the cause of social harmony, there were large numbers of people who did not take their religion too seriously.

Religious warfare had raged in Europe because for a long time it was assumed that a country could have only one religion. From the eighteenth century onwards liberals argued that this was not necessary. The State need not concern itself about religion, which was essentially a private matter. It could allow any number of religions to operate. Church and State should be separate.

The policy of the State having an official religion ended very early in Australia. In 1836 the liberal Governor Bourke dropped the special privileges of the Church of England and gave government funding on the same terms to the Church of England, the Presbyterians and the Catholics. The separation of Church and State came later when liberals took charge after self-government—in New South Wales in 1862, in Victoria in 1870 (it would have been earlier if the Legislative Council had not opposed it). South Australia was the first colony to separate Church and State—in 1851. This had been one of the aims of the founders of the province.

Liberalism was a strong force in Australia and it underpinned the task of keeping religion from disturbing the peace. But something much more positive was at work in Australian society: people actively worked to keep the peace by making sure that in community organisations there were representatives from all backgrounds and faiths. So there were Protestants and Catholics, English, Irish and Scots on the boards and managing committees of hospitals and charities, lodges, sporting clubs and mechanics institutes. There was always low-level tension between the groups and sometimes spectacular brawling. The way to stop this would have been to have separate organisations for each group. But that's exactly what the colonists wanted to avoid.

This desire for social peace was not a political doctrine; it was not, as the political scientists would say, an acceptance of pluralism. The colonists accepted that there were differences between people that were not going to disappear, but they did not want simply to tolerate differences and live apart from each other. They wanted to find ways to come together; they thought the peace would not be secure unless this happened. Behind this desire was a shared memory of how much bitterness had been caused by religious and ethnic differences in the countries from which they had come:

Our children shall, upon this new-won shore—
Warned by all sorrows that have gone before—
Build up the glory of a grand new World.

In the name they gave themselves the colonists showed their desire for harmony. They called themselves British. This term was used more in the colonies than in Britain itself. In Britain people thought of themselves first as English or Scots. If the English in Australia slipped up and called the colonies English, the Scots would very quickly remind them that they were British.

Rose, shamrock and thistle—of England, Ireland and Scotland—as the name for a hotel at Preston, Victoria, and in the Australian coat of arms, Malvern, in Melbourne

Britain did not include Ireland. However, in Australia the term British was used to include the Irish. The symbol that went with the name were the flowers of the three nations—the rose, shamrock and thistle. The Irish were not altogether happy to be called British. Britain was the country that ruled Ireland against its will. And yet the Irish in Australia were doing well and wanted to be accepted. They hoped that Britain would soon allow the Irish the self-government that Australia enjoyed. Then they could be British in Australia with a clear conscience.

In politics it was harder to maintain harmony. Election campaigns often turned into battles between Catholics and Protestants. On a committee or in a parade, all groups could be represented, but elections were inevitably a contest. If a Catholic ran for parliament all Catholics were encouraged to vote for him. Protestants then became alarmed that Catholics—urged on, they were sure, by their priests—were attempting to take over the country. They tried to rally all Protestants to oppose the Catholic candidate.

At the first elections in Melbourne in 1843 (which were for the Legislative Council in Sydney) the Catholic candidate lost. His Irish supporters then went on the rampage, breaking windows and firing guns. The police could not control them. Soldiers had to be called in to restore order. The Protestant response was to form an association for the protection of Protestantism.

All this happened without there being any issue at the election to divide Catholics and Protestants. Elections could be simply a trial of strength: on the part of Catholics, to uphold their right to take part in the government of the country; on the part of Protestants, to uphold the religion they associated with liberty and constitutional government.

Many people did not care about the religion of candidates; they voted on other issues. And Catholics and Protestants who fought at elections might cooperate in community organisations.

There was one political issue that involved the churches and came to divide Protestants and Catholics—education.

The churches ran the first schools (which were all primary schools) with government assistance. They opposed any plan to start up government schools. In New South Wales the first government school did not open until 1847. The government schools did not neglect religion. The teacher could teach the points that all Christians agreed on and the ministers of the different

CREATING A HARMONIOUS SOCIETY: HENRY PARKES ON STATE EDUCATION

Whether we are Englishmen, Scotchmen, or Irishmen, or whether we are the sons of some foreign land, over and above every other consideration we ought to be Australians. He is no friend to building up a free, enlightened, and prosperous people in this land, who seeks to cross the path of any child of tender years by imposing some mere figment of an old-world story that is to debar him of the best means of education.

I think that our Roman Catholic fellow citizens may well afford to drop the word Roman and call themselves Australian Catholics, and, whilst clinging to their faith with all the zeal of their fathers, they may well trust that faith to their clergy, to themselves, and to the example of their own lives, and allow their children to be instructed in the ordinary duties of citizenship with the children of their fellow citizens.

NSW
Debates,
1879–80,
Vol. 1,
pp. 274–5

churches could attend before or after the normal lessons to instruct their children in their special doctrines.

This was not good enough for the churches. They wanted to have full control of their children. They were strong enough to keep government funding flowing to their own schools. In the 1850s and 60s most children at school in eastern Australia were attending church schools. The parents were not as particular as the church leaders. Many sent their children to schools run by a church that was not their own.

Liberal politicians wanted children to be educated to live harmoniously by attending the same school, which must be the government school. They disliked the churches being involved in education. They were not opposed to religion; they were opposed to the ministers and priests keeping old differences and hatreds alive. The leaders of the churches turned education into a battlefield. If one church opened a school, the minister of another religion would open a rival school and try to lure pupils away from the first one.

It was inefficient to have rival schools in small centres which could really support only one school. In the 1860s the government of New South Wales and Victoria brought the government and the church schools under one administration. Its job was to prevent duplication and spend funds efficiently.

The liberals wanted more than this; they wanted the churches removed altogether. The efficiency argument was not enough to achieve this. In the capital cities and large towns there was no inefficiency in having a number of church schools.

The churches themselves were changing their views on education. The Presbyterians and Methodists dropped their opposition to government schools. The bishops of the Church of England wanted to continue their own schools with government funding, but their people were not willing to follow the bishops. They had staged a mini-revolution to reduce their power over the church.

That left the Catholic Church as the only strong opponent of a government education system that would take all children. It was hard for Irish bishops, with their experience of government oppression in Ireland, to accept that the government should run all schools. To them it looked as if education was being handed over to Protestants, who were bound to take the opportunity to attack their faith. In line with the Church's official position, the bishops insisted that religion had to be part of education, all through the teaching day. It was not enough to have a special session of religious instruction at a fixed time.

As they saw opinion moving against church schools, the Catholic bishops issued savage denunciations of government schools, calling them 'godless' and 'seedbeds of immorality'. They surely knew this would not help their cause. They were talking more to their own people, many of whom did not think it was necessary to send their children to a Catholic school. If government aid was withdrawn, the bishops intended to keep their schools going.

The Catholic bishops roused everyone else against them, not just firm Protestants but all those who wanted to avoid Old-World conflicts. In this atmosphere, the liberals could achieve their aim. Victoria removed government funding from church schools in 1872, New South Wales in 1880. This was the policy adopted by all the colonies.

The Catholic bishops did create an alternative Catholic education system. They brought nuns and brothers from Ireland to staff it. They pressured their own people into supporting it. Parents not sending their children to the Catholic school were told that they would be denied the mass. The bishops' aim was to withdraw

DEFENDING THE FAITH:
CATHOLIC CONDEMNATION OF STATE EDUCATION, 1879

It is self-evident that education without Christianity is impossible; you may call it instruction, filling the mind with a certain quantity of secular knowledge, but you cannot dignify it with the name of Education; for religion is an essential part of Education; and to divorce religion or Christianity from Education is to return to paganism, and to reject the Gospel of Jesus Christ. Thus it is that the Church condemns those schools, and that method of teaching in which the religious element is divorced from the secular.

Such, then, being the emphatic teaching of the Catholic Church, we, the Archbishop and Bishops of the colony of New South Wales, with all the weight of our authority, condemn the principle of secularist education, and those schools that are founded on that principle. We condemn them, first, because they contravene the first principles of the Christian religion; and secondly, because they are seed-plots of future immorality, infidelity, and lawlessness, being calculated to debase the standard of human excellence, and to corrupt the political, social, and individual life of future citizens.

R.B. Vaughan,
Pastorals and Speeches on Education,
Sydney, 1880

Catholics from the community. They built their own hospitals and started Catholic lodges and Catholic associations for young people. They were very strongly against Catholics marrying non-Catholics. The more the Catholics withdrew into their own world, the more suspicion they aroused. The bishops kept asking for government funding for their schools, but this was always refused. Every time it was refused, the Catholics were more inclined to think of themselves as a persecuted minority.

The liberals had pursued a noble ideal in wanting to educate all children together and put an end to Old-World feuding. In dealing with the Catholic Church, they faced the dilemma of how to respond to an anti-liberal force. The Catholic Church was officially opposed to the separation of Church and State and to the State running education. The bishops were not prepared to agree to anything that did not provide a full Catholic education for Catholic children, supported by government funds. Against this resistance, the liberals pushed on and stopped aid to church schools. They achieved their object, but at the expense of their ideal. They created a long-lasting and bitter division.

When it was clear that the Catholics would continue with their schools, there was no rethinking. Protestant opinion stood in the way of sympathetic treatment of Catholic requests. Protestants, having given up their own schools in favour of government schools, would not allow public money to go to the nuns and brothers.

The bishops thought they had some hope of reversing the decision when Catholics became an important part of the Labor Party. But that party, having to keep Protestant and Catholic workers together, was not going to reopen the State aid issue. Around the time of World War I the bishops set out to punish the Labor Party for receiving Catholic votes and not supporting Catholic schools. They set up Catholic parties and told Catholics to vote for them. Nearly all of them refused to desert the Labor Party.

Catholics reconnected with the wider community by becoming staunch Labor people. They preferred to keep that position rather than follow their bishops. But their strong presence in the Labor Party and their near absence from the Liberal Party gave the party divide a religious character. Some Protestants would not vote for Labor because it was too Catholic. Catholics would not vote Liberal because it was too Protestant.

A school system and a party system divided on religious lines: this was not the harmonious society that the nineteenth-century liberals had hoped for. But Australian cities did not turn into a Beirut or Belfast, where the two warring sides have their own areas. The conflict in politics and public life remained at a distance from the community. It did not so much reflect community division as save the community from division.

Protestants and Catholics still lived among each other. They interacted in the neighbourhood, at work and in playing and following sport. They interacted in the unions and the Labor Party. Intermarriage continued despite the opposition of the priests. There were still many people on both sides wanting to set aside their differences. The Australian style of dealing with difference did not disappear. It is the social foundation of the peacefulness of Australian democracy.

The divide between Catholic and Protestant ceased to be important in the 1960s. It had no deep roots in the structure of society, so when both sides decided to treat each other as fellow Christians the dispute disappeared.

After World War II Australian society had to deal with new differences on a vast scale. A mass migration program began which brought to this British society non-English-speaking people, at first from Europe, later from Asia, Africa, Latin America and the Middle East. Australians applied to this new challenge the formula that had brought peace to their mixed society. The government, supported by the people, wanted the new migrants to mix in with the old population and not form separate enclaves. The government knew that this would happen only if migrants were welcomed. It told the Australian people to call the migrants New Australians and it set up the Good Neighbour Council, which arranged for old Australians to help the new Australians settle in.

Old Australians were suspicious of the newcomers and a few were openly hostile, but on the whole Australians accepted them. If the newcomers wanted to make a go of it here and did not make a nuisance of themselves, they could be Australians. Migrants found that Australians were generally friendly, but they were puzzled that Australians were not interested in their culture and experience. They were encountering the Australian style of mixing, where people remain friendly by not exploring differences.

The migrants did not mix in as rapidly as the government had hoped. In the inner cities they did form something like enclaves. But within 10 years they were buying houses in the suburbs and scattering themselves widely in the process. After 20 years their children were marrying old Australians. Australian society was again being rapidly integrated from the bottom up.

From the 1970s governments promoted a new name for Australia—multicultural Australia—and migrants were encouraged to retain their culture under an official policy of multiculturalism. These terms recognised the new diversity of Australia, which most Australians accepted, but they met opposition. Some people feared that if migrants were encouraged to retain their own culture, the nation would be too divided. Often they were not aware of those parts of the policy that declared that migrants' first loyalty must be to Australia and to its principles of democracy, equal rights for men and women, toleration of differences and the rule of law. The name 'multiculturalism' helped to create this confusion because it referred only to diversity.

Though official names and policies changed, the dynamic of Australian society continued as before. With intermarriage, the boundaries of ethnic groups became blurred. A few groups, strong

Young migrant family in the suburbs

in the 1950s, disappeared. There was still a widespread determination that old-world disputes should not disturb the social
peace. In the 1950s migrants were told their disputes threatened
the Australian way of life. From the 1970s they were told their
disputes threatened multicultural Australia. It was the same
message.

Nation

People who live in colonies know that the mother country looks down on them. Australian colonists faced this problem in an acute form because they knew that the British looked down on them as the descendants of convicts.

Colonists can respond in two ways. They can claim that they are as good as the mother country. With this option they run the risk of making themselves ridiculous. In a rough colony, only 50 or 80 years old, can you really say that its art, literature and architecture match the great achievements of the mother country? The alternative is to agree with the outlook of the mother country; to run down all things colonial as inferior and second-rate. With this option the colonists run the risk of becoming spineless.

It is hard for colonists to put away the boasting and the cringing and to be calmly confident about themselves. A colony can reach this maturity by a political revolt against the mother country. By overthrowing the mother country's power, the colony becomes an independent nation and the equal of the country that previously controlled it. This is how the United States became a nation. Its sense of nationhood is tied up with its Declaration of Independence and the writing of its constitution.

Australia did not gain its sense of nationhood through politics. The colonists did not have to push very hard before, in the mid-nineteenth century, the British allowed them to become self-governing. The British thought that the next step would soon be that the colonists would demand full independence. British policy makers were resigned to accepting this; some looked forward to it because they thought the colonies were more a burden than a benefit.

But the opposite happened. Once the colonists had been allowed to control their own affairs, they became more loyal to Britain. They wanted to retain their British identity and be part of a worldwide empire which would protect them. To be British did not mean that they could not be Australian as well. Until the 1960s most people thought of themselves as Australians and Britons.

By the late nineteenth century Britain was much more interested in its empire, as it was facing competition from Germany and the United States. The British quietly encouraged the formation of Australian federation, though they knew that Australians had to be in charge of the project. A united Australia would be a stronger element within the Empire than six colonies.

This was an empire like no other. How could you rebel against an empire that allowed you to be self-governing and to take the status of nationhood? But Australians still had the psychological need to assert themselves against the British. Until they did that, they would not have the self-confidence to be a nation.

The Australian colonists boasted that they had created a society much better than Britain's. There was no grinding poverty, no-one forced to beg on the streets. There was no privileged upper class, taking its position because of birth. Opportunity was open to all, and those who had acquired wealth had worked hard to get it. Socially, Britain was the standard of what Australia was not to be.

The pretend battle of sport took the place of a war of independence against Britain. When Australian teams first took the field against English cricketers, they had 22 or fifteen players. In 1877 an Australian eleven beat the English for the first time. Australians were overjoyed to beat the English at their own game. It showed that neither convict blood nor the hot sun had led to a degeneration of the race. Australians could believe that they were as good as or better than their British forebears.

The first period of Australian mastery over the English at cricket began with the Test series of 1897–98, when Australia won four tests to one. This series coincided with the final debates on the

WHICH IS THE BURNING QUESTION?

1. THE INTEREST IN FEDERATION. | 2. THE INTEREST IN CRICKET.

Melbourne's Punch *in 1895 shows Australians' real interest*

constitution for the Commonwealth of Australia. There was much
more interest in the cricket than in the constitution.

Australians were keen to test themselves in real battles. They
fought not against the Empire but for it—in the Sudan in 1885, in
the Boer War in 1899, and in the two world wars. In fighting for

Supporting the Empire: crowds in Sydney farewell troops for the Sudan in 1885

the Empire they were not defending another country—the Empire was their country; and they hoped their soldiers would show the British that they were worthy to belong to this empire.

Australians first fought as a separate unit on the Turkish peninsula of Gallipoli in 1915. Though landed in the wrong spot, and under heavy fire, they advanced into a tangle of cliffs and gullies and held on. When British military experts saw the terrain, they were amazed that the Australians had not been thrown back into the sea. Everyone praised the Australian soldiers. Back home Australians were relieved and elated. No-one could look down on them now. Their soldiers, by their courage and their sacrifice, had shown that they were worthy to be a nation. By the end of the war Australians believed that the Australian soldier was not only as good as the British soldier—he was better.

Officially the nation was born in 1901, but the saying developed that the nation was born at Gallipoli. The date of the landing, 25 April, was celebrated as Anzac Day (ANZAC was the name of the fighting unit—the initials of the Australian and New Zealand Army Corps). Anzac Day became Australia's unofficial national holiday.

BORN AT GALLIPOLI

This report of Australian and New Zealand soldiers landing on Gallipoli was the first detailed news Australians at home received of the event. It was written by the British war correspondent Ellis Ashmead-Bartlett.

The boats had almost reached the beach, when a party of Turks, entrenched ashore, opened a terrible fusillade with rifles and a Maxim machine gun. Fortunately the majority of the bullets went high. The Australians rose to the occasion. Not waiting for orders, or for the boats to reach the beach, they sprang into the sea, and, forming a sort of rough line, rushed at the enemy's trenches.

Their magazines were not charged, so they just went in with cold steel. It was over in a minute. The Turks in the first trench were either bayoneted or they ran away, and their Maxim was captured.

Then the Australians found themselves facing an almost perpendicular cliff of loose sandstone, covered with thick shrubbery. Somewhere half-way up, the enemy had a second trench, strongly held, from which they poured a terrible fire on the troops below and the boats pulling back to the destroyers for the second landing party.

Here was a tough proposition to tackle in the darkness, but those colonials practical above all else, went about it in a practical way. They stopped for a few minutes to pull themselves together, got rid of their packs, and charged their magazines. Then this race of athletes proceeded to scale the cliffs without responding to the enemy's fire. They lost some men, but did not worry. In less than a quarter of an hour the Turks were out of their second position, either bayoneted or fleeing.

But then the Australasians, whose blood was up, instead of entrenching, rushed northwards and eastwards, searching for fresh enemies to bayonet. It was difficult country in which to entrench. Therefore they preferred to advance.

Argus, 8 May 1915

It did not mark a political event. The date of the formation of the nation, 1 January, was not celebrated at all. It was simply New Year's Day.

The nation formed on 1 January 1901 was not fully independent. Britain was still in charge of defence and foreign policy, though it consulted with the Australian government on these matters. No Australian government blindly followed Britain. All governments did their best to make sure that the policy of Britain and its empire would benefit Australia.

It is difficult to say when Australia became fully independent. In 1931 Britain passed the Statute of Westminster, which allowed the self-governing nations within the Empire (the dominions) to be fully independent. They could develop their own defence and foreign policies. Their only tie with Britain would be their allegiance to the King.

Australian governments had not pressed for this change. Canada, South Africa and Ireland wanted it. Australia had more need of Britain's protection than these countries and would have been happy for the existing arrangements to continue. Australia did now want to see the ties of Empire weakened; it wanted the Empire to remain strong to protect it against Japan.

Australia requested that the Statute of Westminster not apply to Australia immediately. It would come into force only when Australia adopted it. So when independence was offered to Australia, it refused to take it. That's why 1931 cannot definitely be the date of Australian independence.

Australia adopted the Statute during World War II, in 1942. Is that when independence was secured? Perhaps, but in 1940 Australia had appointed its first ambassadors to foreign countries, which is one test of independent status. If that is the test, perhaps Australia was independent as early as 1919, when it sent its own representatives to the League of Nations.

The experts can't agree. It is not surprising that ordinary people have no idea when their country became independent. They know they are a separate and independent people, but that does not relate to the political independence of their nation. They felt themselves to be a separate and independent people even when they were firmly part of the Empire. They were 'independent Australian Britons'.

Not everyone was equally strong in their loyalty to the Empire. Irish Catholics and their children looked on the English as the oppressors of Ireland. Socialists thought of the Empire as a system of capitalist oppression. The Catholics and the socialists in the Labor Party made the party wary and suspicious of the Empire.

However, it was never opposed to the connection with the Empire. When Labor was in office, it supported the Empire connection. It was a Labor prime minister, Andrew Fisher, who said at the beginning of World War I that Australia would stand by Britain 'to our last man and our last shilling'. But in the course of the war opposition to it within the party grew, and the party refused to follow its leaders and accept conscription.

In World War II, Britain could not protect Australia against the Japanese. The great naval base at Singapore that was meant to defend Australia fell easily to the enemy. A Labor prime minister, John Curtin, looked to the United States to defend Australia, 'free', as he said, 'of any pangs as to our traditional links or kinship with the United Kingdom'. But this did not mean he was abandoning the traditional links. By the end of the war Curtin was trying to get the British dominions to cooperate more closely and strengthen the Empire. He thought Australia had more chance of influencing the policy of the British Empire than that of the United States. Ben Chifley, who followed him as prime minister, was a firm supporter of the British connection.

Because it had misgivings about the Empire, the Labor Party was more interested than the Liberals in the symbols of Australian nationhood. It wanted an Australian rather than a person from Britain to be governor-general. Prime Minister Scullin in London during the Depression in 1930 stood up to George V and insisted that the King appoint Sir Isaac Isaacs, chief justice of the High Court, as the first Australian-born governor-general.

From its beginnings the Labor Party was opposed to the award of imperial honours. In practice, Labor governments recommended people for imperial honours—but not knighthoods that allowed you to put Sir before your name. The Whitlam government (1972–75) introduced the Australian system of honours, the Order of Australia, to replace the imperial awards. No award under this system carried the title Sir.

The Whitlam government also made 'Advance Australia Fair' the Australian national anthem, to replace 'God Save the Queen'. The British anthem would still be played when the Queen was present or any of her representatives, the governors and the governor-general.

The Liberal Party opposed all these changes. It went on choosing British governors-general until it appointed an Australian lord, Richard Casey, in 1965. Since then all governors-general have been Australian. The Fraser government restored imperial honours. It kept the Order of Australia but added knighthoods to it. The Hawke Labor government again dropped imperial honours and scrapped the Australian knighthood. They have not returned. The Liberals criticised Whitlam for imposing a new anthem on the people. When they returned to power, they held a referendum to choose not an anthem but a song. 'Advance Australia Fair' won. The Hawke government made it the national anthem.

All these changes are now fully accepted by the Australian people, who could not imagine an Englishman in Yarralumla or 'God save the Queen' being played when an Australian won an Olympic gold medal. It might be thought that the Liberals would have suffered for opposing the adoption of these national symbols. Are they not marked forever as the un-Australian party? They are not. There was more passion against these moves than enthusiasm for them. Most people who voted for 'Advance Australia Fair' had no idea of its words.

Labor's appointment of Isaacs in 1931 was ahead of public opinion and was widely condemned as an atttack on Australia's British allegiance. The Liberals suffered no harm in reverting to British appointments. Curtin made a British appointment in 1945—the Duke of Gloucester, the King's brother, the only royal to hold the office. Whitlam's moves were not completely overturned by Fraser and gained acceptance sooner. They were a sort of housekeeping made necessary, not by the emergence of the Australian nation but by the weakening of the allegiance to Britain.

Australians never chose to break their allegiance to Britain. Rather, Britain decided to join the European Union and abandon her connections with the people around the world who called themselves British. Britain made its decision to join Europe in 1961 (though it was not admitted until 1973). Once she was part of Europe, Britain could no longer have special trade arrangements with the dominions overseas and no longer lead them as a British force in world affairs.

The failure of Britain to defend Singapore and protect Australia in World War II is sometimes called 'a betrayal'. That did not disturb Australia's allegiance to Britain. It was the British decision to join Europe that finally persuaded Australians that their double life as Australians and Britons had come to an end. They did feel betrayed when on arriving in the mother country they were asked to join the 'foreigners' queue.

One link with Britain remains. The governor-general is still appointed by the Queen on the recommendation of the prime minister. A republican movement began in 1991 with the aim of creating an Australian head of state. A referendum to establish a republic was defeated in 1999. Many issues were in play here. Half the No vote came from people who wanted to elect the new president directly rather than the president being appointed by parliament on the recommendation of the prime minister. Republicans hoped they would carry the day by appealing to Australian nationalism. To them it is offensive that the Queen plays any part, however small, in Australia's affairs. But for most people their sense of Australianness is not linked to politics. The yobbo who yells 'You Pommy Bastard!' at the cricket is happy to accept a 'Pom' as his Queen. However, he would become a violent revolutionary if the Australian cricket team were to be chosen in Australia but appointed by the Queen.

Distinctions

Some people think there is a very obvious explanation for the Australian colonies becoming democracies. Their explanation goes like this. The first settlers came from very unequal societies, where inferior people had to show respect to superior people. Most of the migrants to Australia did not come from the superior upper classes; they were middle-class or working people. They wanted to get rid of Old-World distinctions and create in the colonies a world in which people did not have to know their place. Anyone in Australia who tried to pretend they were upper class was just laughed at. The old distinctions simply could not be re-established in the new land. People began to treat each other as equals, and so democracy was the only form of government that would suit them.

This is very misleading. Society was not democratised first and then politics. It was the other way about. Politics was democratised long before society was.

It is true that the migrants rejected some aspects of the old society: they did not want position to depend on birth or education or knowing the right people. But those who came to the colonies to better themselves wanted to show off their success in the old ways. What other signs did they know? What other signs would be recognised?

So those who made money in Australia built mansions like the houses of the rich landowners in England; they drove around in carriages; they put on red jackets and went hunting; they established exclusive clubs; they sent their sons to private schools, which copied English private schools. The best sign of success was to receive an honour from the Queen. There was such a demand for these from Australia that the British government had to start a new system of awards for the colonies—the Order of St Michael and St George. The highest awards in the order were knighthoods that allowed you to use the title Sir and Lady for your wife. There were degrees of knighthood. You could be a Knight, a Knight Commander or Knight Grand Cross.

The migrants did not want dukes and lords in Australia, but successful migrants claimed the title of gentleman. This was a unique English position. Gentlemen were at first the large landowners who were not noble. They had to be men of good breeding: that is, descended from other gentlemen or, better still, from a lord. They had to be men of leisure. They lived on the rents collected from the farmers who worked their land. If they were making money from other businesses, they could not be actively involved in running them.

A gentleman also had to possess certain moral qualities. He was a man of honour, who kept his word and showed consideration for others. A man who did not behave like this was 'no gentleman', even though he might own land and be well bred. But what if you passed the moral test—did this make you a gentleman, even if you did not fully meet the other tests? Perhaps. This was how more people were becoming gentlemen in England.

Gentleman was an excellent title for export to the colonies. It was not quite definite; the qualifications were elastic and could be stretched. They were stretched a long way. The test of not being involved in business was easily dropped. Even true gentlemen in Australia—and there were some—were very closely involved in money-making. So that made it acceptable for others to be making money. But the test was not dropped altogether. It was shifted. If you made money as a merchant, that was alright; if you ran a shop and served the public, you could not be a gentleman. As to good breeding, the new gentlemen in Australia pushed their ancestors as far up the social scale as they dared.

The final result was that, in Australia, most men who had made money could be gentlemen. This was a huge change in the rules,

GENTLEMEN

Gentlemen! How that grand old word has been prostituted. 'Gentleman' once meant an honest, courteous, brave and liberal man—a man who had an arm to strike at oppression and vice, and a heart to pity the repentant and weak. Now it means—money, for one thing, good clothes for another, social distinction for another; an ability to read, write, dance, and run into debt for a fourth; a certain style of speaking, looking, walking and eating for a fifth; but it means principally—money. Any low-minded, ignorant ruffian who has suddenly accumulated wealth calls himself a gentleman.

The sham aristocracy of a country like this is pitifully absurd.

Marcus Clarke, 'Democratic snobbery', in *The Peripatetic Philosopher*, 1869

and it was not reached without great social turmoil. The air was full of bitchinesss and gossip. *He* made his first money selling sly grog; *she* was only the daughter of a coal-heaver; and of course you've heard why they *had* to leave England? People who could not meet the true tests themselves attacked others for being low-bred or making money in dodgy ways. That might look as if they were claiming that the idea of a gentleman in Australia was a nonsense. Not at all. They did not want those who had successfully established themselves to keep others out. Men on the make in Australia believed in equality, but only in equality down to their level. That is, they would not admit that anyone was superior to themselves, but they wanted to be superior to those beneath them.

It is surprising that, with so much change and dispute, the category of gentleman did not implode. It didn't. The one definite test for a new gentleman in Australia was that he should be wealthy, and a wealthy man could look like a gentleman once he had a large house and a carriage and dressed like a gentleman.

There was a uniform for the gentleman, copied from England: a long frock coat, a top hat, kid gloves. It survived until the end of the nineteenth century. When it went out of fashion in England, gentlemen kept wearing it in Australia. The dress was more important here, where the other tests of gentlemen had been set aside. It is understandable that the gentlemen were reluctant to give it up. By putting on this uniform they had announced to the world that they were now gentlemen. It must have been a proud and awkward moment.

In England, parliament was a gathering of gentlemen—true gentlemen. The largest group in parliament was the country landowners. Those few members who were not gentlemen were treated as if they were.

The first partly elected Legislative Councils in Australia were made up of landowners and squatters along with a few merchants and lawyers. They thought of themselves as gentlemen and were treated as such. As at Westminster, the Councils were gatherings of the rich and well-educated.

All this changed with the rapid move to a democracy in the 1850s. The rich found it hard to get elected and were forced to retreat to the Legislative Councils. Poor men of little education replaced them. Members heaped vulgar abuse on each other, and some were only in parliament to benefit themselves.

Parliamentarians still dressed as gentlemen and hoped to be treated as gentlemen, but now there was an implosion: no-one believed that parliamentarians were gentlemen. The new democratic institution did not dress itself in its own clothes; it set itself up for a fall by putting on a distinctly undemocratic uniform.

Rich and educated people now regarded politicians as a low-class bunch of incompetents. They made fun of those who could not speak or write properly, who had done lowly work before they became MPs, and who had wives who could never be accepted into good society. If a rich and well-educated man did get into parliament, he was always apologising for keeping such low company. It did give him a lot of good stories to shock and amuse his friends.

AN MP WITH POOR SPELLING

Morris Asher had been an MP briefly in 1859–60; he was thinking of returning to parliament.

Sydney Morning Herald, 26 May 1863

Having heard you are about to resighn your seat in the Assembly, may I take the Libety of asking wither such is the case; and if so wither you would assist me in case I stand for the Electorate?

HENRY PARKES, ESQ., CARRIED IN TRIUMPH TO THE " EMPIRE" OFFICE.

Henry Parkes, former working man, winning his first election dressed as a gentleman, Sydney 1854

These very ordinary parliamentarians had been elected by the votes of ordinary people. Their votes gave them the opportunity to show that they did not want parliamentarians to be just the rich and the well-educated. They elected parliamentarians who could not look down on them and whom they did not have to look up to. They too believed in equality down to their level. But they had not got rid of the idea that parliament was a place they should be able to respect. By their votes they had produced parliaments that they too despised.

Respect for parliament evaporated very quickly. In the Supreme Court in Sydney in 1861, the chief justice at the top of society and a criminal at the bottom shared a joke at the politicians' expense. The criminal was being tried for escaping from jail. Before the case began he asked that he be given another judge because it was the chief justice who had given him the harsh sentence that had put him in jail. The criminal said the chief justice might have 'prejudicial feelings' against him. The judge, thinking he had said 'political feelings', asked 'Why should I have political feelings

257

WHO IS PREFERRED AS AN MP?

James Inglis,
*Our
Australian
Cousins*,
London,
1880, p. 363

The man who can talk loudest, make the boldest protestations, and promise most, is the man the electors prefer. If he can out-swear a bullock-driver, and out-drink a distiller's drayman, he is almost certain of a seat in parliament.

against you. Are you a member of parliament?'. To which the criminal replied 'Not yet'.

When the parliaments acted to protect their reputation, they discovered how little respect they enjoyed. The big man behind the bribing of the Victorian parliament in the 1860s was the squatter

IN SYDNEY DOMAIN.

" EXCUSE MY INTERRUPTION, BUT MAY I ASK IF YOU ARE A MEMBER OF PARLIAMENT?"
" NO, SIR; I AM A GENTLEMAN."

A Bulletin *cartoon of 1887*

Hugh Glass. When the parliament committed him to prison, he became a popular hero. The Supreme Court set him free and the parliament took no further action. The most corrupt member of parliament was C.E. Jones, the member for Ballarat. While he was a minister, he took money to organise opposition to his own government. When this was discovered, the parliament expelled him, but Ballarat re-elected him.

The Ballarat voters thought he was no worse than the men who had expelled him, so they were not going to see him punished. A vicious cycle had set in. Parliament was despised, but voters continued to elect men who kept its reputation low.

In recent years the reputation of politicians has fallen even further. This change has been small compared to the catastrophic collapse that can be dated precisely to the introduction of democracy in the 1850s.

Dignity

At the time Britain first settled Australia, working men in England and Scotland were campaigning for the vote. They wanted the vote to make things different—a better standard of living for workers—and so they could be someone different, not the poor or the lower orders but equal citizens.

Working men in Australia found decency and dignity without needing to have the vote. They were living well and calling their souls their own before democratic politics began.

For most of recorded history the common people worked to grow food under the close watch of their masters. The production of food constituted nearly the whole of the economy. Britain was the first country to move to a modern economy, where trade and industry are more important than food production and most people live in towns and cities. This great change—the industrial revolution—was happening in Britain just at the time it was founding colonies in Australia.

These British colonies jumped straight into the new age. They did not pass through the stage where most people were growing food and living in villages. The land in Australia was used to run sheep and cattle. The wool went to the new factories in England, the cattle to feed the people in the cities on the coast. Wheat and flour were shipped in from elsewhere.

Cities were big in Australia from the beginning because they were the centres for the export trade, which was the heart of the economy. More people were employed in carting, loading and shipping the wool than in producing it. The country was sparsely settled. The squatter employed a dozen shepherds scattered in huts around his run or a few cattlemen mounted on horseback.

South Australia was different. The land was used to produce wheat, which was shipped to the eastern colonies. But within six years of its settlement a machine had been developed to harvest the wheat—the stripper. Here, too, not many people were needed in the countryside.

So, in this new country, economic life was far from primitive. This was a dynamic, flexible, highly efficient economy trading with the world. It produced a very high standard of living for its workers. They were not living in traditional ways closely watched by masters. They moved readily from job to job; those who lived on the job in the country were well out of the boss's eye.

Wages stayed high because there was a shortage of labour. Except in the goldrush of the 1850s, migrants did not flood into the country as they did into the United States. The Australian worker was protected by distance. Workers could make the journey to Australia only if the government paid for their fares.

In this environment workers feared the boss less and became more independent and self-confident. They did not have to be humble before their 'betters'. These attitudes probably had little to do with the first workers being convicts. They had more to do with all workers, convicts and free, coming from a society where workers had long had civil rights, where traditional ties were breaking down and where workers were beginning to claim political rights. This did not mean that workers were to be great activists in Australia. It meant rather that they were ready to think of themselves as more than the 'lower orders'. With prosperity they grew tall.

The new independent spirit was evident in women as well as men. Visitors noted that Australian girls were more forthright and adventurous than English girls. They were very reluctant to become domestic servants and work under the close control of a mistress. As mistresses had trouble getting servants, servants were not so much under the control of their mistresses as they were in England.

In the 1850s male workers got the vote without any struggle. There were no memorable words, no key moments, no heroes. The Eureka rebels had demanded the vote, but Eureka could not be

---

THE INDEPENDENCE OF WOMEN WORKERS

Unfortunately, but a very small proportion of the daughters of the poorer colonial working-class will become domestic servants. For some inexplicable reason, they turn up their noses at the high wages and comparatively light work offered, and prefer to undertake the veriest drudgery in factories for a miserable pittance.

So great is the love of independence in the colonial girl, that she prefers hard work and low wages in order to be able to enjoy freedom of an evening. It is in vain that the press points out that girls whose parents do not keep servants are accustomed to perform the same household duties in their own homes that are required of them in service; that work which is not degrading at home cannot be degrading in service; and that they will be better wives for the knowledge of housework which they acquire in service. They might as well preach to the winds; and there are more applications for employment in shops and factories than there is work, whilst mistresses go begging for lady-helps.

R.E.N. Twopeny, *Town Life in Australia*, London, 1883, pp. 56–7

---

honoured by colonists who remained loyal to Britain. There was a workers' struggle in the 1850s that left a memorial behind—the gaining of the eight-hour day. This was won by building workers in Sydney and Melbourne after short, sharp strikes. Their slogan was eight hours' labour, eight hours' recreation, eight hours' rest. Their wages were so high that some of the workers agreed to take a cut in pay in order to gain the eight-hour day.

These workers were the first in the world to work such short hours. This was an Australian achievement to celebrate. On the anniversary of the first victory, the trade unions paraded through the streets behind their colourful banners. In Melbourne the procession was limited to the workers who had gained the reduced hours. The eight-hour day movement was an ongoing struggle. Only slowly did other workers gain the reduced hours of the stonemasons and bricklayers.

'Eight-hour Day' became a public holiday. The rest of the community turned out to watch the unions parade, and took pleasure in their success. The strikes called to win the eight-hour day did not inconvenience the public. They were short strikes in factories, not in services on which everyone relied. A coachbuilder

NATIVE *versus* IMPORTED.—No. 4.
Our Riding Master, whose courtesy is superior to every other consideration, dismounts to open the gate.
Alice to Mary.—THE OLD MUFF! HOW HIS POLITENESS IS THROWN AWAY.

The English riding-master opens the gate but the Australian girl jumps her horse over the fence (though she is still riding side-saddle)

or a harness maker might have to be brought into line after the rest of the trade had agreed to a reduction of hours. Working men parading in their best Sunday clothes on Eight-hour Day was the sign that life for ordinary people was better here. Good working conditions were worth more than the possession of the vote.

The chief political issue in the 1850s was opening up the land. This aroused great enthusiasm in Sydney and Melbourne, but most of the working men who turned out to meetings probably had no intention of settling on the land themselves. Already in these two cities working men were landowners, a development even more amazing than the limiting of working hours to eight. The inner suburbs were taking shape, not rows of identical dwellings but a jumble of short terraces and freestanding cottages. Workers were among the owners of these houses; some of the worker-owners had built their homes in their spare time.

In the second half of the nineteenth century Australia became known as a working man's paradise. By our standards, of course,

Eight-hour Day parade in Melbourne in 1866

it was not; by world standards at the time it was. Part of the opportunity Australia offered was that a working man could better himself; it was often said that a skilled man should soon be running his own workshop. But the most revealing part of this slogan is the message that you can live well even if you remain a working man. Americans were very boastful about their land of opportunity, but they very definitely associated living well with 'getting on'—with not being a worker.

In the Australian cities a working man could be accepted as a respectable citizen. As well as belonging to a trade union, he might

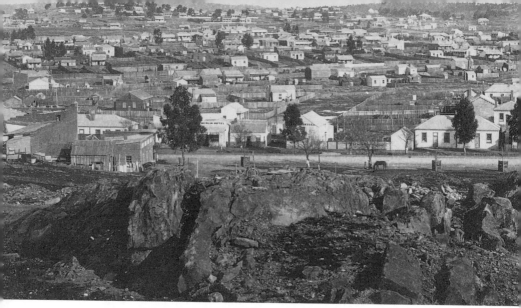

Miners' houses at Bendigo, often built by themselves on land held under miner's right

save with a building society so that he could become a home-owner; he might be a member of a lodge so that his family would have free medical attention if any of them fell ill; he might borrow books from the Mechanics Institute Library.

When working men entered politics it was to protect and entrench what they had already gained. In the early years of democratic politics very few working men sat in parliament, but workers exercised a definite influence. Candidates had to take notice of what they wanted. They did not want governments to spend money on bringing out more immigrants. That would drive wages down. Some colonies stopped assisted immigration altogether; others cut back their programs.

Workers also wanted the eight-hour day system to be made law and to apply to all workers. Governments refused to do that, but

THE FIRST RIGHT OF WORKING MEN

This declaration was made in a petition of the unemployed to the governor of Victoria, 1855.

The first and great primary right of all others—the right to live by our labour, and support our wives and children in moderate comfort and decent respectability.

Argus,
18 August 1855

they did adopt the eight hours for their own workers and required government contractors to do the same.

Workers suffered a huge setback in the 1890s, with economic depression and defeats in big strikes. Wages went down and unemployment up. The socialists in the Labor Party hoped that socialism would eventually replace capitalism. The immediate job of the Labor Party and later of Labor governments was to create jobs with decent wages; to restore workers to the good conditions they had enjoyed before. As governments were so heavily involved in development works, there was plenty of opportunity for them to influence the labour market. The government railways were by far the biggest enterprise in each colony.

The bitter strikes shocked many Australians. They did not like union standover tactics; but equally they did not like employers refusing to negotiate with workers and driving them to a humiliating defeat. They thought Australia was to be free of this Old-World class hatred.

The distinctive Australian solution to industrial warfare was compulsory arbitration. Workers and bosses would take their disputes to a court which would make a binding ruling. Strikes would no longer be necessary. Arbitration was looked on with suspicion by both unions and employers. They did not want their hands to be tied and to be subject to official control. It was the middle-class, progressive liberals who were the chief advocates of arbitration—men like Kingston in South Australia and Deakin in Victoria. The unions came round to supporting it because they were so weak after the strikes. Employers remained opposed. Deakin's government introduced an Arbitration Bill into the Commonwealth parliament in 1904. There was dispute over how many workers it should cover, but eventually it was passed with the support of all parties.

The arbitration system gave the workers an official status equal to that of the employers. They both came to the Arbitration Court with their lawyers and the judge decided the rights and wrongs of their disputes. In settling disputes, the Court set wage rates and working conditions. This was the 'Award', which then controlled how an industry was to be run.

Deakin's government also linked the protection of local industry to the payment of 'fair and reasonable' wages. Justice Higgins of the Arbitration Court was asked to decide what was a 'fair and reasonable' wage for an unskilled labourer. In 1907 he ruled that it must be enough for the 'average employee regarded as a human

THE AFFILIATION OF JUSTICE AND LABOUR.

The radical George Higinbotham, Chief Justice of Victoria, gave generously to support the workers in the Maritime Strike: the drawing prefigures the worker being aided by the law in the Arbitration Court

being living in a civilised community', and enough for him to support a wife and three children. He carefully examined household budgets and set the rate at 7 shillings a day. The amount was not overly generous; it was the same as had been paid as 'a living wage' on government work in the 1890s depression. But there was now an official guarantee that wages could not fall below this amount. This became the 'basic wage'. No man in work could be paid less.

The one thing that every worker knew about public affairs was the amount of the basic wage. For 50 years it was used to calculate all wages. The unskilled received the basic wage; everyone else got the basic wage plus a margin fixed according to the skill and responsibility of their job.

The Australian worker came to think of the state as an arrangement not primarily to secure his rights or to govern the community but to deliver to him the wage to which he was entitled.

The basic wage was dropped in 1967. The Court then set a total wage for each job. From the 1980s governments have encouraged the setting of wages by direct negotiation between employers and employees. But though under threat, the 'Award' system of wages and conditions being set by a court is still in place.

Welfare

In many modern democracies the welfare system binds citizens together as equals. Everyone contributes to the welfare scheme and everyone can draw benefits from it. Australia is unusual in that its social welfare system is not based on contributions from the people. Nor can everyone benefit from it. It is a system where some people pay, somewhat reluctantly, for the welfare of others.

The Australian colonists of the founding generation were so determined not to have a class of poor people that they decided it was dangerous to have a government program to help them.

In England, providing for the poor was an important part of official policy. The landowners in each parish paid a tax on their land to support the poor. The sick and the old received cash payments and pensions. But men in work were also given assistance if their wages were low. The employers of labour saw a chance here: if they lowered wages even further the parish would come good with the money to keep their workers alive. So the taxes for the poor went up and kept on going up. In the early 1800s the policy was in crisis.

In 1834 the government took a new hard line. No payments were to be made to people living at home and certainly not to those who were working; the only way to get help was to go into new workhouses, where life was to be made so tough that people would go there only as a last resort. This would reduce the number of poor people looking for help and bring the tax for the poor down. The workers hated the new workhouses. In hard times there were demonstrations and riots outside them. The workers refused to accept that a free-born Englishman who could not get a job had to go into the workhouse to stay alive.

It was this English poor law that the colonists did not want to see re-established in Australia. Landowners did not want to pay a tax to support the poor; working people did not want to end up in workhouses. Both hoped that in a new country there would be enough work so that there would be no need of a poor law.

But an abundance of work could not prevent the emergence of poor people—the sick, the old, widows and deserted wives with children to support. As there was no poor law, they were totally reliant on charity. So charity became more important in the colonies than in England. In England the poor law provided basic protection, and charity was directed at special deserving cases. In Australia there was only charity. As charity was all that kept the poor from starvation, governments gave subsidies to the charities.

The charities gave aid to people in their homes; they also ran institutions for orphans and old people. The people they helped were not called paupers and the institutions were not called poorhouses—these were the hated English terms. Old people in an institution were called inmates of the Benevolent Asylum.

The chief workers for charity were women or, as they called themselves, Benevolent Ladies. They raised money and visited those needing help in their homes. They would assess the needs of a family, make payments, offer advice and return to check up on what was happening.

Able-bodied men were not meant to need help in Australia. But work was not always abundant. In downturns and in depressions men out of work demanded that governments provide work. They did not want to take charity. They held meetings and marched through the city streets to the government offices. The premier or the minister of works would agree to see a deputation. The delegates and the minister might argue over how much unemployment there was and how many jobs were available in the country. But if unemployment persisted, governments generally did start new works to provide jobs.

The most vulnerable: women and children at a night shelter

Sometimes unemployed men could not avoid taking charity. Or their wives took it so that their men avoided the shame. Until the 1930s government jobs or charity was the method for dealing with unemployment.

That charity should survive so long in a progressive democratic country at first sight seems odd. Didn't the Labor Party denounce this system and work to get an unemployment benefit instead? No. The unemployed themselves and the trade unions stuck to the policy that governments should provide work. They argued that if there was an unemployment benefit, the pressure on governments to provide work would not be as strong.

Labor's position was that the right to work was much to be preferred to the right to welfare. They did not want to follow other countries that had developed a comprehensive welfare system. If all men were in work and no-one got less than the basic wage, a welfare system was not needed. This attitude asssumed that everyone would have a male provider. Of course some women did not. If women had to provide for children they were in deep difficulties. Women's wages were set much lower than men's on the basis that a woman had to provide only for herself. That was true of single girls living at home, who were the great bulk of female workers, but not of sole mothers with children to support, who were regular recipients of charity.

UNEMPLOYED MEN DEMAND WORK, MELBOURNE 1878

A deputation from the unemployed waited on the Premier yesterday at the Treasury buildings, to request that further steps might be taken to provide employment for men out of work. About 150 men walked up to the Government offices with shovels in their hands, prepared to set to work at once if opportunity offered.

Three of their number were appointed to see Mr Berry, and after waiting about an hour they were enabled to do so. They represented to him that a large body of men who had been employed for the first three days at the St Kilda drainage works had, according to the half-time system adopted, then been put off, on the understanding that they would again be employed at the beginning of the present week. On going to the works yesterday morning, however, they found a large number of new men had been engaged.

They pointed out that it would be impossible for men to maintain themselves and their families working only three out of nine days, and they asked that more men be taken on to those works.

Mr Berry advised the men to go up country for work, where he believed it might be easily obtained. Mr Foley said the country was worse than the town, and that men were coming to Melbourne in search of employment.

Mr Berry said he would consult the Commissioner of Public Works as to whether more men could be taken on, but these men must bear in mind that no Government could undertake to give every man work.

Charity for the unemployed rather than benefits survives until the Great Depression

In the 1930s Depression, with unemployment peaking at 30 per cent, the charities simply could not cope. Nor could governments provide jobs, for they no longer had funds for development works. For the first time they had to give benefits to the unemployed. At first these were food vouchers, then money payments.

No-one was happy with hundreds of thousands of men being idle. Governments made extraordinary efforts to provide the unemployed with work. In these hard times, new taxes were levied on all those in work to provide funds to employ those out of work. The work was rationed so that men with wives and children got four or five days' work a week, a single man one or two. In Australia much more than in the United States and Britain, jobs were found for the unemployed. Work was preferred over welfare.

Between the wars the Nationalist and United Australia parties took an interest in the comprehensive welfare schemes operating in Britain and Europe. These were insurance schemes. Workers made a weekly contribution out of their pay to the insurance fund. Their employers and the government also contributed. The fund provided old-age pensions, unemployment, medical and sickness benefits.

The Nationalist and United Australia parties liked the principle that workers contributed to the welfare fund. They stressed the need for self-reliance rather than reliance on government. The

The unemployed are set to work—on the Yarra Boulevard in Melbourne

one welfare payment already operating in Australia—the old-age pension, introduced in 1908—was not based on contributions. The pension was simply paid out of ordinary government revenue. The Treasury did not like this. It was afraid that as the population aged, too much of the budget would have to go to this unfunded benefit. The advocates of contributory schemes tried to turn people off the pension arrangement by calling it charity.

Australia almost got a national insurance scheme. Bruce's government tried to introduce one in 1928 and the Lyons government in 1938. Both governments faced considerable opposition and did not proceed.

The lodges and friendly societies, which ran the existing schemes for medical benefits, and the doctors were opposed. The unions did not want unemployment benefits. The Labor Party would support a welfare scheme only if the wealthy were made to pay for it. They would not support the workers having to make contributions. If contributions were levied, the unions said they would ask the Arbitration Court for a wage rise to cover the cost. The employers very much feared that this might happen and in any case were not keen about the payments they would have to make.

During World War II, Curtin's Labor government introduced a comprehensive welfare scheme. True to Labor's policy, it did not require people to make contributions. The benefits were to be paid out of normal government revenue. However, for the first time workers were to pay income tax. They would be making extra contributions to the government revenue from which the benefits were to be paid. The workers were to pay for the welfare system.

One of the most difficult problems facing the government in the war was to limit consumer spending. Resources had to be directed to the war effort. Imposing income tax on workers to limit the amount they had to spend was not going to be popular. The Labor government sweetened the pill by saying that the taxes would go to the new welfare system.

During the war everyone had a job, so there was not much need for welfare payments. The new money raised could go to the war effort.

Welfare coming out of general revenue has been the Australian system ever since. As govenments seek to control their spending, they naturally want the welfare to go only to those who need it. So welfare benefits are subjected to a means test. The government has to check up on people before they receive a benefit and while they are drawing it. Those on welfare resent the meanness and nosiness of the government. Those who are not eligible for benefits, but who pay the taxes to fund them, resent the generosity of the government. The system creates a lot of bad feeling.

The one major exception to the Australian welfare pattern is Medicare, which provides medical and hospital services. It was introduced by the Hawke Labor government in 1984, reviving a similar program of the Whitlam government. There is a Medicare levy, so all contribute according to their income. Everyone can and does use the service. The system has very broad support. For a long time the Liberal Party planned to limit or abolish it but by the mid-1990s accepted it.

A welfare program in which all participate produces a different feeling from targeted welfare. Australians have had little experience of welfare promoting a sense of common citizenship.

Citizens

A citizen is a person with a political identity. Citizens are not simply inhabitants of a place; they take part as equals in its government. As democracy is a system of equal political rights, citizen is a good name for people living in a democracy.

In Australia some people have at different times thought of themselves as citizens, but it has never been a term that all Australians have taken seriously. Australian men developed a sense of being equal, but it did not come from being equal as citizens.

The Australian democracies in which all men had the right to vote were colonies of Britain, which was a monarchy. Officially these men were not citizens; along with the women and children they were subjects of the Queen. Democracy was still suspect. When the vote was extended to all men, no-one spoke of all men now being citizens. However, the term citizen was commonly used. It was given to people who took an active part in public life and worked for the common good. There was a strong moral element in being a citizen. A citizen was a respectable, responsible person. A drunken no-hoper was quite definitely a subject of the Queen; he might in Australia have the right to vote, but he was not called a citizen.

There were plenty of opportunities for good citizenship. The Australian colonists formed associations to run libraries, community halls, charities and lodges that ran medical benefits schemes. Here they learned how to be good citizens: to listen to opposing arguments, to respect the rulings of the chairman, and to accept that voting decided issues. Some of them learned to take responsibility as members of the managing committee and be office holders—a chairman, secretary or treasurer.

The rules of meetings were taken from the rules of parliament at Westminster. There could be no discussion unless there was a motion before the chair; a motion needed a mover and seconder; amendments could be put to the motion and these were voted on first, and if they were accepted they became part of the motion. All this became second nature. The smallest organisations were run by these rules. It was only from the 1960s that people began to think of this as too formal and artificial.

The colonial parliaments took their rules from Westminster. But these parliaments, especially those of New South Wales and Victoria, did not stick to the rules so well. Their roughhouse behaviour did not set a good model for citizenship. Those who cared about good citizenship still looked to Britain for inspiration. They knew the history of parliament's battles with the king and they admired the great parliamentarians of their own time. They were not looking to Britain as outsiders. They too were Britons, citizens of the empire, enjoying British freedom and the protection of British law. The disgraceful goings-on in the local parliaments were not the summit of their world.

The moral qualities of the good citizen were at first middle-class values. But more and more working people were taking on these values and becoming respectable citizens, which meant they worked hard, kept clean, did not become drunk, saved for a rainy day, brought up their children properly—and took part in community life. Their own associations, the trade unions, were not thought of as being very different from the rest. They had a distinctly moral element: they ran schemes like the lodges to provide sickness and unemployment benefits to keep the worker and his family from falling into poverty and having to rely on charity.

With the campaign for real democracy at the end of the nineteenth century, democrats began to speak of all those who had, or were to be given, political rights as citizens. Australians no longer took so seriously their official status as subjects of the Queen. They could be citizens of a democracy.

The Labor Party was a supporter of real democracy, but Labor men did not talk much of being citizens. The bitter strikes of the 1890s and the Depression had made the unions think of themselves as workers first and foremost. They supported 'one man, one vote' and an end to upper houses to increase their political power and their chance of securing economic and social change.

The Labor Party certainly did not look to outsiders like an organisation of citizens. A citizen was a responsible individual. This party put loyalty to the cause above individual judgement. It made its politicians vote the party line no matter what their own views. Many people who were sympathetic to its cause were upset at the new methods it brought to public life.

The progressive liberals were the democrats who linked democracy to citizenship. They wanted all voters to become true citizens, interested and active in public life. With the founding of the new Commonwealth they thought that politics would have a fresh start. There would be higher standards in public life, and citizens would join the task of building a new nation.

The Commonwealth was formed on a true democratic basis. The people elected the delegates to the federal convention and voted on the constitution. John Quick, who drew up the scheme for involving the people in constitution making, was a delegate to the 1897 convention. He wanted it to put a definition of Australian citizenship in the constitution.

The delegates were not opposed to doing this, but they found a great obstacle in the way. The legal position was that the Australian people were British subjects. If the constitution declared that British subjects in Australia were Australian citizens, then some of the Chinese in Australia would be Australian citizens. But liberals and democrats did not want them to be accepted as citizens and treated equally. In Western Australia, Chinese could not mine for gold. In Victoria, factories subjected to inspection were defined as places where six or more people were employed or where one Chinese was employed.

The desire to maintain discrimination on grounds of race got in the way of the desire to proclaim the equality of citizenship. The constitution finally did not define Australian citizenship. Officially there was no Australian citizenship until 1949.

The progressive liberals were the most influential force in the new Commonwealth, but very soon they were being replaced by that other progressive force, the Labor Party. They worked with

Labor but were upset at the class divisions it encouraged between workers and bosses. That set people apart instead of bringing them together as citizens. They saw Labor as a selfish party, caring for the interests of workers instead of those of the whole community.

But the rise of Labor could not be stopped, and in 1909 the progressive liberals were forced into an alliance with conservative liberals. Against their will, almost, they had to help in the creation of the two-party system, based broadly on class differences. That was far from their ideal of citizens being actively involved in public life.

The great democratic advance around 1900 was the granting of the vote to women. The campaigners for women's rights took citizenship very seriously. Unlike men, they had to struggle to get the vote. One of their arguments was that they were already citizens because of the work they did in the home and in helping people in the community. They had the moral quality of citizens, so they should not be denied the political rights of citizens.

Long before women gained the vote, they had taken on more responsibility in the home. They ran the household and brought up the children. It was mothers rather than fathers who taught children how to be neat and tidy, to be polite, and to know right from wrong. The women's campaigners talked of women as more moral and

---

LEAGUE OF WOMEN VOTERS: OBJECTIVES

In 1945 three women's organisations in Victoria—the Women Citizens' Movement, the League of Women Electors and Women for Canberra—combined to form the League of Women Voters.

1. To support all reasonable reforms and to encourage women to become better fitted for citizenship by the study of social, political and economic subjects.
2. To safeguard the interests of women and children in legislation.
3. To promote the candidature of approved women for Federal and State Parliaments and Municipal Councils.
4. To further the appointment of approved women as Justices of the Peace and to press their claims as members of Boards, Commissions, Juries, the diplomatic Service and wherever they may share in the making and administration of the Law.
5. To work for World Peace and better International Relationships.

League of
Women Voters,
*Women's
Sphere,*
Melbourne,
1989

more responsible than men. They were the true citizens, and men were just—men. Men were a threat to good family life. Too often they wasted their money on drink, were violent to their wives, and insisted on having sex with them and so wore them down with constant pregnancies. The women's movement was not in favour of contraception. It wanted men to control their sexual desires.

Women claimed a key role in society as citizen-mothers. Women needed to be protected as bearers of the next generation of white Australians, and their values could transform society as a whole. They would make sure the laws looked after the health and welfare of children; they would protect women from the sexual demands and violence of men; they would limit or prohibit the sale of alcohol.

After they had acquired the vote, women formed organisations to use their new political power. They were designed to bring together Protestant and Catholic women and to be neither Labor nor Liberal. One of their first jobs was to educate women about the political system, something which had not happened when all men got the vote. The women were opposed to the party system.

Enid Lyons and Dorothy Tangney, first women members of federal parliament, 1943

They thought that women would lose their influence if they allowed themselves to be swallowed up by the existing parties. These were run by men, and the women had issues to push that were against the interests and habits of men. They also thought that parties were divisive and that good citizens, men and women, could combine to build a better world.

Women's non-party organisations regularly ran non-party women candidates for parliament. Only one of them was successful. She was Ivy Weber, elected for Nunawading in the Victorian parliament in 1937. She was supported by the Woman's Christian Temperance Union and the League of Women Voters. Her campaign slogan was 'Mother, Child, Family, Home and Health'. The rest of the handful of women elected in the 60 years after women got the vote were representatives of parties. The first was Edith Cowan, in Western Australia in 1921. She was a Nationalist but upset the party by not toeing the party line. The first women elected to the federal parliament took their seats in 1943, Dorothy Tangney (Labor) and Enid Lyons (United Australia Party).

Souvenir

South Australian
Women's Reception
In Honour of the Visit of
Miss Amy Johnson, C.B.E.

Exhibition Building, Adelaide
Tuesday, July 1st, 1930
Price . . . Threepence

The following Societies are represented:—

(Under the auspices of the National Council of Women of S.A.)

National Council of Women.
Adelaide Hospital Auxiliary.
Adelaide Rescue Society.
Army Nurses Fund.
Australian Nursing Federation.
Australian Board of Missions—Women's Auxiliary.
Baptist Women's League.
Catholic Women's League.
Congregational Church Women's Society.
Council of Jewish Women.
Country Party Association—Women's Section.
Country Women's Association of S.A.
District Trained Nursing Society.
Girls' Friendly Society.
Girl Guides' Association.
Glenelg Women's Service Association.
Housewives' Association.
Infant Schools' Mothers' Clubs Association.
International Peace Society, Adelaide Branch.
Jewish Women's Guild.
Kindergarten Union.
Kingswood Women's Guild of Service.
Lady Victoria Buxton Girls' Club.
League of Loyal Women.
Liberal Federation—Women's Branch.
Liberal Women's Educational Association.

Methodist Women's Auxiliary, Foreign Missions.
Minda Home Association.
Mothers' and Babies' Health Association.
Mothers' Union of South Australia.
P.G.C. Old Collegians' Association.
Presbyterian Women's Missionary Society.
Prisoners' Aid Society.
Queen's Home Incorporated.
Royal British Nurses' Association.
Salvation Army.
Sailors, Soldiers, Nurses Relatives' Association.
Seacliffe Women's Service Association.
Sisters' Sub-branch Returned Soldiers' & Sailors' Imp. League.
South Australian Mothers' Union.
Thebarton Women's Service Association.
Theosophical Society.
Travellers' Aid Society.
Unitarian Women's League.
University Women Graduates' Club.
University Women's Union.
Wattle Day League.
Women's Christian Temperance Union.
Women Teachers' Association.
Women Teachers' Progressive League.
Young Women's Christian Association.

Amy Johnson, the woman flyer, welcomed by Adelaide's female citizens, July 1930

WHY THE WOMEN'S POLITICAL ASSOCIATION IS NON-PARTY

Women Voter,
Melbourne,
August 1909

At the outset we desire to remove a false impression as to our non-party policy. It is not to be supposed that we are a body of gelatinous creatures, who have no definite political views. We have all got very decided views as to the merits of the various political parties—some of us are protectionists, some are free-traders, some are single taxers, some are labourites, some are socialists, some are anti-socialists, but we differ from those organised on party lines in one important particular. We believe that questions affecting individual honour, private and public integrity and principle, the stability of the home, the welfare of children, the present salvation of the criminal and the depraved, the moral, social and economic injustice imposed on women—we believe that all these questions are greater than party, and that in 9 cases out of 10 they are sacrificed to party interests.

So women failed to break the mould of politics. However, they were still influential, chiefly by lobbying politicians on their causes.

The crisis of the 1930s Depression briefly broke the party mould. Middle-class people were frightened by what Labor was planning or talking about, but they did not look to the Nationalist Party to save them. Overnight they formed new organisations of concerned and decent citizens. They felt the party system, both sides of it, did not reflect their values. The revolt of the citizens was short-lived. The new organisations were gathered together in the United Australia movement, which become another party.

Aboriginal people, like women, had to struggle to gain their rights. From the 1930s their demand was that they should be citizens, equal in rights and responsibilities with everyone else. Their rights were gradually restored and they took their victory in the 1967 referendum as a sign that they had become citizens. But soon afterwards Aborigines dropped the talk of being citizens. They referred to their human rights and insisted more on their special separate identity as the indigenous people of the nation. They demanded that their traditional lands be restored and their special culture be recognised.

In the 1960s the women's cause came alive again when it called itself women's liberation. Now women did not make their claims as citizen-mothers. On the contrary, they wanted to be able to avoid being mothers by having cheap and good contraception and the right to have abortions. If they were mothers they wanted to be able to leave their children in the care of others so they could work. Nor did they say they were purer and more moral than men. They wanted to enjoy sex as much as men and to be as free as men in their sexual lives.

They gained many of their new demands by lobbying. One of their most successful organisations was the Women's Electoral Lobby, formed in Melbourne in 1972. It sent off questionnaires to parliamentarians asking their views on women's issues. Few bothered to fill them in. So the women decided to track down and interview all the candidates running for the federal election late in 1972. The newspapers were so interested in the women's movement that they published, for no charge, charts showing the candidates' answers. Women could now decide how to vote on the basis of women's issues.

However, there was less interest, in this new women's movement, in breaking the party system. Instead, women demanded that the parties should run as many women candidates as men and in seats that women could win. By these means the number of women in parliament did rise. Women were still hopeful that when women were present in large numbers, the nature of parliament would change. They believed women would be less interested in abusing opponents and more interested in cooperation. The party battle, they said, was a boys' game.

Australia's political history has not produced a strong Australian ideal of citizenship. When Australians were Britons, they had an identity with a strong civic element. They were citizens of the Empire. They knew that Britain gave parliamentary government to the world and that to be British guaranteed you certain rights and freedoms. This was the central theme of British history, which until the 1960s Australians knew better than their own.

Civic themes are not usually an important part of the Australian history Australians know—convicts, gold-diggers and bushrangers. The political victories of the excluded are remembered—1894 when women first got the vote; 1967 when Aborigines became citizens. But how European men in Australia became citizens, few people know.

EIGHT

Soldiers

In Europe kings often used soldiers to shoot down democratic reformers. Democrats developed the idea that if all citizens were soldiers, governments could not use the army against the people. Making citizens serve for a time in the army was not taking away their freedom; it was the way to preserve it.

The founders of the US constitution gave to the citizens the right to bear arms, not so they could own guns to use against criminals but so the citizens could form the militia, a part-time army, which would be the defence of the citizens if the government ever tried to use an army against them.

Making everyone serve in the army was democratic in another sense. The rich would have to fight as well as the poor. After all, the rich had more property and hence more to lose if their country were defeated. They should not be able to stay at home while sending poor men to do the fighting.

In Australia the democratic arguments in favour of conscription did not take a permanent hold. Australia is the only democracy in the world where there has been a strong movement against conscription on the basis that conscription is antidemocratic.

The principle of conscription was accepted at the foundation of the nation. Under the first Defence Act of 1903 all men between the ages of 18 and 60 could be called up to defend the country. The parliament did not want to pay for a regular army and was suspicious of showy uniforms and of militarism. In fact, there were to be no regular full-time foot soldiers. As good democrats, the politicians did not want an army that was to be set apart from the citizens.

Conscription was to apply only to service in Australia. The British would have preferred that the law allow for Australian soldiers to be sent overseas to fight in the Empire's wars. No Australian government before World War I would agree to this. The standard answer was that if Britain were in danger men would volunteer to fight—as they had done in the Boer War (1899–1902).

In 1905 Japan defeated Russia. This was the first time an Asian country had defeated a European one. Australian governments decided that Australia was in danger. The British navy was meant to defend Australia from invasion, but what if Britain was busy fighting Germany and could not send assistance? Compulsory military training for all young men was introduced in 1909. They were already liable to be called up if there was a war; this was to ensure that they would be trained and ready.

All parties supported compulsory training. The Labor Party took most persuading. It was formed to improve the lives of the workers, not to prepare the workers for wars, which Labor believed were battles between capitalists for economic gain. But Labor was the strongest supporter of the White Australia policy. It too was frightened by Japan's new strength.

Billy Hughes, later prime minister in World War I, led the campaign within the Labor Party in favour of compulsory military training. He took Switzerland as his model—a democratic country with a proud military tradition, where every man was trained to fight. He explained to the party that, in a democracy, training all men to fight would not produce the sort of army they feared. This was an army that could not be used against the workers; it was in tune with Labor ideals, not against them, to make all men serve the common good.

The young men training for war became part of what was called the Citizen Military Force. Citizenship and soldiering were now firmly connected. In World War I they became separated.

Labor won the election that was held just after the outbreak of the war. The Labor leader Andrew Fisher promised to support Britain to 'the last man and the last shilling'. A few Labor people

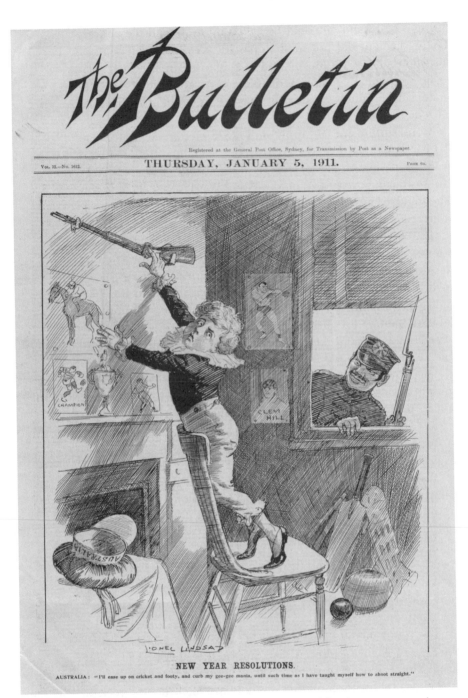

New Year resolutions: Australia: 'I'll ease up on cricket and footy, and curb my gee gee mania, until such time as I have taught myself how to shoot straight.'

Young men as citizen soldiers: senior cadets at Mount Morgan in Queensland

were against the war from the beginning and as the war dragged on, killing millions of young men, the opposition within the party grew. The overwhelming majority of the people, however, remained supporters of the war.

Before the war a gap had developed in the labour movement between the radical leaders of the unions and the parliamentarians. The union leaders thought the parliamentarians had not done enough in government to implement the Labor platform. They wanted a radical party based firmly on the workers and more hostile to capitalism. Now they saw their Labor government devoting all its efforts to fighting in a dreadful war on the other side of the world. That is not what the Labor Party was formed to do.

In 1915 Billy Hughes took over from Andrew Fisher as prime minister. He was happy to devote all Australia's strength to the war effort. He told those who complained about Labor's program being neglected that this was the great crisis in the nation's affairs. If Labor squibbed on running the war, it would lose its hold over the people. If Labor could command the nation during the war, it could then reshape the nation in the peace.

In 1916 the number of men volunteering to serve in the war fell off. When Hughes declared for conscription, the radical union leaders got the Labor Party organisation to declare against conscription for service overseas. Hughes argued that the distinction between service overseas and at home no longer made sense. The British Empire that guaranteed Australia's safety was in danger; if the Empire were to be defeated, Australia would be at the mercy of the victors.

The opponents of conscription did not base their case on opposition to the war. That would have been fatal. They had to argue that conscription in itself was wrong—wrong in all circumstances. They claimed that no government should have the power to make men fight against their will. This argument made the liberty of the citizen the most important principle. Conscription was undemocratic because it took away human freedom.

This was a very odd argument for the Labor Party to use. Labor had been the party that had argued that making liberty the prime value damages society. Labor men had said that an employer should not be at liberty to set wages and conditions to suit himself. Nor should large landowners be at liberty to hold onto their estates while small men were looking for farms. In their own organisations they stressed solidarity, not liberty. They compelled all workers in an industry to join the union. They made all their parliamentarians vote the same way.

Labor's position on conscription had led it into defending extreme selfishness. When the country was in danger, only volunteers should fight. If other men wanted to stay safe at home and let the volunteers take all the risks, the government should not disturb them. In the debate over conscription, it was the Liberal Party that stressed public spirit and cooperation, that all should contribute to the common good. Usually it was the party that defended individual liberties against the threat of Labor's socialism.

In the conscription referendums Labor used many arguments to persuade people to vote No—such as that Australia had already done enough, and that a few more men from Australia would make no difference in a huge conflict—but it took its argument of principle seriously. After the war it changed its platform to total opposition to conscription. It was wrong to train men compulsorily, wrong to conscript men to serve overseas, and wrong to conscript men for the defence of Australia, even if the country was being invaded.

Labor turned anti-conscription into an article of a faith. It was the test of whether you were a true Labor man. It was this issue on which the party had purified itself by throwing out most of its parliamentary leaders. And as the people had followed Labor's call and voted No, it felt that anti-conscription was its bond with the Australian people. It needed to believe this because when the people had the chance between the two conscription referendums to decide who should govern Australia, they had decided very definitely that it should not be Labor.

There is no reason to think that the Australian people were deeply opposed to conscription. If conscription had been introduced as it was everywhere else without a referendum, Australian men would have accepted their obligations. Conscription makes people more willing to serve because they know that everyone is being made to serve. It is a fair system. But if people are asked at referendum if they want conscription introduced, all sorts of other considerations come into play. A No campaign can raise innumerable fears and bogeys—as these ones did.

Australia had a referendum on conscription because it had a Labor government that was at odds with its party organisation. Hughes appealed to the people at referendum because he could not persuade his party to accept conscription. The reason why the party was opposed to conscription involved much more than that issue. Some of the radical union leaders were opposed to the war; more of them were dismayed at a Labor government being caught up in this monstrosity; all of them wanted to show that they decided party policy, not the parliamentarians.

It was for these reasons that one of the major parties became so firmly opposed to conscription. Once conscription no longer enjoyed bipartisan support, it became difficult for the other party to introduce it. This gave Australian democracy its anti-conscription bias.

The men who came home from the war had all gone as volunteers. They were Australia's new heroes, who had made Australia's name in the world. The nation honoured them on its most sacred day, Anzac Day. The honour was theirs—and no-one else's. No honour flowed to democratic government. They were diggers, not citizen soldiers.

The organisation of the returned men, the RSL, became the most powerful in the country. It pressured governments to look after the diggers and made pronouncements about defence policy. It claimed a special place in the nation's affairs because its members had voluntarily fought for the nation. The Labor Party often resented its special standing, because politically it was more

IS CONSCRIPTION A THREAT TO LIBERTY?

John Curtin was a leader of the anti-conscription campaign in World War I. As prime minister in World War II he introduced conscription.

John Curtin

The seeds of Liberty which were sown in the blood-stained soil of Eureka have created an Australian environment which is responsible for the bold, couragous, and self-sacrificing characteristics which have made our sons admired by all the world. If you would preserve these freedom-loving aspirations, which are the very soul-force of true patriotism, then fight to the last gasp against the introduction of conscription into your country, because conscription is the very foundation of the servile state.

John Curtin,
Fight as Free Men,
Melbourne,
1917

H.V. (Bert) Evatt supported conscription in World War I when he was a student at Sydney University. He later joined the Labor Party and was Curtin's foreign minister in World War II.

H. V. Evatt

Compulsory service would not violate our liberty unless it were imposed on us by an external authority. An obligation which we voluntarily impose on ourselves is the highest possible form of moral duty. The whole modern movement towards state interference is an example of this, and we have gradually come to see that we are part of the state, which is no longer a great Leviathan outside ourselves. We are gradually giving up the idea that we can be in or out of the social order as we please.

Tens of thousands of young men of military age would welcome compulsory service abroad as a tremendous relief, resolving an almost hopeless and impossible position. We would be asking that we be honoured with the distinction of service—a service of perfect freedom.

H.V. Evatt,
St Andrew's College Magazine,
No. 13,
Sydney, 1915

---

sympathetic to the Liberals than to itself. But Labor was chiefly responsible for its standing because it had insisted that only volunteers should fight.

When the nation was again at war, Labor had to give up its policy on conscription. In 1940 it agreed that men could be trained compulsorily and conscripted to fight on Australian soil. It was still opposed to conscription for service overseas. Its opposition to that was so ferocious that the Menzies government had to go along with it in order to get bipartisan support for the war effort. Two armies were created: one of volunteers that could fight anywhere; one of conscripts that could fight only in Australia and its territories.

When the Japanese occupied the islands immediately to the north of Australia, the distinction between defending Australia and fighting overseas disappeared. It was clearly part of the defence of Australia to push the Japanese out of the islands and drive them back to Japan. But only one of Australia's armies could do that; the other could not leave Australian territory.

The Labor Party took office just as Japan entered the war. Very soon the Opposition and the press were urging it in this extreme emergency to create one army and make Australian conscripts liable to serve anywhere. The Labor government refused.

The distinction between overseas and local defence had been developed when the fighting was in Europe. The Japanese were certainly 'overseas', except that the seas were Australia's coastal waters over which they were flying to bomb Australia's northern towns. Still Labor refused to conscript men for service 'overseas'. There has never been an idea with such power in Australian history; nothing, it seemed, would make Labor give it up.

The Americans made Labor give it up. They were sending conscripts to Australia to fight the Japanese. When the American newspapers became aware of Australia's strange policy on conscription, they started running stories about Australia not pulling its weight. The American commander in Australia, Douglas MacArthur, became alarmed. He was struggling to get supplies and equipment for this sector of the war and did not want it to be painted as a place where the war was not being fought properly. He told Prime Minister Curtin that he would have to change his government's policy on conscription.

Curtin could not buck this pressure. In 1942 he asked a Labor Party conference to change the policy. There was still considerable opposition. Curtin had to give up his plan of making one army. He secured only a limited extension of the area beyond Australia where conscripts could serve. To the north its boundary was the equator, so Australian conscripts could not take part in an attack on Japan. That did not worry MacArthur. He planned to use only American troops for the important fighting. He wanted Australia to change its policy for public relations purposes. In fact very few Australian conscripts did fight in the extended area.

After the war Labor returned to its traditional policy of opposition to conscription for overseas service. When Menzies returned to power in 1949, he refused to accept the distinctions Labor took as important. He said there should be one army ready to fight anywhere in Australia's interests. He achieved the changes he wanted in two stages. In the early 1950s all regular soldiers were sworn in to serve anywhere; they were no longer to volunteer to serve in a particular war. In the early 1960s, when conscription was introduced, the conscripts were to be part of the regular army and so liable to serve anywhere.

Under these rules conscripts first fought in Vietnam. Labor opposed the Vietnam war and the use of conscripts in it. These were the central issues of the 1966 election. The Labor leader Arthur Calwell was in his element. He had come to prominence in the anti-conscription campaign in World War I. He was campaigning in defence of Labor's traditional policy. It was easy for him to overlook that Curtin had been forced to change

Young men burning their registration papers in protest at conscription in Sydney, 1966

the policy because he had been one of Curtin's most savage opponents.

At the election Calwell was comprehensively defeated. But it cannot be said that the Australian people had put paid forever to Australia's anti-conscription tradition. The Vietnam war was lost, and in the aftermath was commonly regarded as a war that should not have been fought. That conscripts were sent to fight in it makes it even more reprehensible. Labor people still honour the anti-conscription cause.

Australia has a strong military tradition. But it is not a tradition associated with the State, with its form of government. Men have volunteered to fight. Other men have been conscripted, but since

REMEMBER 1916-17?

The Australian people defeated conscription!

WHAT ABOUT 1969?

318 Australians killed,
1,560 Australians wounded,
and **3,338** National Service conscriptees fighting in the undeclared war in Vietnam.

IF WE WERE STRONG ENOUGH TO DEFEAT THE CONSCRIPTION ORDER IN 1916 . . . WHY AREN'T WE STRONG ENOUGH TO DO IT NOW! OR ARE WE?

ON OCTOBER 25

STOP CONSCRIPTION OF AUSTRALIA'S YOUTH FOR OVERSEAS SERVICE

DEFEAT THE LIBERAL-COUNTRY PARTY CANDIDATES

VOTE FOR LABOR AND PROGRESSIVE CANDIDATES PUT THE D.L.P. AND LIBERAL-COUNTRY PARTY LAST

Authorised by E. V. Elliott and printed for the Seamen's Union of Australia, 289 Sussex St., Sydney, by Apollo Printing Pty. Ltd., 53-55 Liverpool St., Sydney.

Calling up the anti-conscription tradition

1916 the two major parties have been at odds over where it is proper for them to fight.

The guardian of the nation's military tradition was not the State but the organisation of the returned soldiers themselves, the RSL. Even here distinctions between soldiers were drawn. After World War I the RSL would allow only those who had gone overseas to fight to be members, a mirror image of Labor's policy of making 'overseas' the place where men could not be compelled to go. The men who had manned the guns defending Australia's ports in World War I were not allowed to join the RSL.

That defence of the nation is a single project, and that the State should have the power to command all men to serve—these commonplace ideas have not been accepted in Australia.

Schools

A n educational expert from the United States visited Australia in 1954 to advise on its school system. He was always being told what a democratic, egalitarian society Australia was. Why then, he wondered, did the private schools hold such a strong place in the education system?

An expert from France, Germany or Sweden would have wondered the same. An expert from England would have felt more at home.

Government schools in some democracies are places where students of all backgrounds come together and learn that they are future citizens of the one country. The common experience of attending the one school prepares them to live together and symbolises their shared citizenship.

This is not to say that private schools are undemocratic. Democracy preserves freedom, and individuals and groups must be free to run schools and parents to send children to them. But if private schools become numerous, the experience of a common education is lost. Whatever the government schools teach or do, they cannot in themselves be symbols of a common citizenship.

Australia's first government schools were intended to bring all children together and to be symbols of a new harmonious society. They were called at first 'national schools' to show they were

> ### EDUCATION AND EGALITARIANISM
>
> Australians are proud of their tradition of egalitarianism and lack of social snobbishness and class stratification. When I see how strong a place the private schools have in the educational scene, I wonder how strong the tradition really is, and how long the tradition can be maintained.
>
> There is undoubtedly a deep ground swell of democracy in Australian life that serves as a check on the building up of class stratification and privilege. It has prevented great extremes of wealth and poverty. It has even penalised initiative and originality in some respects in the great desire for equality. But the real question is whether the dual schools systems are eating away at the foundations of democracy or whether they are building sturdily upon them and strengthening them.

R. Freeman Butts, Assumptions Underlying Australian Education, Melbourne, 1955, p. 22

designed for everyone. The supporters of these schools saw religious differences as the chief threat to social harmony. They wanted Catholic and Protestant children to be educated together. Differences in wealth were less threatening, but some supporters also welcomed the new schools as places where the children of the rich and poor would sit together.

The government schools failed to bring children of all religions together. When state aid was withdrawn from the church schools, the Catholic bishops kept their schools going. Many Catholic children continued to attend government schools, but gradually the bishops persuaded more of their people that they had to send their children to the schools of the brothers and nuns.

The government schools did better at bringing together children of different social classes. Parents from a much wider range of income groups sent their children to government schools in Australia than in England. Many small private schools closed, unable to compete with the government schools that were free or charged only very low fees. The governments made sure their new schools looked good. In the cities and towns they built great temples of learning to which anyone would be pleased to send their children.

Small numbers of rich Protestant parents continued to send their children to private primary schools. These were schools run

Temples of learning: the new government school at Bendigo

by the Protestant churches which offered both primary and secondary education.

In the nineteenth century the colonial governments ran few if any secondary schools. They were under little pressure to do so. There were many ways of getting on in the world without having a secondary education. The government offered a few scholarships so that very bright children from its primary schools could go on to a private secondary school.

In the early twentieth century Australia had the reputation of being a highly progressive country, a social laboratory. In education, however, it was backward. In the primary schools teachers taught a narrow range of subjects, cramming information into students who had to sit up straight and remain silent. Secondary education was in the hands of the private church schools and available to only a tiny minority.

An educational reform movement began which aimed to bring Australia up to the best practice overseas. It wanted primary and secondary education to be available to all, a wider range of subjects to be taught, children to be encouraged to be more active and expressive, and for schools to provide an education in citizenship. The reformers argued that education was important for national prosperity. They wanted education to give students skills they could use. They planned technical, domestic science and agricultural high schools as well as more academic schools. But nowhere should the education be narrow, and it must prepare students for citizenship.

The creation of the Commonwealth of Australia was a spur to the reformers. They linked the changes they wanted to the building of a new nation. If it was to be a great nation, they said, it must have a skilled workforce and its citizens must be well-informed and responsible.

This was the one time in Australia's history where the idea of citizenship had real force. Boys and girls were to be educated to be citizens, and boys and young men were to be trained to defend their country. However, the idea did not have enough force to transform education. The churches opposed the building of government secondary schools that would compete with their own. State governments struggled to find money for new projects in education. More government high schools of different sorts were built, but not enough to provide schools for all. The strongest high schools remained the academic.

Theoretically the high schools ensured that all bright children could get a good education. However, it was much harder for working-class parents to allow their children to go on to secondary school than for middle-class parents. They needed their children to start supporting themselves and helping out with family expenses.

The Labor Party, which represented working people, did not have a strong interest in education. It was most interested in wages and working conditions. It assumed that most children of workers would also be workers. However, Labor did insist that the way be open to bright working-class children to continue their education. It supported bursary schemes, free books and the abolition of the fees that some of the early high schools charged. Some individual Labor politicians were strong supporters of education, but the party generally did not regard secondary education for all as important or see schools as places to build a more open and democratic society and foster a common citizenship.

The progressive liberal thinker, Walter Murdoch, wrote this book for school children in 1912

The politicians most supportive of that ideal were the progressive liberals. However, in the early twentieth century they were being elbowed aside by Labor and were being forced into alliance with more conservative liberals, who were less interested in expanding government education.

The government high schools were overshadowed by the older private schools. In some states they were more numerous than the government schools, and everywhere the private schools defined the style of the school. The private schools in Australia were imitating the great public schools of England and so they had uniforms, prefects, hymns, and school houses that competed in sport. The government schools in turn imitated the Australian private schools.

The curriculum of the state high schools and the private schools was controlled by the requirements of the universities. Only tiny numbers went on to the university—more from the private schools

The new education encouraged free expression in children, but old methods survived in this drawing class

than the government—but all students studied as if the university was their goal. The exams run by the universities were regarded as the test of quality.

Administrators of the Australian schools knew of the very different American practice. There, the junior high schools gave a general education to all children. They taught a wide range of subjects, not all of them academic. The Australians thought this made education a joke and tut-tutted about the lowering of standards. The American idea of educational democracy was that government schools should take in everyone. The Australian idea of educational democracy was that any bright child should have the opportunity to receive a high-quality, academic education in a traditional English setting.

After World War II the demand for secondary education rose rapidly. Soon all children were spending some time at secondary school, the great majority at government schools. The government system became more like the American. Separate schools for technical or domestic science education were closed. All students attended high schools. They were no longer separated according to ability into different streams. They received together a general education, and in the early years at least were less controlled by the demands for university entrance. The prefects were dropped, but not school uniforms.

As these changes were taking place, a fundamental shift in government policy towards private schools occurred. In 1963 the Menzies Liberal government announced that it would give aid to private schools for science laboratories. Then came aid for libraries, then regular government grants simply for the running of the schools.

Most of the private schools were Catholic. By the 1960s the Catholic system was close to collapse under the pressure of coping with the rapidly growing numbers of students. Some people in the church were beginning to doubt whether the system could survive and whether the church gained much from having its own schools. That rethinking stopped when the government aid began to flow.

Some of the Protestant private schools had doubts about accepting aid, fearing that it might threaten their independence. A few even declined. Soon all were accepting it. Government aid allowed their rapid expansion.

The move towards a more inclusive and less academic education in the government schools occurred just as university was becoming the destination of more and more students. To do well in the exam that determined university entrance was becoming more vital. The old government academic high schools had done well in preparing students for these exams. When government high schools were taking children with the whole range of abilities and interests, they did less well.

The private schools, taking only children whose parents could pay their fees, had an easier task in preparing students for exams. Between the wars parents sent their children to private schools so they would make appropriate friendships and useful connections, and perhaps become ladies and gentlemen. Now the greatest attraction of the private schools was a good score in the university entrance exam. From the 1980s there was a drift of enrolments away from government and towards private schools.

Since the late 1960s both major parties have supported government aid to private schools. Labor is unwilling to fund the wealthiest private schools; the Liberals support them all. Labor worries about the drift of enrolments away from government schools; the Liberals encourage it.

In the 1990s the chief argument the Liberals advanced in support of private schools was that parents should have a choice in their children's education. Of course only those who have the money to pay the fees can have the choice. The Liberals accepted this and worked to give more parents the choice by increasing aid to keep fees down and allowing new private schools to open.

Democracy has many elements. The democrats of the French revolution had a three-part slogan: liberty, equality, fraternity. Choice for parents in education stresses liberty; a common experience for all students stresses equality and fraternity.

It was not unreasonable for the visiting American expert in 1954 to expect an egalitarian society to be more committed to equality and fraternity in its school system. His mistake was to think that egalitarianism is genuine only if it shows itself in formal institutions like schools.

Equality

Australians treat each other as equals. This is the egalitarianism they have perfected. Australian democracy is first of all a democracy of manners.

Some people claim that Australian society is not egalitarian because there are wide differences of income, which may now be getting wider. This misses the point of Australian egalitarianism. It is the way Australians blot out those differences when people meet face to face. They talk to each other as if they are equals and they will put down anyone claiming social superiority. It is the feel of Australian society that is so markedly egalitarian, not its social structure. The democracy of manners was established when differences in income were much greater than they are now.

The democracy of manners was developed and long practised solely by men. Women's chief business was the keeping of the home, and homes were places which showed off differences in wealth and social standing. Men met each other as equals outside the home. In family and social life, wives maintained social distinctions that husbands might claim they did not take so seriously, without actually overruling their wives.

Several circumstances prepared the way for a democracy of manners. First, there was no class of dirty and degraded paupers. Nearly everyone was respectable and hence able to be respected.

Second, working men were prosperous and self-confident and did not have to show special respect in order to get work. Third, there was no great difference in tastes and interests between working men and the rest of the male population. There was only a very small group of cultivated and well-educated people. Most of the rich were self-made men, who were not going to look down on a working man because he did not know Latin and Greek.

One of the things that impressed outside observers about nineteenth-century Australia was the interest in sport: not simply the level of interest, but that people of all sorts were interested and present at the big events. The whole society was talking about the same thing. The interest in sport—racing, cricket, football—was a very important bond between men of different classes.

Drink was another bond. The pub in Australia was a man's place. By custom and—in some places—by law, women were excluded from bars. The women's movement opposed the pub as the enemy of the home. It would have been less so if men were drinking in the pubs with their wives and girlfriends. But the women campaigners saw pubs as impure places, not fit for women. Men agreed with them. The diggers in World War I were shocked to find women in English pubs.

In England working men and women went to the pubs, which middle-class people avoided if they were 'a common public house'. In Australia a wider range of men went to the pubs, and then sooner or later went home to their wives. From the time of World War I in most states they were forced to go home at 6 pm, because the temperance campaigners, men and women, had succeeded in their campaign to limit drinking hours.

Drinking became a ritual act of equality. To decline to join a group of men for a drink was to insult them. A group of men drinking would take it in turns to pay for a round of drinks. The drinking could not stop until each man had paid for his round. The larger the group, the more drink that had to be consumed. This was 'shouting', different from the English 'treating', where someone with money would pay for others. 'Shouting' required absolute equality. Women could not understand it: 'Why can't you have just one or two drinks and come home?'. A man might prefer to do this, but he could not break the code.

On his visit to England in 1900, Henry Lawson was shocked to find women at work in the fields. The Australian practice was that women did not work out on the farm or station. Their work centred

Upper-, middle- and lower-class people at the one event—the Melbourne Cup in 1882

on the homestead and what was close by, the veggie garden and the dairy.

The idea that women were purer and more refined than men took a very strong hold in Australia. It led to a firmer separation

A SQUATTER AT A WORKING-MEN'S PUB

John jumped on the verandah. He was well known and very popular in the district, and was instantly greeted by a dozen individuals, all wanting to have a drink with him.

'What are you going to drink, Mr West?'

'Come along, Mr West,' another shouted; 'I'm a-goin' to shout; what's yours?'

A drunken, long-legged stockmen, in boots and breeches, his cabbage-tree hat hanging far back on his head, lurched up and asked—

'Izay, yunkplo', avyou washyoneck jishmorn?'

John, who had much tact and good-humour when managing men under all circumstances, and never stood on his dignity foolishly, replied laughingly—

'I believe I have. Does it look particularly dirty?'

'Not s'hout'shide, yunkplo', 'shin'shide, I meant. Comenave a b-b-ball.'

John was not a teetotaller, although a disapprover of the vice of drinking, and the men knew it. He was aware that most of them take a refusal as a direct personal insult; and accordingly, on the principle of doing in Rome as the Romans do, he agreed. 'Drinks all round' are ordered for those in the room.

C. Grant,
Bush Life in Queensland,
Edinburgh
1881, Vol. 2,
pp. 50–1

of the sexes in all classes of society. The distinction between rough and polite behaviour did not coincide with a division between lower and upper classes; it lay in the difference between men on their own and men when they were with women and children. Men were fluent in two languages. Out in the paddocks and in the pubs their talk was laced with swear words. At home the swearing would disappear, more or less. 'No language', the wife would say, if her husband forgot himself. 'Language' was another bond between men.

Gentlemen presented themselves as different from other men, but they were not as refined as the English original. The gentleman squatter herded sheep and mustered cattle. On the goldfields gentlemen dressed and worked like the other diggers. If a coach became bogged, the gentlemen pushed it and waded through swollen streams with the rest of the passengers. Gentlemen did not

Members of the Woman's Christian Temperance Union demonstrate outside the South Australian parliament, September 1938

have valets to dress them and run their baths. Male servants inside the house were very rare. A lady had her lady's maid. A gentleman looked after himself.

Democratic manners developed only slowly. Old-world social distinctions, prejudices and ways of interacting shifted and softened a long time before they were dropped. Australian society did not gain its present-day egalitarian tone until after World War I. The dress of the gentlemen, a badge of inequality, did not disappear until the late nineteenth century. Tipping did not become rare until all workers received a living wage in the early twentieth century.

The democracy of manners had its classic expression on the goldfields in the 1850s. Men of all types did hard work, dressed alike, and called each other 'mate'. They were all fellow conspirators in keeping the gold commissioners from extracting too much from them for licences. The diggers complained about the commissioners, but this autocratic rule made their free and easy

> ## A LINE HAD TO BE DRAWN: THE YERING RACE-CLUB BALL
>
> All the ladies of the neighbourhood attended, as well as those of the town. It was unfortunately quite impossible to keep the gathering as select as the more aristocratic of the ladies would have wished, on account of their small number as compared with that of the gentlemen. Since the success of the affair depended upon the largeness of the attendance, it was arranged that, as usual, one portion of the hall should be reserved for the 'nobs', and the other part for the public generally. Still a line had to be drawn. Discrimination had to be shown somewhere. A number of Chinamen, who had persuaded white women to live with them, had settled in the little town, and the committee were strict in refusing to issue entry tickets to the mottled population.
>
> All enjoyed themselves greatly. The bar-girls, bullock-drivers' wives, and servants, kept themselves at the lower end of the room, where perhaps the dancing was more vigorous and less formal. Still the utmost decorum prevailed. However, some of the more select were irritated because after supper two or three of the gentlemen sought relief from the conventionalities of high life among the less fastidious classes.

C. Grant,
Bush Life in Queensland,
Edinburgh, 1881, Vol. 2, pp. 60–1

democratic manners possible. If the diggers had been governing themselves, they would have had to give authority to a few and then they would all no longer have been the same.

'Mate' was an English word that came into much wider use in Australia. It was used first for a man and his mate working together, with the mate often being an offsider rather than an equal. Then it was used for men who were definitely equals and who were strongly attached to one another; this applied only to small groups—two or three men would be mates in this sense. On the goldfields, first of all, it became a term that all men used in addressing each other. It was casual, yet friendly, carrying the warmth of the deeper bond. 'Mate' could also be used aggressively towards men who were resisting equality. Some men on the goldfields did not want to be called mate and went along with it to avoid mockery or robbery. They looked forward to making their fortune and getting back to a properly ordered society.

In the years immediately after the goldrushes, the rushes were remembered as a time when all social distinctions were overturned, but not as a time when they came to an end. No doubt many men after their goldfields experience were more willing to treat each other as equals, but in the 1860s and 70s not all men were calling each other 'mate'.

Equality also flourished in the outback pastoral country among the bushmen. A bushman was a man who lived and worked confidently in the bush. He could ride, muster cattle, herd sheep, find his way, look after himself in all conditions, cope with all emergencies. Both bosses and workers in the bush were bushmen. In economic terms there was a great gulf between them. The squatter leased or owned huge tracts of countryside; the worker-bushman might own only his horse. Yet they were brought together in this man's world by the bond of work. Bosses in the bush could not run their properties from the office of the homestead. They had to be able to do the work themselves and be a match for their men. They were more like a chief than an employer.

Watercolour with traces of pencil 15.9 x 24.1
Presented by Mrs. J. Bradstreet, 1979
National Gallery of Victoria, Melbourne

The squatter dressed in working clothes, cabbage-tree hat, shirt worn outside trousers and thigh-length boots

Throughout the ages, those who did not work looked down on those who did. Work itself—getting your hands dirty—was thought demeaning. That attitude still existed in Australia, but not among the squatters and their men. This gave a huge boost to the self-confidence of the worker-bushman. No other man could look down on him because he had the skills that they all valued.

Riding well was the chief of these. Australia's best-loved poem, 'The Man from Snowy River' by Banjo Paterson, tells of a great feat of horsemanship. It begins:

There was movement at the station, for the word had passed
    around
That the colt from old Regret had got away,
And had joined the wild bush horses, he was worth a thousand
    pound,
So all the cracks had gathered to the fray.
All the tried and noted riders from the stations near and far
Had mustered at the homestead overnight,
For the bushmen love hard riding where the wild bush horses are,
And the stock horse sniffs the battle with delight.

Whether the riders were owners or workers is immaterial; skill is what brings them together.

The stories and poems of Banjo Paterson and Henry Lawson, published in the 1890s, made the bushman into a national hero. Usually the bushman is a working man. There is an easy democratic assumption that he is as much a man as any other and that his affairs are equally interesting. It is here, rather than in a political document, that all men are proclaimed to be equal.

This first national literature carried the message that an Australian man is one who treats other men as equal. From now on, in stories, poems and histories, the equality of the goldfields was honoured and held up as a model.

Lawson and Paterson were very popular in the 1890s, but their influence must not be exaggerated. There were plenty of middle-class people not ready to take shearers or gold-diggers as models of good behaviour. To accept them as the typical Australian would feed the prejudice of the British that Australians were a common sort of people.

But what if the common sort of people turned into heroes of the Empire? The diggers of World War I gave Australia the honoured place it craved in the Empire and the world. No-one could quarrel with the diggers, and their reputation as larrikins, unwilling to salute officers, simply had to be accepted. They fixed the national style as casual, egalitarian and disrespectful.

Armies are made up of officers and men, but in Australia after World War I that distinction was overlooked. On the memorials to the Boer War (1899–1902), officers are listed first with their rank and then ordinary soldiers and troopers. On the World War I memorials, there is one alphabetical listing with no mention of rank. Within the RSL the same equality was practised. Rank was not to be mentioned. Officers and men were to treat each other as equals, as comrades. Eventually everyone who went to the war gained the title of the ordinary soldier—digger.

Egalitarianism remained male until the 1960s. The women of women's liberation attacked this form of equality because it excluded women and they saw it as encouraging attitudes in men that were demeaning to women. They promoted their own form of equality—sisterhood. 'Sister' has not taken off as a form of address. But in the 1990s 'mate' began to be gender-free. A few men used the term in addressing women. A few women used it in talking to each other and to men. This distinctive mark of Australian egalitarianism may survive into a new age.

The democracy of manners owes nothing to democratic politics, but it has implications for politics. Politics is necessarily about power, about inequality. In democracies, those who exercise power gain their authority by the votes of the people. That inequality Australians are reluctant to recognise. Their egalitarianism is a bond of equals, in part directed against the disruption of authority. Australians will recognise that a boss or a military officer must have power, though they will respect him only if he exercises power properly. But politicians have no excuse for wanting power; they have wilfully put themselves above the rest. They will have trouble therefore in gaining respect, no matter who they are or what they do. Many Australians seem to think politics exists only because there are a few egomaniacs wanting to be politicians.

The democracy of manners is a precious achievement. One of the reasons people fought for democracy was that they wanted respect for ordinary people, that they should not be humiliated and scorned by their 'betters'. Australians achieved that outside politics, and their egalitarianism is more deep-seated and genuine

The digger sets the
Australian style

Officer: "Why do you not salute?"
Anzac: "Well, to tell you the truth, digger, we've cut it right out."

because it is not a political doctrine. But so that all men can be equal, politicians have to be dishonoured.

Government

Australians think of themselves as anti-authority. It is not true. Australians are suspicious of persons in authority, but towards impersonal authority they are very obedient.

This is the country which for a long period closed its pubs at 6 pm and which pioneered the compulsory wearing of seatbelts in cars. Its people since 1924 have accepted the compulsion to vote. Its anti-smoking legislation is so tough that smoking is prohibited in its largest sporting stadium, the Melbourne Cricket Ground, though it is open to the skies. At an Australian Rules football match, the fans yell obscenities at the umpire and then at half-time walk quietly outside to have a smoke.

Australian government was not created in Australia. The government came off the boat, in the person of the governor and his officials, carrying all the authority of the government in Britain. With only one exception settlers never had to come together and form a government. The authority which secured to them the benefits of their pioneering was not of their making.

Melbourne was the exception; it alone of the colonial capitals was an unauthorised settlement. For a few months the settlers did govern themselves. Then the governor in Sydney visited and installed a magistrate responsible to him.

The founding governments of the Australian colonies had the virtues of the British government that created them: they provided a secure world, in which all people enjoyed protection of their property and liberty and the opportunity to start enterprises and make money. The convicts of course did not have their liberty, but they were deprived of it by the law, which also set the term for their release and protected the property and persons of ex-convicts as if they had always been free.

A secure environment for private enterprise was an important factor in Britain's rapid economic growth. The economic certainty provided by the British governments in the Australian colonies also aided their economic growth. This is the silent factor in the Australian story. It's only when economic growth is hindered by uncertainty and instability that this factor gets the recognition it deserves.

The early Australian governments were actually better than the British. The British government was run by the aristocracy and gentry, who rewarded their followers with government jobs. The job might pay well but have no duties. If the job did have duties, the holder was not obliged to perform them himself. He hired a deputy to do the work, but kept most of the proceeds for himself. Jobs often did not have salaries: the holder made his money by the collection of fees, which he could manipulate to his own advantage.

This system was being reformed just as Australia was settled, and so the new rules applied here from the beginning. All jobs had to be real jobs; the work could not be done by a deputy; the reward would be a fixed salary rather than fees. So the British officials who ruled under the governor's control were efficient and honest.

Government did not begin with taxation. The funds of the first governments came from the British taxpayer. The job of the Colonial Office was to get the governor to limit his spending and to raise money by local taxation. It was some time before the colonists in Australia were paying the full cost of their government. For the first 100 years they never really did that, because their defence was provided free by the British navy. For most of human history defence spending has been the biggest item in government budgets. In the Australian colonies it was one of the smallest, which allowed government funds to be spent on the internal development of the colony.

Usually in empires, governors of colonies taxed the people and sent the proceeds back to the mother country. In the Australian colonies taxes were not sent to Britain. After the revolt of the American colonies Britain resolved not to tax its overseas settlers. Britain got its benefit from the colonies through the growth in its trade and the returns on the private funds invested in Australia. The governor's job was to promote the development of the economy, which would enable the colony to pay its way and bring more benefit to Britain. There was a basic harmony between what the British government wanted of the governors and what the settlers wanted.

Governors and their officials built roads and bridges, improved ports, encouraged exploration, surveyed land for settlement, and provided settlers with their labour force, at first convicts and later free immigrants. The British government which sent the governors did none of these things in its own country. So the function of government changed in Australia: it was not primarily to keep order within and defeat enemies without; it was a resource which settlers could draw on to make money.

The best service that government could provide: the first train at Upper Chapman in Western Australia

The social character of the government changed too, or rather it did not have a social character. In Britain, government was closely linked to the social order; the richest people were the great landowners and they and their friends ran the government. In Australia the government was one person, the governor, who was detached from, and superior to, all groups in the local society. Yet government was much more than the person of the governor; he embodied the full authority of the British government and was the representative of the monarch. So government was both more singular and more abstract.

Settlers of course attempted to influence the governor. The richer settlers had more influence than others, and they occupied the positions in the Legislative Councils, which were at first appointed and then partly elected. But the councils never controlled the governor and the governors did not rule simply in the interests of the wealthy settlers. Several governors clashed with the wealthy settlers. The demand for self-government in New South Wales in the 1840s came from the rich squatters, who objected to Governor Gipps attempting to make them pay more for their land.

In the mid-1850s governors and officials were replaced by premiers and ministers responsible to parliament. The transition was smooth. The public servants remained in place. The regular business of government remained the same: to provide the infrastructure for the development of the economy. Democratic government made it easier for more people to make demands for roads, bridges and local services. If people wanted something done, they went in a deputation to the minister, escorted by their local member. If the local member could not get results out of ministers, he lost his seat at the next election.

The democratic governments, like those run by the governors, were omni-competent; they took on everything. They ran the school system and the police, which in Britain and in many other countries were the business of local government. Local government in Australia was weak; it was established late and did not cover the whole country. Its chief job was the making of local roads, and in the towns the collection of rubbish. Where there was no local government, the colonial government did all that was necessary. In most of the countryside of New South Wales there was no local government until 1906.

The colonial governments did all their work without imposing direct taxation. Until late in the nineteenth century there was no income tax and no company tax. All the money you earned, you kept. Government was not a burden that you had to pay for: it was a magic pudding; you could cut slice after slice and there was always more.

The magic was performed by the government collecting its revenue from taxes that you were unaware of—duties collected on imported goods—and from the sale of crown lands—which was not a tax at all. Local government did tax directly; its revenue came from rates collected on land. This was the chief reason why it did so little and why in many places it did not exist at all. No-one wanted to give local government more responsibilities because that would increase direct taxes.

The first government schools were built only when local people raised some of the cost of the building. That gave them some say in the running of the school. But from the 1870s the colonial governments, without raising any new taxation, were able to cover the full cost of school building. Local control of education disappeared. Who could quarrel with this when schools came for nothing?

The democratic governments were responsible for huge undertakings. The government railways were the largest businesses and biggest employers in colonial times. The provision of teachers and policemen throughout the colony and the sale and management of crown lands required large government departments.

Colonial politics did not look as if it would manage these large undertakings well. Members were concerned with getting benefits for their electorate and willing to trade their support to do so. Governments were short-lived and always had only a precarious hold on power. But though politics was confused and unstable, administration was honest and efficient. Frequent changes of government did not matter much because there was no fundamental disagreement over what government should be doing. The senior public servants had tenure, and many of them were of outstanding quality. Ministers appointed public servants to reward supporters, but incoming ministers did not sack existing public servants.

To their credit, politicians did not use politics to enrich themselves. A railway might be built to please constituents though there was little real need for it; a railway might even be built to run close to the property owned by members of parliament; but the money for railways did not go directly into MPs' pockets. The

Great public servants and their work: Charles Todd, postmaster-general of South Australia, erecting the first pole in the Overland Telegraph at Darwin

governor, still appointed from Britain, was a guarantor that proper standards were maintained.

Though the colonists had little respect for their politicians, their faith in government grew in the nineteenth century. In the twentieth century they created a national government, which was meant to have limited powers but quickly came to be used as an all-purpose facility, like the colonial governments. It was to protect and foster industry, ensure that workers received a living wage and that farmers got a good return for their crops.

Government in Australia has been continuous; it has never broken down and had to be reconstituted. Except in the treatment

Great public servants and their work: C.Y. O'Connor, engineer-in-chief of Western Australia; the pipes being laid from Mundaring Weir to the eastern goldfields

of Aboriginal people, government has never been an oppressive force, something that large numbers of people feared. Government has never been simply a means of fleecing people; it has always been a supplier of services that people wanted.

There has been strong government but no ruling class. When the governors ruled, the rich landowners and squatters thought they would take over when self-government was granted. But when that happened, they were quickly defeated and democratic politics began. The democratic politicians were a very mixed bag indeed, not identified with any one group in society, so distinct that they were a group in themselves—the despised politicians.

Government is without social character; it is an impersonal force. That makes it possible for Australian egalitarians to give it the great respect which its record deserves.

319

TRUSTING IN GOVERNMENT

This is an extract from the novel Jacob Shumate *written by Henry Wrixon, who was for many years a member of the Victorian parliament.*

The first thing that attracted the attention of the new MP, when he came down to breakfast a few mornings after election day, was the large heap of letters that lay upon the table awaiting his attention.

He was surprised to find what a number of Cricket Clubs, Rowing Clubs, Tennis Clubs, Racing Clubs, Hare and Hound Clubs, and General Sports Committees were anxious to do him honour.

Then there were the letters which came from people who had learned to cherish a comprehensive trust in their Government. The settlers in the Cote Cote Valley wrote to ask when the Government was going to drain their land; or were they to leave the land after the Government had put them on it? The members of the Tum Tum Fox Club informed the Member that the Department had sent them down rifles to help to destroy the foxes, but where was the ammunition? Did they expect them to kill the foxes without? An indignant parent complained that he did not get the full allowance of sixpence a week per child for bringing his children to school over the limit fixed by law for the allowance—though the road was so bad that he had to put a pair of horses in the trap to carry them. A comparatively poor widow wanted a place for her daughter as a typist, or something respectable, as she could barely make ends meet now with the price of things and the high wage for the house-help. The Art Association of Brassville wanted slight assistance from the Government, or somebody, to enable one of their number to make a painting of the charming copy of Raphael's 'La Giardiniera' that was in the Public Gallery of Miranda.

Henry Wrixon
Jacob
Shumate,
London, 1903,
Vol. 1,
pp. 168–9

Voters

In democracies the people are sovereign; they create the
government that is to rule them. That is the theory. In Australia
that has not been the practice. The people in their sovereign power
do not create governments; the people are forced to take part in
the creation of governments. From 1911 it was compulsory to enrol
for federal elections. From 1924 it was compulsory to vote in federal
elections.

Compulsory voting is firmly enforced. Those who don't vote are
asked for an explanation. If it is unsatisfactory, they are fined. If they
are unable or unwilling to pay the fine, they are sent to jail for one
or two days. After the 1993 federal election 41 people were sent to
jail.

The first Commonwealth elections in 1901 were conducted on
the franchise of the different states, using the state electoral rolls.
A uniform Commonwealth franchise was set in 1902. It included
votes for women (at that stage law in only two of the states), and
in other respects was for the white population more generous than
state law. The electoral rolls of the states clearly could not be used
for the next Commonwealth election. The Commonwealth had to
create its own.

The new Commonwealth law did not make enrolment to vote
compulsory, but the government was worried that too few people

would enrol. It was anxious to get the people involved in their new Commonwealth. The government decided itself to enrol the people. The prime minister got the agreement of the state premiers for the police to be used for the job. Over several months in 1903 policemen went from house to house, to every house in the island continent, collecting names for the first Commonwealth electoral roll.

To use the police for this job was not unusual in Australia. The police were the only officers of the colonial governments who were located in every district. Those omni-competent governments turned the police into omni-competent administrators: they collected statistics, inspected dairies, checked on school attendance, and buried paupers. In some states they had also collected names for the electoral rolls.

The police did a good job. But of course they missed some people. The lists went on public display and if your name had been missed you could apply to be included. Few bothered to check; people assumed that it was the job of the police to secure them the vote. On election day there were always some people complaining that they had been denied the vote because their name was not on the roll. These mistakes were not simply due to the police. The lists were redone every year, but before they had been collected and printed thousands of people had moved house. The population was very mobile. Much of the work in the country was seasonal and in the cities a large proportion of the population moved house every year.

The Electoral Office wanted to make people responsible for reporting changes in their address. It recommended that enrolment become compulsory. The Labor government of Andrew Fisher accepted the recommendation and passed a law for compulsory enrolment in 1911. To get the new system started, the police were called in again. They visited every house and got electors to fill in an electoral card with their personal details. The cards were now to form the master roll. When electors moved house, they had to send in a new card. If they did not do so, they were to be fined.

But how would the Electoral Office know if people had moved house? It appointed spies. In cities and towns they were the postmen, in the countryside the police. They sent regular reports of comings and goings to the Electoral Office. They also distributed electoral cards to newcomers on their beat and encouraged them to send them in. When the Electoral Office got reports from their spies, it checked to see whether newcomers had sent in their card. If they had not, they were asked to explain why. If they did not offer a good excuse, the Electoral Officer fined them.

Once government had taken the responsibility of enrolling the people, it was only a small step to force the people to supply the information to make the government's records as accurate as possible. It was only another small step from compulsory enrolment to compulsory voting. In 1911 several politicians were ready to take it. They asked what the point was of getting everyone on the roll if they did not bother to vote. If parliament was ready to force people to do their civic duty regarding enrolment, why not force them to perform the higher duty of voting?

In Australia, no new matter of principle was involved in moving from compulsory enrolment to compulsory voting. It was said again and again that the second was the 'natural corollary' of the first.

So the idea of compelling people to vote was born. Its birth was not related to changes in the proportion of people voting. Compulsion was discussed as an option in the federal parliament in 1911. At the 1910 federal election the proportion of people voting had jumped to 62 per cent, from 51 per cent in 1906 and 50 per cent in 1903. People thinking about this issue were not focusing on changing turnout figures but on the huge numbers of citizens who, if left to themselves, would never enrol or vote.

The idea of compulsion was born in Australia. It was not copied from anywhere else. There were a few European countries that had attempted compulsion in the nineteenth century, but these were not the spur to action. There was, and is still, no precedent for compulsory voting in the English-speaking countries with which Australia usually identifies itself. The idea was generated in minds that accepted a commanding role for government. Government could produce a near-perfect electoral roll and it could complete the job by engineering a near-perfect turnout. Governments could do anything—even make apathetic men and women into citizens.

Compulsory voting was adopted first in Queensland for state elections. In 1914 the Liberal government in Queensland faced almost certain defeat at the 1915 elections. Labor looked set to win a majority of seats for the first time. The Liberals considered that one of their disadvantages was that Labor was better at getting its supporters to the polling booths. It decided to make its supporters turn out in equal force by making voting compulsory. Again, this move was not related to overall turnout figures. At the previous election 75 per cent of the people had voted, a quite respectable figure and the best for state elections around that time.

Labor in Queensland did not oppose the introduction of compulsory voting. It went on to win the 1915 election, which made it think quite well of compulsion. Compulsory voting quickly became part of Labor's national platform. Just at the time the two political parties were becoming divided over military conscription, they were coming to an agreement that voting at elections should be compulsory. The advantage to the parties of compulsory voting was that they would not have to spend money and effort in getting people to the polls. 'Getting out the vote' would become the government's business.

At the 1922 federal election the turnout fell to 58 per cent after being above 70 per cent for the previous four elections. The Nationalist government was returned and took no action on compulsory voting. In June 1924 at the Victorian state election the turnout was only 50 per cent and the Labor Party for the first time became the largest party in the parliament. This was more worrying for the Nationalists, who faced a federal election in the following year. A week later Senator Payne, a Nationalist backbencher, introduced a Bill for compulsory voting into the federal parliament.

The backbencher was not acting alone. The parliamentary Nationalist party supported the move. The government, however, did not want to take responsibility for the change. It reached an agreement with the Labor Party that compulsion would pass rapidly through the parliament as a private member's Bill.

In introducing the Bill, Senator Payne spoke of compulsion making Australia more democratic. If democratic government was meant to represent the people, it would be improved by representing all the people: 'we must force those who live under that form of government to see that it is democratic, not only in name, but in deed'. There was very little discussion. No leading members of the government or Opposition took part. Only one member spoke strongly against the measure as a denial of liberty. No votes were recorded; the Bill passed both houses on the voices. It took only 52 minutes in the Representatives and 86 minutes in the Senate for compulsory voting to become law.

Australian voters accepted compulsion, and turnout figures rose to above 90 per cent. Compulsory voting was adopted for state elections in Victoria in 1926, in New South Wales and Tasmania in 1928, in Western Australia in 1936, and in South Australia in 1942. At the first federal elections held under the compulsory voting law, Ernie Judd refused to vote because as a socialist he could not support any of the candidates, who were all capitalists. The High Court held that this was not a valid excuse and that he had to pay his fine. All such excuses have been rejected by the courts. Objectors have been told they have to vote even if they do not prefer one candidate over another, and even if they don't know enough about the candidates to distinguish between them.

The defenders of compulsory voting dismiss these protests as 'grandstanding'. Though the law declares that voting is compulsory, all that can be enforced is attendance at the polling booth and the acceptance of a ballot paper. No-one has to vote against their principles or conscience; the elector can vote informal or leave the ballot-paper blank.

In the 1990s there was a movement within the Liberal Party against compulsory voting. It was now commonly accepted that the poor were the least likely to vote if voting were voluntary, and so compulsory voting aided the Labor Party. In 1993 the Liberal Party of South Australia won an election with voluntary voting in its platform. It introduced a Bill for voluntary voting but this was defeated in the Legislative Council by the Labor Party and the Democrats.

The Liberal Party was by no means united on this issue. In the 1990s a Liberal government in Victoria, controlling both houses, made no move against compulsion. Under voluntary voting there is the possibility that the Liberal Party might do better but the certainty that it will have to spend much more money on elections in order to get out its vote. Public funding for elections is made on the basis of the number of votes a party secures. Unless those rules were changed, voluntary voting would give the parties less government funding.

There is no broader movement against compulsion. Opinion polls record that over 70 per cent of the people are in favour of compulsion. If all those people voted voluntarily that would be a respectable turnout. However, compulsion remains not because there is convincing evidence that Australians would not vote under a voluntary system but because it suits the interests of the parties.

How far would the use of police extend? As large numbers of people still did not vote
at the first compulsory federal election, it was suggested that the police in future
might be sent to fetch them

COMPULSORY VOTING

If democracy exists to give expression to some presumed basic right to choose our political leaders, then voluntary voting is imperative. If, however, as I would argue, democracy exists to protect and promote the common good, then the tendency of voluntary voting to disenfranchise the poor is a decisive argument against it.

Stephen Buckle,
philosopher,
Australian,
3–4 February
2001

The parties are fortunate to have a compliant electorate. The Australian people want to be compelled to vote.

Those who write and comment on politics are overwhelmingly in favour of compulsion. In defending compulsion, they make a distinctively Australian contribution to political philosophy. They argue that with compulsion governments have to pay attention to the interests of everyone and particularly of the poor, which they could ignore under voluntary voting. That may be so, but they go on to claim that to move to voluntary voting would 'disenfranchise' the poor. This is double-speak. To allow people the freedom to vote or not would be to take the vote from them!

Australian writers and commentators are scathing about the low turnout for American presidential elctions and boast that in Australia governments have greater legitimacy because all the people take part in their creation. They do not think their case is weakened because the people are compelled to take part.

To the objection that compulsory voting is a denial of liberty, they argue that governments regularly make citizens do things— serve on juries, pay taxes, fight in the defence of the country. Of course governments compel citizens, but compulsory voting relates to another issue altogether: how governments themselves are created. Are citizens to be forced to create governments?

These arguments have been developed in a society where the value placed on personal liberty and the responsibilities of citizenship has shifted markedly from that in other English-speaking democracies. The existence of government is taken for granted and the people can be forced to be citizens.

327

THIRTEEN

Finale

Our enquiry into the relationship between democracy and society in Australia is at an end.

Australian democracy is certainly distinctive. There has been strong opposition to military conscription, but not to compulsory voting. Egalitarianism has not led to a universal welfare system nor prohibited the growth of private schools. Politicians have been held in contempt, but governments have been omni-competent and efficient. The people have been scornful of British snobbishness, but loyal to a British monarch. Men have been keen about mateship leaving women to take citizenship seriously. There are no grand Australian statements about democracy, but the values that underpin it flourish in society at large.

All these characteristics have their causes. Taken together, they account for that strange gap, that lack of attachment, between a democratic society and its democratic institutions of government, with which our enquiry began.

Another way of approaching the matter is to say that the movements for political democracy were not strong enough to command the society and to set its ideals. Manhood suffrage was achieved in the mid-nineteenth century when the word democracy could not be safely uttered. Democratic practice thus began without a democratic ideology.

A democratic ideology was certainly present in the second democratic movement at the end of the nineteenth century. Its carriers were at first the progressive liberals. The Commonwealth of Australia, founded on the direct vote of the people, is their lasting monument. Their most creative work in government at colonial and national level was performed with the support of the new Labor Party. But in the early twentieth century, the Labor Party grew amazingly rapidly and squeezed out the progressive liberals. It looked for a time that Labor could carry forward its ideal of an enlightened, self-governing citizenry shaping a new social order. Labor projected itself as the true national party and boasted of its moves to give the nation a strong defence force and to support compulsory military training. But in the Great War those who wanted Labor to be a class party for the workers took control, threw out the parliamentary leaders and gave Labor the pyrrhic victory of anti-conscription. Labor now carried the tag of being the disloyal party.

Labor recovered and was able on several occasions to govern well, but only as one party in a two-party system. It was not the standard-bearer of a wider democratic movement as it had been before the war. Indeed, the party system came to discourage wider democratic involvement. The small women's movement tried valiantly to keep alive the ideal of good citizens acting outside the party system. Briefly in the Depression citizens' leagues flourished, but were just as quickly absorbed back into the party system.

In the 1850s and in the 1890s the democratic movement was associated with the claims of colonists to rule themselves. On both occasions those claims were met without disrupting the ties of Empire. On the contrary, those ties strengthened as Britain allowed the colonies to be self-governing in the 1850s and to form themselves into a nation in the 1890s.

Australians defined themselves against the British, but not in the political sphere. Their nationalism does not have a strong political component. There was never a time when they attached themselves to their political system as the embodiment of the nation.

Australia still awaits the moment when its natural democrats will become self-conscious citizens.

Appendices

O N E

Timeline

(Note: Democratic principles and institutions are noted here only for the colony or state in which they are first established; for information on all colonies, see table of Democratic Landmarks.)

1786   Britain, assuming New South Wales is *terra nullius*, plans convict settlement without recognition of Aboriginal ownership

1788   Convict settlement at Sydney, with Governor Arthur Phillip in charge

1823   Governor to be advised by nominated Legislative Council; Supreme Court established

1824   *Australian*, first independent newspaper

1831   Assisted migration of free working people

1833   Ex-convicts eligible to serve as jurymen in criminal trials

1836   Governor Richard Bourke funds Catholic Anglican and Presbyterian churches on equal basis

1838   Myall Creek massacre of Aborigines; Governor George Gipps puts offenders on trial; seven hanged

1840   Transportation ceases to mainland Australia

1842   Two-thirds of members of Legislative Council to be elected on property franchise, ex-convicts eligible to vote and stand

333

1847	First government ('national') schools
1849	Attempt to revive transportation
1850	Legislative Councils, two-thirds elected, for Victoria, Tasmania, South Australia
1851	Australasian League for the Abolition of Tranportation formed; South Australia separates Church and State; discovery of gold
1852	Britain abandons transportation (except for Western Australia) and allows New South Wales, Victoria, South Australia and Tasmania to prepare constitutions with two houses of parliament for self-government
1856	Victoria adopts secret ballot; South Australia includes secret ballot and manhood suffrage (without plural voting) for Assembly in its constitution for self-government
1856–57	Self-government begins in four southeastern colonies, with ministers responsible to parliament
1859	Queensland separates from New South Wales and follows its constitution
1861	Land selection on time payment begins in New South Wales and Victoria
1865	Deadlock between Assembly and Council in Victoria over tariff
1870	Victoria adopts payment of members; Western Australia acquires partly elected Council
1872	Victoria stops state aid to private schools
1877	Deadlock between Assembly and Council in Victoria over payment of members
1884	Women's Suffrage Society established in Melbourne
1890	Western Australia becomes self-governing; trade unions defeated in Maritime Strike in eastern Australia
1891	Labor Party formed; federal convention draws up constitution for the Commonwealth of Australia (not adopted)
1894	South Australia adopts female suffrage
1896	Tasmania adopts Hare–Clark proportional representation for Assembly seats of Hobart and Launceston (and for whole state, 1907)
1897	Elections for second federal convention
1898	Referendum on Commonwealth constitution carried in New South Wales, Victoria, South Australia and Tasmania (but with insufficient Yes votes in New South Wales)

1899	Referendum on revised Commonwealth constitution carried in all colonies except Western Australia
1900	Referendum on constitution carried in Western Australia
1901	Commonwealth of Australia inaugurated
1902	Adult suffrage (except for Aborigines) in both Houses of Commonwealth parliament
1903	High Court established
1904	Australian Women's National League forms (supporting non-Labor parties)
1907	Harvester judgement of Arbitration Court establishes basic wage
1909	Compulsory military training; Commonwealth old-age pensions; parties opposed to Labor combine as Liberal Party
1910	Labor Party wins majority in both Houses of Commonwealth parliament
1911	Labor government's attempt to increase powers of federal parliament fails at referendum
1913	Country Party begins in Western Australia
1915	Australian troops land at Gallipoli
1916	Referendum on conscription for war in Europe fails; Labor Party splits on conscription
1917	Labor conscriptionists combine with Liberals to form Nationalist Party
1918	Preferential voting for Commonwealth elections (allowing the new Country Party to compete with Nationalists without advantaging the Labor Party)
1920	Communist Party formed
1921	Edith Cowan first woman to be elected to an Australian parliament (in Western Australia)
1922	Nominated Legislative Council abolished in Queensland
1924	Compulsory voting for Commonwealth elections
1927	Commonwealth parliament sits for first time at national capital, Canberra
1929	Great Depression begins
1931	Statute of Westminster gives British self-governing dominions power over foreign policy and defence (Australia not adopting it until 1942); Isaac Isaacs appointed first Australian-born governor-general; Jack Lang, premier of New South Wales, defaults on payment of interest on loans to Britain; Lang and his party expelled from the Labor Party; New Guard, a private army opposed to

communism and Lang, forms in Sydney; United Australia
Party replaces Nationalist Party; Premiers' Plan is joint
government response to Depression (cutting spending,
wages and pensions and requesting bondholders to accept
lower interest)

1932   Francis de Groot of the New Guard opens Sydney Harbour
Bridge ahead of Lang; Lang dismissed by Governor Game

1933   New South Wales nominated Legislative Council replaced
by one for which members of the Assembly and Council
elect one-third of Council members every three years

1936   Lang Labor and official Labor combine in New South Wales

1938   Aborigines mark 150th anniversary of European settlement with day of mourning and request for Commonwealth control of Aboriginal affairs; legislation for
National Insurance (contributory welfare scheme) passes
parliament but United Australia government decides not
to proceed with it; communist trade unionists attempt to
stop export of pig iron to Japan

1939   New South Wales Labor parliamentarians remove Lang
as leader; conscription for home defence

1940   Australia appoints first ambassadors (to Japan and the United
States); Communist Party banned for opposing the war

1941   B.A. Santamaria forms secret organisation, 'the movement', to combat communism in the trade unions

1942   Australian forces in Pacific put under command of
General Douglas MacArthur of the United States; ban on
Communist Party lifted (as it now supported war)

1943   Conscription for overseas service (but only for defined
zone to Australia's north)

1944   Labor government fails at referendum to increase greatly
the powers of Commonwealth parliament; Labor government introduces welfare payments on non-contributory
basis; Liberal Party replaces United Australia Party

1945   Communist Party reaches maximum membership

1947   Immigration program accepts non-British people; Labor
government attempts to nationalise the banks

1949   Senate elected by proportional representation; communist-
led miners' strike defeated by use of troops; Australian
citizenship established

1950   Victoria's upper house the first in the states to be elected
by adult suffrage

1951	Referendum to give Commonwealth power to ban Communist Party fails
1954	Labor Party splits when its leader H.V. Evatt denounces the anti-communist movement; Democratic Labor Party forms
1962	Aboriginal people gain right to vote in Commonwealth elections
1963	Commonwealth government gives state aid to private schools
1964	Conscription reintroduced (to include service overseas)
1966	Conscripts sent to Vietnam War
1967	Referendum carried to give Commonwealth power over Aboriginal affairs and for Aborigines to be counted in census
1970	Moratoriums to protest at Vietnam War
1971	Western Australia establishes ombudsman
1972	Women's Electoral Lobby forms; Arbitration Court establishes principle of equal pay for work of equal value
1973	South Australia's Legislative Council elected by proportional representation (with state voting as one)
1975	Commonwealth Racial Discrimination Act; Whitlam government dismissed by Governor-General Sir John Kerr
1977	Foundation of Australian Democrats; referendum on National Anthem won by 'Advance Australia Fair'; Queensland government bans street marches
1978	Referendum carried in New South Wales to make Legislative Council directly elected by the people (with proportional representation and the state voting as one); Northern Territory becomes self-governing
1981	Commonwealth Human Rights Commission established
1982	Commonwealth establishes freedom of information
1984	Commonwealth Sex Discrimination Act; Country Party everywhere now known as National Party
1987	Western Australia's Legislative Council elected by proportional representation (with state divided into regions)
1988	New Parliament House opens in Canberra; Australian Capital Territory becomes self-governing
1989	Fitzgerald commission recommends new institutions to ensure democratic government in Queensland
1992	High Court overturns doctrine of *terra nullius* in Mabo case
1999	Referendum on republic fails

337

Democratic
Landmarks

Australian colonies/states, Commonwealth of Australia, United Kingdom

	NSW	VIC	SA	TAS	QLD	WA	Aust	UK
Secret ballot	1858	1856	1856	1858	1859	1877	1901	1872
Adult male suffrage for lower house	1858	1857	1856	1858	1872	1893	1902	1918
No property qualification for members of lower house	1858	1857	1856	1901	1872	1893	1901	1858
Separation of Church and State	1862	1870	1851	1869	1860	1895	1901	
Payment of members	1889	1870	1887	1890	1886	1900	1901	1911
No plural voting	1893	1899	1856	1901	1905	1907	1901	1948
Female suffrage	1902	1909	1894	1903	1905	1899	1902	1928
Adult suffrage for upper house	1978	1950	1973	1968	*	1964	1902	
Ombudsman	1974	1973	1972	1978	1974	1971	1976	1967**
Freedom of information	1989	1982	1991	1991	1992	1992	1982	2000
Votes for Aborigines	Officially Aboriginal people had the same rights as others, but from 1902, because they were denied the right to vote in Commonwealth elections, they were often illegally denied the vote in state elections.				1965	1962	1962	N/A

* Legislative Council abolished in 1922.
** All complaints to be directed through MPs.

THREE

Australian prime ministers

Prime Ministers	Party	Period of office
Barton, Edmund	Liberal Protectionist	1901–03
Deakin, Alfred	Liberal Protectionist	1903–04
Watson, Chris	Labor	1904
Reid, George	Liberal Free trade	1904–05
Deakin, Alfred	Liberal Protectionist	1905–08
Fisher, Andrew	Labor	1908–09
Deakin, Alfred	Liberal	1909–10
Fisher, Andrew	Labor	1910–13
Cook, Joseph	Liberal	1913–14
Fisher, Andrew	Labor	1914–15
Hughes, Billy	Labor	1915–17
Hughes, Billy	Nationalist	1917–23
Bruce, Stanley	Nationalist	1923–29

Prime Ministers	Party	Period of office
Scullin, James	Labor	1929–32
Lyons, Joseph	United Australia	1932–39
Page, Earle*	Country	1939
Menzies, Robert	United Australia	1939–41
Fadden, Arthur	Country	1941
Curtin, John	Labor	1941–45
Forde, Francis*	Labor	1945
Chifley, Ben	Labor	1945–49
Menzies, Robert	Liberal	1949–66
Holt, Harold	Liberal	1966–67
McEwen, John*	Country	1967–68
Gorton, John	Liberal	1968–71
McMahon, William	Liberal	1971–72
Whitlam, Gough	Labor	1972–75
Fraser, Malcolm	Liberal	1975–83
Hawke, Bob	Labor	1983–91
Keating, Paul	Labor	1991–96
Howard, John	Liberal	1996–

*Caretakers.

Guide to political labels

In Britain, early nineteenth century

Conservatives

Conservatives appeared as a response to the social and political upheaval of the French revolution (1789–1799). They wanted to preserve the monarchy, a state church, and a social order in which aristocrats of noble birth were at the top. Intelligent conservatives were not opposed to all change; they wanted change to be gradual, not driven by ideology or a program, and always respectful of the customs and institutions of the country.

Liberals

Liberals favour freedom; they take their name from the Latin word 'liber', free. Liberals opposed the old social order and wanted a more open society without special privileges (especially those of birth). But they were opposed to democracy. They thought the test for political rights should be property ownership or education. They believed that the people who were fitted to be citizens could govern themselves; good government did not depend on a strong monarch or leadership from a noble aristocracy or a state church. Liberals opposed tyranny, oppression and arbitrary rule. They believed in education and progress. Liberalism was supported by middle-class and professional people, growing in numbers with the growth of cities.

Democrats

Democrats wanted political rights for all people, usually only for all men. Democrats gained their support from working people. In Britain from the 1830s the Chartists, a mass working-class movement, advocated a complete program for a democratic parliament. Both conservatives and liberals opposed democracy. As democracy allocated political rights without reference to birth or property, it was a very radical doctrine. As the mass of the people were poor and uneducated, liberals and conservatives assumed that democracy would lead to an attack on property, to chaos and bloodshed.

In Australia

Liberalism was used by those who wanted to limit the power of governors and to give equal rights to ex-convicts (who could be depicted as an oppressed group). By the mid-nineteenth century liberalism was used to attack the claims of the squatters, who were accused of wanting to turn themselves into a landed aristocracy. Liberals came from the middle class—merchants, traders and professional people. They used democratic support in their campaigns against the squatters, though they were opposed to democracy. However, the liberals were coming to realise that manhood suffrage (votes for all men) did not mean the people would actually rule, and that perhaps it could be agreed to without danger. The liberals were less frightened of the people in Australia, as there was not a large group of very poor people and property ownership was more widespread. Conservatives, on the other hand, opposed all democratic change, and believed that democracy would be as disastrous in Australia as it would be if it were introduced in Britain.

By the 1860s the conservatives were defeated. Manhood suffrage was law. Liberals now accepted manhood suffrage and the ballot,

343

even if they did not accept democracy in principle. They still called themselves liberals and not democrats. Liberalism was the ruling philosophy in the first 30 years of responsible government. Divisions between parliamentarians at this time were divisions between liberals. Free traders and protectionists were both liberals. The most radical liberals were in Victoria. Their opponents called themselves constitutionalists.

In the late nineteenth century progressive liberals were open supporters of democracy and of a more active government. The Labor Party, formed in 1891, was more radical than the progressive liberals: it wanted a completely democratic constitution (with no upper house) and was keener about state intervention. Some liberals would not accept the need for further democratisation and were now called, and sometimes called themselves, conservatives.

Within the Labor Party there were many who hoped that eventually the private ownership of businesses would be replaced by socialism. In a socialist society enterprises are not owned by private individuals or companies. Socialists had different ideas about who should own them. Some thought the government; others thought cooperatives of workers.

As the Labor Party's strength grew, all other groups came together to oppose it. At the national level this 'fusion' occurred in 1909. The new party called itself the Liberal Party. It argued that Labor threatened freedom by being too ready to expand government power and that its ideal of socialism would take away all freedom.

Committed socialists were soon critical of the Labor Party. There had been Labor governments but no real move to socialism. Disappointed socialists founded the Communist Party in 1920. Communists followed the teachings of Karl Marx, who argued that socialism would never come peacefully. There was no democratic path to socialism. The workers had to seize power, stamp out private ownership and destroy anyone who got in their way. The Labor Party was very anxious to distance itself from the communists. The Liberals attacked Labor for not distancing itself enough.

Twice the party opposed to Labor has taken in leading parliamentarians from the Labor Party. On each occasion it changed its name—in 1917 to the Nationalist Party and in 1931 to the United Australia Party. When the United Australia Party collapsed during World War II, Robert Menzies brought together the groups opposed to Labor in a new Liberal Party. The various changes of name make it difficult to refer to this continuing organisation. It would be convenient if its members were referred to simply as Liberals, the name they have gone under for most of their history.

The Country Party first contested federal elections in 1919. It wanted to protect the interests of farmers and was often ready to expand government power to do so. Usually it formed a coalition with the Liberals, when the two parties together held a majority of seats in parliament. Starting in Queensland in 1974, the Country Party changed its name to the National Party in order to win a wider group of supporters.

For nearly the whole of the twentieth century there were no politicians calling themselves conservative who got elected, though Labor often called its opponents conservatives. It was only in the 1980s and 90s that a few members of the Liberal Party and National Party called themselves conservatives. They were of course democrats, unlike earlier conservatives. They were social conservatives thinking that too much freedom was damaging society—so they wanted to preserve the traditional family and were tough on drugs. On the economy, however, they were thorough-going liberals, wanting to reduce government ownership and control.

Further reading

General

Grattan, Michelle, ed., *Australian Prime Ministers*, New Holland, Sydney, 2000
Mcminn, W.G., *A Constitutional History of Australia*, Oxford University Press, Melbourne, 1979
Manne, Robert, ed., *The Australian Century: Political Struggle in the Building of a Nation*, Text, Melbourne, 1999

Rights without votes

Hirst, J.B., *Convict Society and its Enemies: A History of Early New South Wales*, Allen & Unwin, Sydney, 1983
Melbourne, A.C.V., *Early Constitutional Development in Australia*, 2nd edn, University of Queensland Press, Brisbane, 1963
Neal, David, *The Rule of Law in a Penal Colony: Law and Power in Early New South Wales*, Cambridge University Press, Melbourne, 1991
Reece, R.H.W., *Aborigines and Colonists: Aborigines and Colonial Society in New South Wales in the 1830s and 1840s*, Sydney University Press, Sydney, 1974

Votes for men

Hirst, J.B., *The Strange Birth of Colonial Democracy: New South Wales 1848–1884*, Allen & Unwin, Sydney, 1988
Jaensch, Dean, ed., *The Flinders History of South Australia: Political History*, Wakefield Press, Adelaide, 1986
Loveday, P. & Martin, A.W., *Parliament Factions and Parties: The First Thirty Years of Responsible Government in New South Wales, 1856–1889*, Melbourne University Press, Melbourne, 1966
Macintyre, Stuart, *A Colonial Liberalism: The Lost World of Three Victorian Visionaries*, Oxford University Press, Melbourne, 1991
Serle, Geoffrey, *The Golden Age: A History of the Colony of Victoria 1851–1861*, Melbourne University Press, Melbourne, 1963

Real democracy

Hirst, John, *The Sentimental Nation: The Making of the Australian Commonwealth*, Oxford University Press, Melbourne, 2000
Irving, Helen, *To Constitute a Nation: A Cultural History of Australia's Constitution*, Cambridge University Press, Melbourne, 1997
Loveday, P., Martin A.W. & Parker, R.S., eds, *The Emergence of the Australian Party System*, Hale & Iremonger, Sydney, 1977
Oldfield, Audrey, *Woman Suffrage in Australia: A Gift or a Struggle*, Cambridge University Press, Melbourne, 1992
Rickard, John, *Class and Politics: New South Wales, Victoria and the Early Commonwealth*, Australian National University Press, Canberra, 1976

Threats to democracy

Cathcart, Michael, *Defending the National Tuckshop: The Secret Army Intrigue of 1931*, McPhee Gribble, Melbourne, 1988
Macintyre, Stuart, *The Reds*, Allen & Unwin, Sydney, 1998
Moore, Andrew, *The Secret Army and the Premier: Conservative Paramilitary Organisations in New South Wales 1930–32*, New South Wales University Press, Sydney, 1989
Schedvin, C.B., *Australia and the Great Depression: A Study of Economic Development and Policy in the 1920s and 1930s*, Sydney University Press, Sydney, 1970

Rights and limits

Attwood, Bain & Markus, Andrew, *The 1967 Referendum, Or When Aborigines Didn't Get The Vote*, Australian Institute of Aboriginal and Torres Strait Islander Studies, Canberra, 1997
Bailey, P., *Human Rights: Australia in an International Context*, Butterworths, Sydney, 1990
Dickie, Phil, *The Road to Fitzgerald and Beyond*, University of Queensland Press, Brisbane, 1989
Horne, Donald, *Time of Hope: Australia 1966–72*, Angus & Robertson, Sydney, 1980
Kelly, Paul, *November 1975: The Inside Story of Australia's Greatest Political Crisis*, Allen & Unwin, Sydney, 1995

Democracy and society

Almond, Gabriel Abraham & Verba, Sidney, *The Civic Culture: Political Attitudes and Democracy in Five Nations*, Little Brown, Boston, 1965
Emy, Hugh V., *The Politics of Australian Democracy*, Macmillan, Melbourne, 1974
Hancock, W.K., *Australia*, 2nd edition, Jacaranda, Brisbane, 1961
Lake, Marilyn, *Getting Equal: The History of Australian Feminism*, Allen & Unwin, Sydney, 1999
Rickard, John, *Australia: A Cultural History*, Longman, London, 1988

Illustrations

The publishers wish to thank the following organisations and individuals for permission to reproduce copyright illustration material in this publication:

p. 127 State Library of Victoria

p. 131 Published by—The communist Party of Australia
Borchardt Library, La Trobe University

p. 137 State Library of Victoria

p. 138 Mitchell Library.

p. 139 *The Brisbane Courier,* Tuesday, November 3, 1925 courtesy of
Queensland Newspapers

p. 141 By permission of the National Library of Australia

p. 143 State Library of Victoria

p. 145 Fairfax Photo Library

p. 147 By permission of the National Library of Australia

p. 148 Fairfax Photo Library

p. 151 National Trust of Australia (Tasmania)

p. 153 Mitchell Library, State Library of New South Wales

p. 155 By permission of the National Library of Australia

p. 157 *Communist Review,* January 1939
State Library of Victoria

p. 159 State Library of Victoria

p. 161 By permission of the National Library of Australia

p. 165 Courtesy of the Estate of B. A. Santamaria/Oxford University Press

p. 168 Courtesy: Liberal Party of Australia
Mitchell Library, State Library of New South Wales

p. 172 Mitchell Library, State Library of New South Wales

p. 173 Mitchell Library, State Library of New South Wales

p. 174 Mitchell Library, State Library of New South Wales

p. 178 State Library of Victoria

p. 181 J S Battye Library Pictorial Collection

p. 185 By permission of the National Library of Australia

p. 186 Jack Horner Collection, AIATSIS

p. 190 (insert)Herald & Weekly Times

p. 190 Moratorium march
State Library of Victoria

p. 191 *The Advertiser*/Photograph courtesy of the State Library of South Australia

p. 199 By permission of the National Library of Australia

p. 200 *The Age*

p. 201 Mitchell Library, State Library of New South Wales

p. 208 Commonwealth of Australia/DOFA

p. 210 CFMEU/Queensland Newspapers Pty Ltd.

p. 211 Mitchell Library, State Library of New South Wales

p. 213 By permission of Bruce Dawe

p. 216 Mitchell Library

p. 218 State Library of Victoria

p. 226 Sane Democracy
Mitchell Library, State Library of New South Wales
Speakers' Notes
ALP/Mitchell Library, State Library of New South Wales

p. 236 Hotel, Preston, Victoria
State Library of Victoria
Coat of Arms
Courtesy: J. V. Lindesay

p. 243 Museum Victoria
Collection: State Electricity Commission
Photographer unknown

p. 246 *Melbourne Punch*, 7 February 1895
State Library of Victoria

p. 247 Mitchell Library, State Library of New South Wales

p. 257 *Illustrated Sydney News*, 6 May 1854
Mitchell Library

p. 258 *Bulletin*, 20 August 1887
Mitchell Library, State Library of new South Wales

p. 263 *Sydney Punch*, September 1, 1866

p. 264 *Illustrated Australian News*, 26 May 1866
State Library of Victoria

p. 265 State Library of Victoria

p. 267 *Bulletin*, 11 October 1890
By permission of the National Library of Australia

p. 271 *Illustrated Australian News*, 1 June 1891
State Library of Victoria

Index